THE GOSPEL

OF THE

KINGDOM OF HEAVEN.

THE GOSPEL

OF THE

KINGDOM OF HEAVEN:

A COURSE OF LECTURES
ON THE GOSPEL OF ST. LUKE.

BY F. D. MAURICE,

INCUMBENT OF ST. PETER'S, VERE STREET.

'*Come forth out of Thy royall chambers, O Prince of all the kings of the earth! Put on the robes of Thy imperiall majesty! take up that unlimited sceptre which Thy Almighty Father hath bequeath'd Thee! for now the voice of Thy Bride calls Thee, and all creatures sigh to bee renew'd.*'—MILTON.

the Attic Press, Inc.
GREENWOOD, S. C.

Reprint 1977
ISBN 0-87921-037-0

PREFACE.

I have called these discourses 'Lectures,' not sermons. They are strictly readings on the Gospel of St. Luke. But they were addressed to a congregation. The ordinary rules of preaching were observed in the delivery of them; a text was placed at the head of each. It was chosen because much of the sense of the surrounding passages seemed to be woven into it. That I presume is the meaning of a 'text;' the justification for its use in the pulpit. It should always suggest, and in some sort compel, the study of the book from which it is taken; it should never be forgotten in the disquisition which is appended to it. When I revised the lectures, and prepared them for the press, I might, along with other alterations, have dropped these headings. But I was unwilling to give the book the form of a commentary, or to lose any of the links which connected the Gospel that is written with the Gospel that is preached. Why I felt this reluctance will be evident if I explain the object of the course, and the circumstances which suggested it.

The life of a Jesus who was not the Christ, who is
not the King of Men, who came from no Father in
heaven, who baptized with no Spirit, who did not rise
from the dead, has been written with consummate ability.
Though this Jesus claimed titles which were not his,
though he practised mean deceptions, he has been recognised as a hero both by his biographer, and by numbers
who have read the biography. Men and women, rich and
poor, in all parts of what we still called Christendom,
have been inclined to accept him as a substitute for
the Person whom in their infancy they were taught to
revere. If they could fully accept him, casting away all
their old impressions, a great incubus, they think, would
be taken from their spirits, they would breathe more
freely.

In these Lectures I have endeavoured to ascertain what
is told us respecting the life of Jesus by one of those
Evangelists who proclaim Him to be the Christ, who says
that He did come from a Father, that He did baptize
with the Holy Spirit, that He did rise from the dead.
I have chosen the one who is most directly connected
with the later history of the Church, who was not
an Apostle, who professedly wrote for the use of a
man already instructed in the faith of the Apostles. I
have followed the course of this writer's narrative, not
changing it under any pretext. I have adhered to his

phraseology, striving to avoid the substitution of any other for his.

Can such a task be necessary in our days? Is not every Sunday-school child acquainted with the letter of the Gospels? Is it not our business to consider whence they were derived, how they may be interpreted and modified to suit the temper of our times, what divine and human elements there may be in them, how far they represent exactly the acts and words of Christ, how far they embody thoughts and beliefs of which the Evangelists became possessed after their Master had departed from them? I do not question the wisdom of discussing any of these questions. I am glad to profit by the learning and sagacity of those who take part in them on either side. But I have not found the other task, which requires no learning, superfluous for myself. I think it is not superfluous for our age.

If the children in Sunday-schools understand and accept the letter of the Gospels, their teachers and those who preach to them out of pulpits, I fear, do not. Certain conventional notions mingle themselves with it in all our minds; we read it as if they were inseparable from it. Clergymen receive these notions as sacred heirlooms. They are enforced by public opinion. If an ecclesiastical synod should acquire the power of imposing penalties, spiritual or civil, they will be enforced by those penalties.

They subvert, as it seems to me, the words of the Bible and the principle of the Creeds. They create that wish to be rid of Him who is the centre and subject of the New Testament history which M. Renan's book has developed. At the same time they contain the germs of the new faith. The Jesus of the Frenchman has been formed in orthodox schools and circles.

I purpose in this preface to indicate three or four of these conventional notions. I have done what I could that my reader might be able to test them by the Scriptures themselves. Whatever be his opinions, he will have every motive to expose me. I am about to encounter a set of interpretations which apologists for the Bible take for granted, which opposers of the Bible equally take for granted. I should not dare to dispute them if I were not convinced that God Himself is proving them to be untenable, and is calling upon us to abandon them as the only condition on which we can retain the belief of our forefathers.

I. In these Lectures I have had again and again to consider the question whether the Gospel of St. Luke exhibits to us a Christ who breaks through the order of the universe by strange and irregular acts of power. That He did so is assumed by the writers of our books of evidence. That He could transgress laws is said to be the proof of the truth of His mission. All that reverence for fixed laws which characterises our time—which is the encouragement to our scientific inquiries, and the fruit of them—rebels against such a proof. 'The tokens,' says the objector, 'of One who comes from the God of order 'should be, that He upholds order not that He vio- 'lates it.' That assertion seems to me incontrovertible. Gods made out of men's own thoughts—gods made in the likeness of things in heaven or earth or under the earth— may be capricious as those thoughts are capricious, may be variable as the things which we observe are variable. The proper ministers of such gods are enchanters and magicians, who play tricks with nature that they may prove how great and wise they are. The ministers of a God who gives the sea its bounds that it should not pass, who hath established the earth and it abideth, should take the very opposite course to that of these magicians. They should be witnesses for laws, against anomalies. They should show that there is a living and eternal order which all the changes and vicissitudes of nature obey. They should show that true power is exercised in obedience to this order, that all power which sets it aside is to be broken in pieces.

It seems to me that exactly the claim which the Evan- gelists put forth for Jesus is, that He was the revealer and assertor of the Divine order, that He entered into conflict with the anomalies which disturbed that order.

He came, they say, preaching the Kingdom of Heaven, the Kingdom of the eternal, unchangeable God. The laws of that Kingdom He proclaimed as more fundamental, less capable of any suspension or modification, than the laws that were written on stone and were ratified by thunders and lightnings. This Kingdom of Heaven is a Kingdom over men. But Christ drew His illustrations of it from the facts and the course of nature. *That* He exhibited as another part of the same living order. What we call miracles are said to be the signs and powers of the heavenly kingdom, the signs of its permanent nature, the powers by which it works out its effects. How do they answer to these titles? They are directed against the confusions of the world, against the plagues and torments which distract human life. Is the novelty of these acts the proof of their greatness? The Evangelists' language would lead us to exactly the contrary opinion. Christ is said to do the works of His Father in Heaven. If He was really the Son of God, if He might really claim to manifest His Father's mind and will to men, this would be just the account of them which we should expect, which we should consider most reasonable. And therefore it must be a secret feeling that He was *not* this, that the words which seem to import this are not real but fictitious words, that has led to the theory upon which we are at times ready to rest the whole evidence of the

Gospels. That such a view of things was very reasonable
in the Unitarian apologists for the Gospels in the last
century, that it may not have seemed very unreasonable
to Paley, I quite understand. But can those who adhere
to the words of our Creeds, can those who take the declaration of Christ's Sonship in a strict sense, can those who
think that all human sonship is the image of His, accept
that hypothesis? These are thoughts which I would
suggest to persons who are eager to uphold the popular
notion of miracles. Before they charge any who dissent
from it as heretics, they should consider carefully whether
they are orthodox. At all events, they should ask themselves whether they are adhering to the letter of the
statements in the Evangelists, or are departing from it;
whether there is anywhere to be found in them a hint
of that exaltation of power at the expense of law which
is becoming characteristic of our divinity.

I admit, then, the full force of the objection which the
advocates of the Renan Gospel allege against us who profess to be champions of the old Gospel. But I think that
we have incurred this charge by departing from that old
Gospel, and by practically accepting the premises upon
which the new Gospel rests. We start from the idea of a
natural Jesus : we attribute to Him certain *supernatural*
exercises of power. All such exercises are by the very
assumption irregular, anomalous. The old Gospel starts

from the supernatural ground, assumes a supernatural
Being to be the Author of the universe, to have created it
according to laws which are the expression of His mind.
The tendency has been apparent in human creatures at all
times to make themselves the measures of the universe,
to deduce laws from appearances, to mould the lawgiver
after their conceptions. The revelation of a Creator is the
counteraction of this tendency, the discovery of Him who
preserves the harmonies of the universe, the witness that
its discords cannot be perpetual. 'There is no such
'revelation,' says the new Gospel; 'everything begins from
'phenomena, or from man, the observer of phenomena.'
Then, if the past history of the world is true, there will be
a succession of enchanters like the Jesus of Renan. The
more any man is a reformer—the more impatient he is
of the abuses he sees around him, of the evils which are
besetting his fellow-creatures—the more he will practise
these falsehoods; he has no other chance. He must cheat if
he is to save his fellow-creatures from being cheated. He
must lie, if he has the least care that truth should prevail.

II. The second notion to which I shall allude is this.
'The New Testament is the proclamation of a certain
'religion. It is the true religion, the religion which all
'ought to believe. The Gospels contain the simpler part
'of this religion. The doctrines or mysteries of it are
'set forth in the Epistles.' This statement would strike

a number of readers as too obvious to be disputed.
Whatever may be the evidence which supports the
authority either of Gospels or Epistles, this account of
them—that they announce or embody a *religion*—would
be equally accepted by all parties of Christians, and by
those who reject Christianity.

'But then,' say these last, 'though you are all agreed
' that these books contain a religion, and that it is the true
' religion, the only religion, the religion which all men
' ought to receive, you are not the least agreed what it is.
' Greeks, Romanists, Protestants, are at war upon that
' question. Protestants are split into a multitude of sects,
' each of which declares that its own is the Christian
' religion. When you are brought face to face with Hin-
' doos or Buddhists, they ask you which of your different
' religions you wish them to accept; and you can make no
' answer, or only the most stammering answer. When you
' are brought face to face with Mahometans, they can
' boast that their religion grew up six centuries after
' yours; that it conquered a number of the countries which
' once were yours; that it does not yield at all to the
' force of your arguments.'

These facts are indisputable. If there are any special
pleas to be urged against them, I have no such pleas.
They seem to me just as important as any facts of nature.
I cannot believe in God without regarding them as *His*

facts. I cannot shut my eyes to them without trying to hide from myself some lessons, profound, tremendous lessons, which He is teaching us.

But are the Gospels the announcement of a religion? Is that what they profess to be? Is that the conception which would be formed of them by any one who simply read them as they are written? Does the word 'religion,' or anything which answers to that word, even occur in them? Do they not profess to be the account of One who was born King of the Jews, who did certain acts proving, in the judgment of the Evangelists, that that title was really His, whose claims were rejected by the Jewish priests and rulers? Do not the Evangelists say that Jesus preached the Gospel of the Kingdom of Heaven to all classes and conditions of men—that He claimed all as His subjects? Do they not say that this was the main cause of His rejection; that His greatest opponents were those who professed a strict and exclusive religion, and who drew sharp lines between themselves and the rest of their countrymen? Is not the connexion between the Gospels and the other parts of the New Testament this, that the Apostles proclaimed the son of David to have risen from the dead, and ascended on high, that He might be the King of *all* men? Did not their battle with their countrymen turn upon the question, whether there was a Son of Man who might be announced by that name to Jews and

Greeks, to Barbarians and Scythians, to bondsmen and reemen, whether there was One in whom God had reconciled the world to Himself, One in whom all things in Heaven and earth shall be at last gathered up ?

If we adhere to this language, we must cast aside the other, however plausible it sounds. We must treat it as an invention of men, as their substitute for the message of God. Those who hold the Bible not only to contain, but to be, the word of God, are especially bound to take this course. And if we do take it, the Gospels will themselves explain to us why the attempt to make men embrace a religion must have been, and must for ever be, futile. Men, by their religion, seek to establish some meeting-place or reconciliation between them and God. The Gospel is the news that God is reconciled to man in His Son, that in Him there is a meeting-point between God and man. A religion must always be affected by the local habits, by the individual temperaments, of those who profess it. A Gospel is the unveiling or discovery to men of a common Head. At the message of a Son of Man in whom Jews and Greeks were one, a Church consisting of men with different languages, opposing habits, contrasted educations, hostile religions, started into life. At the message of a Son of Man who had taken the nature of men, Goths rose out of their brutal condition, Latins rose out of a civilization which was worse than barbarism.

Then there grew out of the conceptions which Latins
formed of this Gospel, a Latin religion; out of the conceptions which Greeks formed of it, a Greek religion; out
of the conceptions which Goths formed of it, a Gothic
religion. These religions were at variance with each
other. Within each of them there were elements of
continual strife. They had no force before the Islamite
shout, ' There is one God; a man is His prophet and the
conqueror in His Name.' That mighty and living message
could only be encountered by nations which confessed an
actual King—one with man, one with God—as the bond of
their fellowship. But the Islamite faith lasted on. For
the West, while it could organize its polity and fight its
battles in this Name, must have its religion, its schemes
of drawing nigh to God, its methods of propitiation. In
the Lord's Prayer and the Creed, the name of the Eternal
Father confronted the mere ruler who was represented by
Caliphs and Sultans. He was hidden from the people by
mediators visible and invisible. He from whom all grace
and love proceed was continually presented to the conscience as the great object of its terror, in the very likeness
of the Evil Spirit. His perfect Image was of necessity
darkened, as He was darkened. The Saints or the Virgin
—generally some local virgin—must persuade the Son to
persuade His Father not to punish crimes which it was
infinitely desirable for the order of society, for the cause

of righteousness, that He should punish, to ask toleration for sins by which His children were enslaved. Against this Latin religion came forth the Gospel, ' God has made ' peace with us in His Son. We may trust the Son ' absolutely to put away sins. Indulgences are the devil's ' gifts, not His.' But the Gospel of Luther became the religion of Lutheranism. It was opposed by the religion of Geneva, by the religion of Zurich, by the religion of England. Each nation has been great while it has ac·knowledged Jesus as a King; each sect has been great when it has accepted a Gospel of Christ, and protested against some religion which was hiding Him from men. Each nation has become separate from every other when it has boasted some system of religion, and has rallied round that. Each sect has become narrow and persecuting as it has set up its own religion, and has called that the religion of Christ. And yet every nation has borne witness of the truth by showing that it must prefer its own king, an actual man, to any system whatsoever; each sect has borne witness to the truth by showing that the name of its founder was dearer to it, and a greater security for its continuance, than any system of opinions. The Latin Church has borne witness to the truth by confessing that its religious system must go to pieces if there is not a Bishop who is also a King (it signifies little whether he is the best or the worst man on earth, whether his government is the model of the Divine Government or concentrates in itself all the baseness, tyranny, and corruption that is diffused through the Governments of the world) to declare what the religion is, and to bind those who profess it into one. All these are testimonies to the need of a living Head. Nor till *the* Head of Humanity is proclaimed will the insufficiency of the *partial* heads be felt, will the counterfeit universal head shrink into nothingness.

These facts, then, are indeed of unspeakable value. They show that Religion in the original Roman sense, as expressing obligation to some unseen ruler, is grand, sacred, imperishable. But what the obligation is, must be determined by the character of the ruler. If that is not righteous, or if the righteousness is not declared so that it may be known, the religion will become identical with superstition, with the mere dread of a power which can do the worshipper mischief. It will be supported by the State for its own purposes, the statesmen all the while mocking at its pretences. If the State, as in the case of Rome, becomes a despotism, ruling over many tribes which profess different religions, some of these will be treated as lawful, some as unlawful. Such as obviously interfere with civil order will be put down ; the rest will be protected, as affording a help more or less useful in keeping those who adopt it in subjection to the visible emperor. Only if there should be the announcement of a kingdom based on a foundation exactly the opposite to his, toleration will inevitably be changed into persecution; the kingdoms must fight till one of them fall. Such is the history of the struggle which occupied the first centuries of the modern world. It was not a struggle between a Christian religion and another religion, or a multitude of other religions. It was the struggle between a kingdom which was grounded on the dominion of a man raised to be a God, with the announcement that the true King of men is one who, being in the form of God, took upon Him the nature of His subjects, that He might deliver them from all their oppressors bodily and spiritual. Is there such a one? Is the kingdom real or imaginary? That has been the question in all periods; that is the question now. Mr. Carlyle has taught us how, in every age—in this democratic age as much as any—the demand of men is for a king; how any one who has exercised any influence over his fellows has come forth to meet that demand. He has made us acquainted with some of these kings; the best of them have surely been those who have confessed a kingdom of which they were only ministers; he asks reverence for them as for men who bowed to eternal laws. They died, and left the world, he thinks, very bare and sorrowful. Very bare indeed, if there is not a King who entirely obeyed and fulfilled the eternal laws, and who is not dead but alive. Very sorrowful, if the best message it

can hear is this: 'You have been dreaming for the last
' three-quarters of a century of a common humanity.
' You have been utterly unable to realize it without a
' head, a king. You have been convinced, by evidence
' more and more overwhelming, that he who professes
' to be the Visible Head of humanity has no power to bind
' its limbs together; he cries for the help of earthly
' monarchs to uphold him. Philology, and criticism, have
' been trying to connect the present with the past; every
' man feels that connexion, and confesses one with an inter-
' minable future. And now hear and understand! Criticism
' and philology have clearly ascertained that there is no
' Head of humanity, no one who binds the ages together;
' no Prince of the kings of the earth.' The news may be
very loudly proclaimed. For some reasons I have given
already, for others which I may state presently, it may
eagerly be welcomed. *Our* unbelief has been anticipating
it, and preparing for it. But it will not have the kind of
success which those who send it forth anticipate. Men will
have a Christ of some kind. He may be a mob Barabbas, he
may be a Cæsar. We may make our choice between these
Christs, we may try them alternately. Either must have more
reality and more influence than a Galilean Thaumaturgist,
who feigned to contend with death and was overcome by it.
But the tyranny of each will at last be intolerable. The cry for
deliverance will again arise; God will show who is His Christ.

III. The third of the prevalent opinions to which I shall
refer depends upon the second. 'There being a religion
'which men are required to accept, there must be sanc-
'tions to enforce it. They must consist of the most bril-
'liant rewards for obedience, of the most tremendous
'punishments for disobedience. Pains and pleasures are
'the motives by which men are stimulated to act as the
'human legislator wishes them to act. The pains and
'pleasures which a Divine Legislator holds out cannot be
'limited by the threescore years and ten during which we
'stay upon this earth. They must stretch through illimit-
'able ages ; there can be no term to them.'

'Yes,' the believer in the Jesus of Renan says, 'beyond
'all doubt this must be the opinion of those who accept
'what you call the Gospels, who suppose them to have
'proceeded from a Divine Author ; who think that they
'express the judgment of a Son of God ; of one that rose
'from the dead. The words *everlasting life* and *everlasting
'punishment* are, those Gospels say, His words. Modern
'divines have not introduced them. Rather it has been
'the habit of our time to hide them from view, to explain
'them away. Only a few are honest enough to take them
'in all their horrible significance. Even those only use the
'threatening part of them occasionally for great offenders
'or desperate heretics—even they do not speak of the
'devil and of demons as the Gospels speak continually,

' almost in every page. We are told that we must acknow-
' ledge the existence of such beings ; but in general little
' is said about them. It seems to be thought that they
' had tremendous power in Palestine, while Jesus walked
' the earth, but that their influence is not much exerted
' over us. We are very depraved, of course, utterly de-
' praved. But that is the fault of our own nature. Malig-
' nant spiritual influences were believed in during the
' Middle Ages, were thought then to be present and active.
' What cultivated man dares confess a similar conviction
' now ? Does not a clergyman, going into districts where
' such superstitions exist, labour to discourage them?
' Does not the English Clergyman denounce the Irish
' Priest for making use of them, that the people may
' tremble at his curse, and hope for his exorcism ? '

I acknowledge at once that we have evaded the express
statements of the Gospels respecting eternal or everlasting
life, respecting eternal or everlasting punishment. I acknowledge it as an indication of the same habit of mind,
that we give so little prominence to the story of our
Lord's temptation by the devil, which stands at the very
threshold of the Gospel narrative, to those stories of the
casting out of demons which form one of their capital and
obvious characteristics. I think any objector has a right
to demand the reason of these omissions and prevarica-
tions. No reason seems to me so entirely to meet the

facts of the case as this.   We *have* regarded those phrases about everlasting life and everlasting punishment as the sanctions of a religion.   We have translated the Gospels into Bentham-Dumont *Traités des Peines et des Recompenses.*   We have believed that we were to outdo the Benthamite legislator by producing heavier punishments and greater recompenses than he could produce. And therefore these words have been kept as a reserved force, to be brought forth at the end of discourses, to clench the arguments and rhetoric of preachers.   And the preacher has been supposed to exhibit his discretion in distributing promises and threatenings according to some theory of his as to the persons who might need the one and might not need the other.

Now when we read the Gospels, we find that the first announcement of the Christ is this : ' *He shall baptize with the Holy Ghost and with fire.   His fan is in His hand, and He will throughly purge His floor, and will gather the wheat into the garner; but will burn up the chaff with un- quenchable fire.*' No one can suppose the Gospels to be true and to have any order in them who does not take these words as cardinal words, words of which all the subsequent history is an illustration and fulfilment.   The Evangelists never suffer us to forget them.   The characteristic of the Christ is that which is indicated by the name ; He is anointed with the Spirit.   All His exercises

of power are the works of the Spirit. They are not acts
directed towards the outside of the man, but to the man
himself. If they affect his body, they affect the springs
of life in his body; that which determines its condition,
but which the eye cannot see. And the conflict is always
represented as being with powers which have usurped
dominion over his thoughts, over his will—powers which
have made him a slave. The Holy Spirit is at work to
deliver him from this captivity. What would this regene-
rating baptism of the Spirit be worth if it were not accompanied with a fire to burn up whatever defiles man and
the societies of man? Can that fire be a poor material
fire, which, like all material things, must die out? If it
is to purge an immortal being—a fellowship of immortal
beings—must it not be an unquenchable fire, one that no
evil with which it comes into contact can overcome or
extinguish? Such a divine fire must be that with which
the Son of Man baptizes; even as with such a fire He was
Himself baptized.

But are there not threatenings of an 'outer darkness,' of
'weeping and gnashing of teeth,' of a 'damnation of Hell,'
which it is most hard to escape? Fearful indeed are these
threatenings; fearful in the frequency of their repetition;
fearful in the occasions which called them forth. Oh, let
us meditate them well! Let us observe that they are not
reserved for publicans or harlots, or heretics and heathens;

that they *are* reserved, strictly, carefully reserved, for the
most religious men, for those who were practising the
most exclusive religion, for those who were using the
sanctions of this religion, habitually, perseveringly, against
publicans and harlots and heretics and heathens. Let
us ask ourselves whether the outer darkness is not that
exclusion from the love which was seeking to embrace
publicans, harlots, heretics, heathens; whether the weeping
and gnashing of teeth is not for the loss of the fellowship
with the Son of Man and with the race for which He died
through this exclusiveness; whether the deep hell into which
the Jewish nation and its rulers were sinking was not the
hell of Covetousness, of Hypocrisy, of Malignity, out of
which the Spirit of God was seeking to raise them, which
the fires of God were seeking to consume in them. If we
think over these things, the Epistles will interpret the
Gospels to us. We shall understand how the law of the
Spirit of Life in Christ Jesus delivered Saul of Tarsus
(who had been living under the sanctions of his religion,
and enforcing those sanctions upon all other men) from the
law of sin and death; we may understand what his conver-
sion meant, and what his Gospel to the world meant, and
why that Gospel exposed him to the same bitter persecution
which he had once enkindled.

And then, also, we shall never feel tempted to contract
the meaning of the words eternal or everlasting when

they are applied to the Divine fires, or the Divine punishments. We shall only complain of the contraction and mutilation which they *have* suffered—both in this relation and when they are associated with life—through the refusal to take them in their natural original sense. All through the Old Testament we hear of Him who is, and who was, and who is to come. If we suppose the New Testament to be in very deed the revelation of this God in a man, we must accept St. John's words literally, that in Him the life of the Father, the Eternal Life, was manifested to us. And if so, the eternal fires must be those by which God has in all ages been purging His universe of its corruptions; the eternal punishment must be that which has been, and is, and will be directed to the extirpation of the great curse of moral evil.

Is there, then, no indication anywhere of fires which are not purifying but destructive, of punishments which do not aim at the cure of evil, but at the perpetual prolongation of evil? Such fires, such punishments, we are distinctly warned of. They are connected with those passages, which we are rightly accused of slurring over, respecting the Spirit of evil who tempted our Lord, respecting those demons whom He cast out. Not a part of the message of the Kingdom of Heaven, but every part of it, concerns the struggle of the Son of Man with the Accuser, the Tempter, the Destroyer; concerns the deliverance of men from the physical and moral slavery which he has brought into God's universe. Everywhere the Son of Man is defying his claim to rule; everywhere He is asserting the creation to be the Creator's. I accept this as the most glorious message ever brought to mankind. If I confess that the conflict came to its crisis when the Deliverer appeared in our world—that there is nothing in the Old Testament at all resembling the Temptation in the Wilderness, or the exorcisms of evil spirits—I do not therefore confine the meaning of those records by any limits of space or time. They reveal to us, I conceive, the principle and secret of the war that has been waged in every palace and every hovel from the beginning of the world. They contain the interpretation of that which has been most confused in the language, most radical in the convictions, of every nation, civilized and uncivilized. They give a sense to the most cowardly superstitions, to the cries and confessions of the bravest men. Abstractions about evil have satisfied schoolmen and lazy speculators. Such abstractions have never satisfied workers and sufferers. They have felt evil as a power which was threatening them or holding them in bondage. Take from biography, history, poetry, all that expresses and embodies this conviction, and what a ghastly skeleton of each will be left! Take from us the sense that we are wrestling with actual principalities and powers, and you

turn our existence into a series of shadow-fights. Then
the ghost assumes the place of the spirit; there is a dread
of apparitions which may present themselves to the
eye, because the dread of influences that corrupt the
conscience and the heart has evaporated. We have, in
our days, in the highest circles, even amongst scientific
men, proofs enough that the sense of spiritual power, the
desire for spiritual communications, has not passed away.
But the sense and the desire have become fantastic and
frivolous, and combined with gross materialism, because
they have been divorced almost wholly from any association
with moral good and evil. Far more venerable, pointing
to far deeper human necessities, is the witch mythology
of the Middle Ages, are the superstitions of peasants
in all countries and ages. These may be often blended
with a grotesque humour, but they are not playthings to
fill up a vacant hour, new excitements to supply the place
of old excitements that have been worn out. They have
a dreadful seriousness. They have been the cause of un-
paralleled cruelties, especially when those who should have
met them with the Gospel of a Spirit of Power, and Love,
and a sound mind, have cultivated the servile terrors of
the people, have confounded these terrors with godly fear,
have turned them to the increase of their own influence. To
such blending of light with darkness, to such dishonesty,
whether in the priests of one communion or another,

some of the darkest crimes in human history must be traced. The office of the true minister of God's Kingdom is surely to labour for the extirpation all such superstitions in all countries, Christian and heathen. He has a right to tell the Irish priests, or any priests who are fostering them, that they are doing the devil's work. But his efforts and his denunciations will avail little if he only hovers between the demonology of the old world and the materialism of the modern. He will lose the loyalty to human experience which is latent under the first, the loyalty to the facts of nature which is obvious in the other. When we dare to accept the Gospels as they stand, we shall be able to oppose the Manicheeism which draws from the sense of moral and physical evil the inference that there are two rival *Creators*, each of whom requires some homage, the most malignant the greatest homage ; we shall be able to spoil the occupation of the charlatan, whose art consists in blending the phenomena of the visible world with the terrors of the invisible, and making man the victim and slave of both. For we shall believe in a King of men, who went into death and the grave and hell, that He might destroy him that had the power of death and hell. We shall believe in a Spirit of God who makes us partakers of the deliverance that has been wrought for our race, who gives us power to be children of God and citizens of the Kingdom of Heaven.

What must one who asks this help of Jesus think of the Jesus of Renan? He is simply the Christ stripped of all power to overcome *any* terrors of human beings, to put down *any* superstition or priestcraft, to raise humanity out of *any* of the natural or supernatural miseries which have crushed and tormented it. He is the embodiment of an impotent wish to do men good and conquer their oppressors—a wish which could only succeed in its most partial efforts by practising the cheats which have been the greatest instruments of sacerdotal and imperial tyranny. And yet I see not where we can stop short of such a conception if we do not confess a Christ, who exhibited on earth the power which He has exerted and will exert through the ages till all enemies are put under His feet.*

---

* It has been often suggested that those who object to the notions of future punishment which are popularly adopted, have strong personal motives for their dissent. A prelate of the English Church has recently, I understand, given the weight of his episcopal authority to this suspicion. Some have complained of it as uncharitable. Testing it as I ought to test every such admonition, by my own conscience—since I have no faculty for determining how far it applies to my neighbours—I at once recognise its justice ; I accept it without modification. I *have* a strong personal motive for rejecting these popular notions ; the motive may be exactly the one which the defender of them supposes. I *do* find that I am tempted to those evil states of mind which constitute, as the Bible teaches me, the curse and horror of hell, to which all its outward physical torments, be they what they may, are subordinate. I do *not* find that I have any power to raise myself out of these states of mind. I acknowledge the influence of an evil spirit who would draw me into them and fix me in them. My hope of deliverance from them arises wholly from the belief that it is the will of God manifested in Christ to raise

IV. The last of these notions is one to which I alluded at the beginning of this Preface 'The four Gospels are 'written documents. Before we can give credence to the 'message which they contain, we must be assured of their 'authenticity and inspiration. *When* we are assured 'of their authenticity and inspiration, we must accept 'them absolutely, unreservedly. Therefore,' says the objector, 'if you cannot prove the authenticity and inspira-'tion of these books; if you are not agreed among your-'selves what inspiration means, what is involved in 'authenticity; if questions about the composition of these 'books are giving you ever-increasing trouble, and leading 'you into ever-fresh evasions; if you long to hide these 'questions from the vulgar, and yet confess that you 'cannot hide them—where must your belief go? what 'security have you for its permanence in any class of 'men? There are some who already refuse to accept your 'books of evidence as inspired. With the increase of educa-'tion, will not their number be multiplied indefinitely?'

All that I have said in this Preface implies that I

my will, and the will of those who are tempted as I am tempted, and who have fallen as I have fallen, out of this perdition. Can I have a stronger or more directly personal motive for rejecting the opinion which is proclaimed in so many pulpits, which it seems the object of recent declarations to endorse, that it is the purpose of God to keep men in a state of sin—a continually increasing and deepening state of sin—for ever and ever? That I hold to be the purpose of the devil, whose works Christ came to destroy.

recognise the Gospel narrative as a Divine message to
mankind, and that I ask Christians to receive that
message in a much more direct and simple sense than
they are wont to receive it. *Therefore* do I recognise
the truth of the arguments which I have just recited.
If the Gospel is a Divine message to mankind, it *cannot*
depend for the proof of its veracity, for its influence
over men, upon any theories about the composition of the
books which contain it, upon any arguments about their
authenticity or inspiration, upon any definitions which we
can give of the words 'Authenticity' and 'Inspiration.' A
Gospel to the poor, a Gospel of the Kingdom of Heaven,
never did make its way, never could make its way, to the
hearts, consciences, reasons of those for whom it was intended, by any such process. We deny history, we contradict in terms our own professions, when we assume that
it did. And what has been the effect of that assumption
upon our own minds? I have endeavoured to show in
this Preface what it has been. We give the Gospels credit
for being authentic, inspired, Divine. We lift our voices
loudly against those who doubt their possession of any
of the qualities which we associate or fancy we associate
with these titles. And there our duty to them ends.
What they actually say we do not inquire. We change
their language into language of our own; we efface their
most obvious characteristics; we, in effect, re-write them;

all the while affirming that they not only contain, but are, the Word of God.

And is it not inevitable that we should commit these great contradictions whilst we adhere to that formula? Looked at as documents, what is the great question respecting these Gospels—the question which is at the root of all others? It is this. ' Are not the three so-called ' synoptical Gospels histories mixed with a certain leaven ' of later theology? Is not the fourth Gospel the full ' development of that later theology, with a human history ' artificially and awkwardly grafted upon it?' This is the battle we have to fight with those who dispute the authority of the Gospels in France, Germany, and England. All other battles are child's play to this. But with what weapons do we go into this? We have thrown away our weapons. We have to all intents and purposes admitted the conclusions of our opponents. For we say that St. John uses the expression Word of God in a sense which may be very convenient for a system of Divinity, but which has nothing to do with our habitual language, with our common life. In *these* the book shall mean the Word of God, shall *be* the Word of God. And therefore we cannot hear *the* Person, *the* Word, speaking out of the book. We must regard it as containing a set of letters and notions which we may twist and manipulate as much as we please. The awe of the Word, the power of the Word, has departed, while we are in the very act of asserting its awe and its power. The Word no longer convinces us, governs us. We are its masters, we are to enforce it on the acceptance and obedience of men.

Should this habit of mind continue among us, I believe we shall find more and more of our countrymen who only hesitate between the two opinions, whether the fourth Gospel is a feeble reproduction of Philo's Theosophy, or whether, as Renan thinks, there are in it the footprints of a genuine narrative, which must have been written by a vain old man, jealous of the preference that had been given to Peter over him in the older Evangelists, and full of bitter spite against Judas. It is easy to denounce these as extreme and monstrous notions. It is far better and safer to inquire what has produced them, and how we may be led into either of them. If we do not habitually think of the Word of God as a living Person, it signifies little whether the first verse of the fourth Gospel, and all the rest of the writings which profess to set forth the operations of the Word, were derived from Philo or from any one else. If we think that the Eternal Life which was with the Father has not been manifested, and according to the constitution of humanity cannot be manifested to us, we must treat the apostle who wrote to testify of its manifestation as the greatest of all impostors; that we do not feel the personal bitterness to such a deceiver which Renan feels, must be the accident of our circumstances or the effect of our indifference.

On the other hand, if we do heartily recognise these as the fundamental principles of our faith, the first three Gospels will become clear to us in the light of these; we shall examine their differences, not with trembling, but with satisfaction. The theology of the fourth Gospel will be the key to their history. We shall find that they have had power over men, because the divine Word has been making His Gospel heard in them, when those who were entrusted with it have most darkened it by their fancies, have most used the holy book to shut out the Holy God. We shall read them as the record not of a life which lasted thirty-three years, but of a life which has been the light of men in all ages, which is the source of all that is true and beautiful in human existence now, which will be revealed as the satisfaction of all that men have longed for, all that God has promised. The life of such a Jesus as Renan has described may be written by any one who has learning and artistic skill for the task. The life of Christ can only be contained in a Gospel of the Kingdom of Heaven. If I should succeed in persuading a few readers to study that Gospel as it is written in the

manly and wholesome words of one of those by whom
it was originally declared to mankind, and to forget any
words of mine and of other interpreters which have concealed the import and weakened the power of his, the
purpose of these Lectures will be accomplished.

TABLE OF CONTENTS.

PREFACE.

CONCERNING certain prevalent opinions which hinder those who receive the Gospels from taking them in their simple sense, and which induce many to reject them.

LECTURE I.

THE PURPOSE OF THE GOSPEL OF ST. LUKE.

Subject. ST. LUKE, c. I. vv. 1—5.

LECTURE II.

THE ANNOUNCEMENT OF THE SON OF DAVID.

Subject. ST. LUKE, c. I. vv. 6—80.

LECTURE XIII.

THE GLORY AND HUMILIATION OF THE KING.

Subject. ST. LUKE, c. IX. vv. 1—48.

LECTURE XIV.

THE ETERNAL LIFE OF THE KINGDOM OF HEAVEN.

Subject. ST. LUKE, c. IX. vv. 49—62, and c. X. vv. 1—38.

LECTURE XV.

THE SPIRIT OF THE KING AND OF THE JEWISH RULERS.

Subject. ST. LUKE, c. X. vv. 38—42, and c. XI.

LECTURE XVI.

THE FIRE WHICH IS TO BAPTIZE THE NATION AND THE KING.

Subject. St. Luke, c. XII. vv. 1—51.

LECTURE XVII.

THE CITY OF THE GREAT KING.

Subject. St. Luke, c. XII. vv. 51—59, and c. XIII.

LECTURE XXIII.

THE KING ENTERING HIS CAPITAL.

Subject. ST. LUKE, c. XIX.

LECTURE XXIV.

THE KING AMIDST THE CHIEF PRIESTS AND SCRIBES.

Subject. ST. LUKE, c. XX.

LECTURE XXVIII.

THE KING TRIUMPHANT.

LECTURE I.

THE PURPOSE OF THE GOSPEL.

St. Luke I. 1—5.

Forasmuch as many have taken in hand to set forth in order a declaration of those things which are most surely believed among us, even as they delivered them unto us, which from the beginning were eyewitnesses, and ministers of the word ; it seemed good to me also, having had perfect understanding of all things from the very first, to write unto thee in order, most excellent Theophilus, that thou mightest know the certainty of those things, wherein thou hast been instructed.

Two years ago, on St. Luke's day, I began a series of Lectures on the Acts of the Apostles. This year I commence a series on the Gospel of St. Luke. Am I not reversing the order of these writings ? Does not the Evangelist call that 'the former treatise' which I am considering last ?

Let me remind you that St. Luke was the preacher of a Gospel before he was the writer of one. The book which we call the Acts of the Apostles tells us what he preached, and to what kind of men he preached. It tells us what message St. Peter delivered to those who were assembled, from all parts of the Roman and Parthian empires on the day of Pentecost. It tells us what message St. Paul delivered to Jews and Gentiles both, in different cities of

B

Greece and Asia Minor. The word Gospel, or good tidings᾽ is a word especially dear to St. Paul, whose companion St. Luke was. We are not left to gather from his writings what sense he attached to it. He has defined it carefully in the opening passage of the Epistle to the Romans :—
'Paul, a servant of Jesus Christ, called to be an apostle, separated unto the gospel of God (which he had promised afore by his prophets in the holy scriptures), concerning his Son Jesus Christ our Lord, which was made of the seed of David, according to the flesh ; and declared to be the Son of God with power, according to the spirit of holiness, by the resurrection from the dead᾽: by whom we have received grace and apostleship, for obedience to the faith among all nations, for his name : among whom are ye also the called of Jesus Christ.'

These, then, were the tidings which St. Paul and St. Luke delivered. In answer to these tidings Churches arose. Those who were received into them, Jews and Gentiles, confessed One who was made of the seed of David according to the flesh, and declared to be the Son of God with power, to be their common Lord, the bond of their fellowship. They said that they were held together by that Spirit of Holiness which dwelt in Him. They spoke of themselves as citizens of the kingdom of God.

Those who had received this Gospel and been baptized into this fellowship, had been told by the Apostles of certain acts by which Jesus, while He was upon earth, had shown Himself to be the Son of David and the Son of God. There must have been a multitude of reports concerning these acts floating about, some coming from friends, some from enemies. Could they not be collected? could not the chaff be separated from the wheat, the fancies of men from the Divine discovery ? The answer to this demand is in the written Gospel. How a Gospel should be written, who should write it, those who longed for one could not tell. But they believed the longing to be given them from above; they could not doubt that He who inspired it would in some way gratify it.

As I read the Gospels, I find how this need has been supplied. From the place which they occupy in our Bibles, it has been supposed that they contain 'lives of Jesus,' originally simple, probably derived from a common source, increased and interpolated by degrees as notions of His character and office, which had not been previously entertained, were developed in the Church. Such a notion, it seems to me, is dispelled, if we take any one of them and consider it carefully and regularly. I propose to do this with St. Luke's, not from any preference for it, but specially on account of its connexion with that other treatise of which I have spoken to you already. When we have gone through it, you may reconsider that treatise in what appears its natural order.

(1) The introduction to this Gospel is the highest authority for that account of the purpose of its composition which I have given you. Theophilus, whoever he was, was already a disciple. He had been instructed in the things which were most surely believed in the Church. He desired to know the certainty of those things. St. Luke believed that it was his vocation to give him what he wanted. If Theophilus was an individual, he represented the need of the Church generally. That which was good for him, might, if God pleased, be good for ages to come.

(2) Many, St. Luke says, had attempted this task before him. They had taken in hand, our translators say, *to set forth a* DECLARATION *of the things which are most surely believed* in the Churches. The *declaration,* I conceive, had been made already. That had been contained in the preaching of the Apostles and their helpers. What was wanted was a continuous *Narrative* of the things which made the substance of the declaration; for it was a declaration of *things,* not of *opinions;* of events that had happened, of acts that had been done. The preaching concerned a person, the narrative must exhibit a person.

Who had taken this great enterprise in hand St. Luke does not say. He may or may not have read the narrative of St. Matthew or St. Mark. Those narratives may or may not have been written. At all events, his phrase 'many' will not be satisfied by these two. Nor does St. Luke pronounce on the merits or demerits of his predecessors. That was not his calling. There was a better judge than he of the genuine and the spurious. We may safely affirm that he was not afraid if the experiments to produce a record of our Lord's acts were ever so numerous; if some of them were ever so confused and erroneous. He could not believe the word which he preached unless he had confidence that what was true would live, that what was false would be, sooner or later, divided from it. If God had conferred the highest blessing on the human race, He would take care that the human race should not miss the blessing through any want of means to be acquainted with it.

(3) The next clause of this introduction has perplexed many, perhaps has given pain to some. *As they delivered these things to us, which from the beginning were eyewitnesses.*

What then, are we not about to read the story of an eye-witness? St. Luke does not claim that character; he does not desire that we should invest him with it. He has received these records from those who were. He has examined their reports carefully. He does not say that he ever saw Christ whilst he was walking in Galilee or Judæa. He seems to imply the contrary. Now here is a difference between him and some of the other Evangelists, perhaps between him and all the other three. Is it a difference which puts him below them, which makes his testimony inferior to theirs? According to their own judgment and confession, assuredly it is not. They tell us that they did not understand the words and acts of Jesus whilst they were walking with him, whilst they were eyewitnesses of what He did. They misapprehended the particular words and acts. They misapprehended their relation to each other. They misapprehended the Person who was the speaker of the words and the doer of the acts. They tell us this again and again, in various forms of expression, all natural, all simple. ' *Their eyes were holden*,' ' *Their hearts were hardened*.'

No doubt they would, sometimes, have ventured to reproduce His parables, or His explanation of the parables, to those about them. They must have been conscious that their lips were stammering, that they misrepresented Him when they most wished to be faithful in their reports; that they degraded Him whom they most wished that others should exalt. By degrees, they will have learnt the wisdom of obeying Him simply, by only preaching ' *Repent, for the kingdom of Heaven is at hand*,' as He bade them, and using the powers of that kingdom as He imparted them. What they all say—what no one says so frequently

as the beloved disciple—is, that the things which they could
not understand at first came to them with full power and
revelation when they saw Him no more ; that His Spirit
brought back to them acts which had been hidden in the
cells of their memory, quickened words that had been mere
dead sounds, harmonized precepts which had seemed frag-
mentary or contradictory, discovered to them the divine
source from which they had issued. No doubt to be eyewitnesses of a fact or a person is an honourable distinction :
but an eyewitness may glorify himself on that distinction,
and attribute a worth to it which no careful student of
evidence will concede. There are qualities necessary in an
eyewitness besides his eyes, if he would teach us anything,
if he would impart truth to us ; one who possesses these
qualities, and who faithfully sifts the testimonies of eyewitnesses, may tell us what they do not tell, may open
to us the very sense and purpose of what they do tell. It
is so in all cases : if we believe the Evangelists—those of
them who were eyewitnesses—it is pre-eminently so in
this case.

(4) In connexion with this subject, I would direct your
attention to an expression of St. Luke which is sometimes
overlooked. He speaks of those who were *eyewitnesses and
ministers of the Word.* What does he mean by the *Word ?*
He does not surely mean that a man could be an eye-
witness of sounds, or a minister of sounds. If the expression occurred in St. John's Gospel, it would cause no
perplexity. We should assume at once that he was speaking of the Word which was in the beginning ; whose life
was the light of men ; who was made flesh and dwelt among
men. But it has been customary to assume that no other
of the Evangelists ever fell into this kind of language.

I cannot doubt that the Apostle who survived to the end of the age, was specially appointed to remove confusions which had haunted the readers of the earlier Gospels and which were giving occasion to various partial theories, by declaring broadly that He who healed the sick and cast out demons whilst He walked below, was the eternal Source of all good and deliverance to the sons of men, one with the Father before the worlds were. But every Jew could read, as well as St. John, that the Word of God had come to Isaiah or Jeremiah or Ezekiel. Every Jew who read their prophecies as they were written, believed they had conversed with this Word as with a living person. The thought, 'He with whom *we* have conversed is that same Person—He has in human flesh revealed Himself to us,' was not a strange speculation, the refinement of a later age. It was the simplest way of connecting the old world with their day. It was the great escape from the rabbinical traditions which buried the divine Person under the mere letter of the books. That this thought should express itself naturally—unconsciously, as it were—at the outset of a Gospel concerning a Person, who was an impostor if He were not *the* messenger of God, *the* utterer of His mind, cannot, I think, cause us any surprise. Formally to assert the force of the prophetical phrase—to make it prominent before all others—was not St. Luke's calling. The King, the Christ, is his subject. If we admit any direction of the minds of those who wrote these books—indeed, any special callings of men in this world at all—we can perceive why the tasks of the different Evangelists should be different. We can perceive also why each should inevitably at times adopt forms of speech which appear more characteristic of another.

(5) Many having written, '*it seemed good to me also,*' says Luke, to write. ' It seemed good to him !' Some may cry, ' Was he not then taught to write by the Spirit of God ?' I imagine, my friends, that he who described the day of Pentecost, and referred the whole existence and work of the Church to the Spirit of God, had quite as awful a feeling of His government over himself as any of us can have. The freedom of his language shows me *how* strong his feeling was ; our sensitiveness and unwilling-ness to connect the Spirit with the operations of the human intellect, indicate the weakness of ours. The habitual con-viction that he could not have undertaken such a task as he was now entering upon, if he had not been moved to it by the Holy Spirit—that he could not pursue it faithfully, laboriously, effectually, unless the Spirit were at every moment leading his mind out of its own fantasies to the apprehension of that which is—preserved the Evangelist from a number of subtleties into which we fall, because we have lost that conviction, and rather suppose that we are to protect the lessons of the Spirit, than that He is to protect us. We ask for distinctions about the degrees and measures in which the Spirit has been, or will be, vouchsafed. The Evangelists make no such distinctions. I think they dared not. Could they doubt, that if the Spirit called them to the greatest of all works—to that which would most con-cern the name of God, and the good of their fellow-men for generations—they should have the help and light which they required, that which the Source of all light and help knew that they required ? Would they have wished us to doubt that, in all our works, even the humblest, He will grant us what we require ?

(6) The next clause teaches us much on this subject,

and would teach us more, if it had not been unhappily
perverted in our version. We represent St. Luke as
saying, that he had *perfect understanding of all things
from the very first.* I do not know exactly what meaning
our translators wished us to attach to that statement;
but if any readers have attached *this* meaning to it, that
St. Luke arrived at once, without effort—without any
process of sifting or inquiry—at an understanding of the
facts which he records, they have directly inverted his
words. What he says is, that it seemed good to him to
write, *having followed out all things with careful diligence
from their source,* just as a man traces the source of a
river from its mountain bed through all its windings.
Instead of being absolved from this diligence by the
presence of the divine Spirit, he felt himself obliged by
that Spirit to spare no labour, not to omit the most earnest
and solicitous examination of what he heard from those
who were eyewitnesses and ministers of the Word; not to
give himself credit for understanding it at the first, but to
wait for that clear penetrating light which could distinguish
between his own impressions and the truth of things. And
I apprehend, that the difference between those reports
which many had undertaken to write, and those which
have really stamped themselves on the heart and conscience and faith of mankind, may be traced mainly to
this cause—that the first were the fruits of immature
thoughts and feelings which had a strong hold on the
writers' minds, but which had never been submitted to any
severe process whereby the gold might be severed from
the dross; that the others came from men who remembered
the promise, '*He shall baptize with the Spirit and with
fire,*' and who believed that whatever passed through their

intellects must undergo this divine fire, if it was to last through the ages, and to testify, in them all, of Him who does not change.

(7) There is one word more in this preface which I cannot pass by. St. Luke professes to write to Theophilus *in order*. The narrative is to be an orderly or continuous one. If it does not fulfil this condition, it will not answer its purpose; it will not tell Theophilus *the certainty of those things wherein he has been instructed*. Can we then discover the order which St. Luke has followed ? Clearly, it is very different from that of common biographers, especially different from that which a biographer of Jesus would have adopted, if we may judge from the experience of eighteen centuries. Think how the fancy of painters and of writers of legends has expatiated over the infancy and boyhood of Christ, and then remember how many incidents are recorded by our Evangelist—who yet records more than any other—of all the period before He began to be about thirty years of age. Evidently, his conception of the life must be entirely different from theirs. What with them is most substantial is for him a mere introduction,—a most valuable introduction, as I think,—but one which must become false to us if we lose the Evangelist's perspective, and contemplate it according to some theory of our own. What then is this perspective? What rule does it follow ? The answer to this question will come out, I trust, in the course of our readings. I will only anticipate it thus far. I think you will find that what the Evangelist traces are the steps by which a King claimed dominion over His subjects ; how they were prepared for Him ; how He was prepared for going forth among them ; how He manifested the powers of His Kingdom ; how He illustrated the nature

of it; what kinds of opposition He encountered; what battles He fought; who stood by Him, who deserted Him; how He seemed to be vanquished; how He prevailed at last. The more steadily we keep before ourselves the thought of a Kingdom of Heaven—a kingdom actual in the highest sense, explaining the nature and forces of every kingdom that has existed on the earth, showing what in those kingdoms must abide, what must pass away—the more shall we adhere to the letter of the Gospels, the more shall we enter into their spirit.

This characteristic is common to them all. And it is in the light of that common object we can best examine their specific differences. In general, the hint of a purpose is given very early in the narratives. The title of St. Matthew's Gospel—*The book of the generations of Jesus Christ, the Son of David, the Son of Abraham*—with the genealogy which follows, marks out his design to associate Jesus with the foregone history of his land. Much as St. Mark resembles him, it is evidently his main object to set forth a *Gospel of the Son of God.* He exhibits royalty more in act, less as the fulfilment of past anticipations. In this first chapter of St. Luke we have certain signs of *his* intention, which criticism has often sought to obliterate. The stories of the vision to Zacharias and of the birth of John the Baptist, and of the annunciation to the Virgin, belong exclusively to him. Those who suppose that he was writing the life of a Teacher whom he had preferred to other teachers, to whom he attributed great supernatural powers, of course assume these to be embellishments, introduced for the purpose of magnifying the hero, and of showing that, like other heroes, he had a celestial parentage. On that hypothesis we must at once

concede the extravagance and falsity of that which St.
Luke sets down as true. Were the hypothesis established,
we must abandon the stories of this chapter, and along
with them, I conceive, all the rest of the narrative.

If Jesus was not the Son of David or the Son of God,
the notion that a preacher of repentance was appointed as
the witness of His birth, as well as the notion that a
Virgin was chosen to be the instrument of it, fall naturally
and without an effort. If He was the Son of God and the
King of men, we may feel, we ought to feel, that these
records are not those which *prove* Him to possess His
divine royalty—that He must have had it, apart from all
circumstances of His birth. The evidence for it may be
quite independent of any such circumstances. We may
be very thankful to St. John for setting forth His higher
generation, to St. Mark for fixing our minds on that
evidence of His works on earth which was wholly uncon-
nected with the Virgin. But we shall not feel that such a
narrative as we read here is a startling or inconsistent one.
Theophilus must have asked, ' If such a Person as you
' speak of did come into the world, *How* did He come ?
' Was His birth like another birth ? Was there no prepara-
' tion for it, no announcement of it ? ' An Evangelist who
undertook to tell him the certainty of those things wherein
he had been instructed, could not evade such inquiries.
The answer, it seems to me, which is given is the simplest
that we can imagine. What it is, in what manner the two
gifts to men, of a Prophet and of a Son, were announced
and were received, I propose to consider next Sunday. I
would only allude here to the connexion of these passages
with what we know of the writer. The distinction between
the Old and the New Covenant, the covenant with servants

and the covenant with sons, the covenant with the nation and the covenant with mankind, must have been always present to the mind of a companion of St. Paul. To show how one passed into the other, how one fulfilled the other, must have been a prominent object in his preaching. When he began to examine all the records of his Lord upon earth, would it have seemed to him a strange anomaly, would it not have struck him as an orderly, reasonable commencement of such a history that there should be a birth like that of the son of Zacharias, the climax of those births on which the Old Testament puts such honour, that there should be one like that of the Son of Mary to inaugurate the new age ? May not the evidence of these have come mightily home to him, not being exceptions in the divine method, but as the highest illustrations of it,—as a justification of the past, and a preparation for the future ? Are not these stories witnesses to us of the glory and blessing of human parentage, of our right to claim a divine parentage ?

LECTURE II.

St. Luke I. 46—48.

And Mary said, My soul doth magnify the Lord, and my spirit hath rejoiced in God my Saviour. For he hath regarded the low estate of his handmaiden: for, behold, from henceforth all generations shall call me blessed.

St. Luke's introduction, which we considered last Sunday, is strictly prosaic. He speaks of the carefulness with which he had studied the reports of those who had been eyewitnesses of Christ's acts. He claims no exemption from the ordinary toils of a historian. He seems to think that he is more bound to perform them because his subject is so awful, and because he believes himself divinely called to unfold it.

The narrative begins with a quietness befitting this preface. We hear of two old people, both of the sacred Jewish family, who are walking in all the commandments of the Lord blameless. They are childless. Zacharias punctually fulfils his duties as a priest. At a certain time he goes according to the order of his course into the House of the Lord. It is his lot to burn incense.

Then we arrive, some will say, at the supernatural part of the story.

'*And the whole multitude of the people were praying with-*

out at the time of incense. And there appeared unto him an angel of the Lord standing on the right side of the altar of incense. And when Zacharias saw him, he was troubled, and fear fell upon him. But the angel said unto him, Fear not, Zacharias: for thy prayer is heard; and thy wife Elisabeth shall bear thee a son, and thou shalt call his name John. And thou shalt have joy and gladness; and many shall rejoice at his birth. For he shall be great in the sight of the Lord, and shall drink neither wine nor strong drink; and he shall be filled with the Holy Ghost, even from his mother's womb. And many of the children of Israel shall he turn to the Lord their God. And he shall go before him in the spirit and power of Elias, to turn the hearts of the fathers to the children, and the disobedient to the wisdom of the just; to make ready a people prepared for the Lord. And Zacharias said unto the angel, Whereby shall I know this? for I am an old man, and my wife well stricken in years. And the angel answering said unto him, I am Gabriel, that stand in the presence of God; and am sent to speak unto thee, and to show thee these glad tidings. And, behold, thou shalt be dumb, and not able to speak, until the day that these things shall be performed, because thou believest not my words, which shall be fulfilled in their season. And the people waited for Zacharias, and marvelled that he tarried so long in the temple. And when he came out, he could not speak unto them: and they perceived that he had seen a vision in the temple: for he beckoned unto them, and remained speechless. And it came to pass, that, as soon as the days of his ministration were accomplished, he departed to his own house.'

This narrative of an angelic visitation does not *bring* us into a supernatural region. We are in one already. The

Temple-worship meant nothing if there were not an actual
established intercourse between the visible and the invisible world. The Jew believed that He who dwelt behind
the veil had made a covenant with his fathers and him,
that He had given them a law, that He had appointed
their priests and their sacrifices. In His name they protested against all worship of visible things. And *therefore*
the visits of angels are not in the Old Testament what
they are in Pagan records. The heathen started from the
human ground, was continually feeling after God. Ever and
anon, he was sure that communications from heaven did reach
the earth. Without such, the condition of man seemed to
him utterly dreary, inexplicable, hopeless. But these communications are disorderly interruptions of the course of
human life, even if they confer on it some of its chief
blessings. The Hebrew starts from the divine ground. He
does not want casual appearances to testify that God is
speaking to men. That He should not speak is for him
the perplexing anomaly. Life must cease, according to the
lessons which he had received from his childhood, if God
were withdrawn from His universe ; above all from the
creatures whom He had made in His image.

But there were times when it did seem as if He were
withdrawn from His universe ; when the children of the
Covenant seemed to have lost sight of Him ; when their
worship had been either turned to other objects, or had
become utterly hard and unreal, a punctual observance of
rites, not a living intercourse. At such times we do hear
of angel visits. They come to those who are beginning to
think that the world is deserted by its Deliverer, and given
over to its oppressors. They come seldom to the great of
the earth ; rather to peasants like Gideon, who are threshing

their wheat by the winepress when the Midianites are possessing the land of Israel, and the Israelites are bowing down to Baal. They are sent to break the yoke of some great superstition which has degraded the people. They are never imparted to any man that he may be exalted, but that he may understand God to be the God of his countrymen as much as himself; that he may be a witness to them of their true unchanging Lord; that he may stir them up to defy and mock those who pretend to be their lords. These are almost invariable characteristics of the angelic appearances in the Old Testament. The one which startled Zacharias, and sent him dumb to his house, will bear the test. It told him that he was the priest of a living God, not of one about whom he might read in a book; of a God who directed the minds of His creatures, not of one who merely demanded from them a certain quantity of sacrifice and incense.

We hear that, when the promise of the angel was fulfilled to Zacharias, when his child was actually born, when he had written on the table that its name was to be John, his tongue was loosed. He could not but sing, as his fathers had sung in every great crisis of their history. He had felt, no doubt, that there was some merit in his punctual observance of the commandments, some great distinction between him, the Levite, the descendant of Aaron, and the people who might not enter the Holy Place. Now, when the weight that had crushed his heart and his wife's heart has been removed, all such self-glorifying thoughts disappear. He speaks of the Lord God of Israel, who has visited and redeemed His people. The wonder of a common birth, an ordinary father's joy mingles in his thanksgiving with the belief that God is

accomplishing His purposes to the land, that there is to be
an unveiling of Him, such as all prophets had longed for.
The child is to be a prophet of the Highest, ' *to give knowledge of salvation unto His people by the remission of their
sins, through the tender mercy of our God ; whereby the day-
spring from on high hath visited us, to give light to them
that sit in darkness and in the shadow of death, to guide our
feet into the way of peace.*' See how impossible it is for
any true Israelite to think of God except as a Deliverer
of his nation and of mankind.

But there is another story in this chapter, the scenery of
which is altogether different. We are no longer in Jerusalem, amidst the worship in the holy Temple, amidst the
clouds of incense. We are in a despised city of Galilee,
in the house of a poor maiden. To her, too, we are told,
an angel comes, and thus he speaks : ' *Hail, thou that art
highly favoured: the Lord is with thee, blessed art thou among
women.*' To her he says : ' *Fear not, Mary: for thou hast
found favour with God.   And, behold, thou shalt conceive in
thy womb, and bring forth a son, and shalt call his name Jesus.
He shall be great, and shall be called the Son of the Highest:
and the Lord God shall give unto him the throne of his father
David : and he shall reign over the house of Jacob for ever ;
and of his kingdom there shall be no end.*' She is at first,
like Zacharias, *troubled at the angel's saying, and casts in
her mind what manner of salutation this should be.*   But
she receives it with awe and submission ; ' *Behold the hand-
maid of the Lord; be it unto me according to thy word.*'

The remark seems too obvious to be necessary, that we
have here the announcement of a King and a Kingdom.
But my object in these lectures is to fix your minds upon
those commonplaces in the Gospels, which we overlook, or

explain away, or change for some more refined notions of our own. I wish you to see that, at all events in the judgment of St. Luke, these names, Son of God and Son of David, are not introduced to prove a doctrine or establish a mission; that they are essential to the Gospel, as a Gospel; that it would have no significance apart from them. 'He is to reign over the House of Israel; of His 'kingdom there is to be no end;' are key-notes to all the subsequent history.

The Song of Mary, *when she rose with haste and came into the hill country of Judæa,* and had heard the salutation of Elizabeth, is the hymn at the birth of a King, as the one I have just spoken of is the hymn at the birth of a Prophet. It is the hymn for mothers, as that is the hymn for fathers; not the less the hymn for all mothers because the Virgin felt herself to be *the* mother of *the* Child; the mother in a more eminent sense than any other could claim to be. It is the hymn of the Jewish mother who feels that she cannot be merely that. The promise being fulfilled to Abraham and his seed, all generations of men must call her blessed.

The Life that is to come forth from her is a new life to herself. It raises her wholly out of herself. Her soul magnifies the Lord, her spirit rejoices in God her Saviour. A communion is opened between her and Heaven; she knows that she is not merely a child of earth. And yet she is most truly a child of earth. He '*hath regarded the low estate of His handmaiden.*' She has never understood her own nothingness so much as in this moment of exaltation; there has never been awakened in her such awe of the divine Majesty as now when she is brought so near to it. '*He that is mighty hath done to me great*

c 2

things, and holy is his Name.' And that which I pointed
out as characteristic of the other song is far more
characteristic of this. Instead of feeling more separate
from other creatures by reason of the honour that has
been put upon her, her deepest joy springs from the
sense of union with them; God's care for her is the
pledge of His care for them. *'His mercy is on them that
fear him, from generation to generation.'* All the greatness
is His; what she hopes for is the manifestation of His glory,
and the overthrow of those that exalt themselves into His
throne. *'He hath shewed strength with his arm; he hath
scattered the proud in the imagination of their hearts.'* There
speaks the true Israelite. The downfall of the powers
which men have worshipped to their own misery and
slavery—the manifestation of Him who alone has a right
to the worship of His creatures—this she hails as the
ultimate deliverance to the race. To her, as to Hannah
and every mother of the land in the days of old, the
mystery of birth, its feebleness and its glory, explains the
condition of man and the purpose of his Creator. *'He
hath put down the mighty from their seats, and exalted
them of low degree. He hath filled the hungry with good
things; and the rich he hath sent empty away.'* And she,
in the fullest sense, perceives, what others had perceived
in a lower sense, how the gift of the Child is the
witness of the permanence of the divine Word, so that
nothing which was assured to the times of old could fail of
its fulfilment in the times to come. *'He hath holpen his
servant Israel, in remembrance of his mercy; as he spake to
our fathers, to Abraham, and to his seed for ever.'*

In these hymns there is that union of the Old and New
Testaments, that contrast between them, which I thought

that St. Paul's fellow-worker would be more likely than most other men to recognise and to bring before us. A sense might be given to that remark which I should consider utterly false. It may be said that these hymns are the work of an artist who had a purpose of his own, who composed them to teach the world certain lessons which he deemed important. If they had been devised to express a certain sentiment, I do not believe they could have expressed that sentiment. If they had been written to denote the passage from one period to another, I am sure they would not have helped us to understand that passage. Artificial compositions—(even if they are not dishonest as these must have been)—compositions with a set theme—always fail to make the impression which is left on us by the outpouring of a heart at some great moment of its grief or joy. The actual sufferer, the actual rejoicer, is the spokesman of human beings; the sophist and rhetorician vainly try to expound what human beings might feel or ought to feel. The song of Zacharias is emphatically the song of a man whose tongue is unloosed; who for the first time has entered into the meaning of the books which he has been reading since his childhood, of the services in which he has been engaged ever since he became a priest. A speech may be invented with tolerable success for a general on the eve of a battle, though such as have really come down to us stir the blood far more; but the mimicry of *this* kind of feeling must have been odious and contemptible. I know not where you could find the stamp of fraud more clear and in-effaceable than on a document which attempted it. If the words of Zacharias have lasted to our day, and have been accepted by men of different races as vital and true words—as words which speak to and speak forth the human heart within them—I cannot persuade myself that *they* bear that stamp of insincerity.

The Virgin's song has endured a severer test in the ages through which it has been transmitted to us. It has lived on—it still lives on—through an adoration of her which makes her adoration of Him who did to her great things, her profound lowliness, her identification of herself with the race which was to call her blessed, the strangest contradictions. If it has borne a continual witness against these profanations—if they have not been able to change its letter or its spirit—how much may it have done to keep alive, in a multitude of hearts that have stooped to the most dangerous sentimentalism, even to the vulgarest idolatry, the belief of a great Head of humanity, whom she was permitted to bring forth—of an Everlasting Father, whom she might dare, in Him, to approach. No cold prosaic words, nothing else than a lyrical rapture, could have been a genuine expression of her spirit, could have become an expression for the true spirit of Christendom during eighteen centuries.

I believe, my friends, that if that song has effected something for mankind, its greatest work yet remains to be effected. First, I claim it for the wives and mothers of England. Let those who bind themselves to what they think a holier state—a state more like that of the Virgin—use it as devoutly as they will. I do not grudge it them. I earnestly trust that they will meditate upon it, and enter into it far more deeply than they have ever done. The correction of whatever is mischievous in their theories or their practices lies in it, not in our protests against them. But those who have accepted another condition—who have believed that God called them to it, and sanctifies it—should understand how *the* birth hallows every birth, with what dignity *the* Mother invests all maternity; how her joy is the warrant and example of all joy; how it links the infant that blesses any one household to humanity.

Secondly. Since this century is the one in which this word *humanity* is most spoken of, in which humanity is becoming an object of worship, let us who sing this song consider whether we have ever accepted it in its full sense —whether, if we did, it might not deliver us from the perils of this idolatry, and might not enable us to realize the truth which the idolatry conceals. Is not Mary's song a witness against the disposition of humanity to exalt itself, or to exalt any one of the creatures who share it, into the throne of heaven? Is not her song a witness *for* the redemption and glory of humanity in the person of its Lord? Has not the Church herself fallen into the error which is now reaching its climax in those who renounce the Church? Has she ever fully proclaimed the principle which might subvert that error? Has she ever confessed, as the Israelite did, that God glorifies Himself by raising to a divine life the humanity which, without Him, must sink into utter death.

Lastly. If this song may help us to look on the lowest creatures we see on earth with a reverence which we have never paid them yet, if it should make every child an object of awe to us, may it not teach us also how to think of those whom we remember to-day as having passed away from the earth? They have shared in the adoration which has been bestowed on the Mother of their Lord. Did they not share with her—*do* they not share with her—

that sense of a low estate which God regarded? Are they not a communion, because they give all glory to their Divine Head, and take none to themselves? Shall we not claim our places in their communion just in proportion as we magnify Him—as His Spirit enables our spirit to rejoice in God their Saviour and ours?[1]

[1] Preached on All Saints' Day.

LECTURE III.

BIRTH AND CHILDHOOD OF THE KING.

St. Luke II. 13, 14.

And suddenly there was with the angel a multitude of the heavenly host praising God, and saying, Glory to God in the highest, and on earth peace, good will toward men.

I.—(1) The Birth of Jesus is the first subject which comes before us in this chapter. That He was born at Nazareth, not, as St. Luke says, at Bethlehem, is the opinion of most who suppose the Evangelists to be the biographers of a great and favourite Teacher, an eminent Galilean Reformer. It is difficult to understand how they could arrive at any other conclusion. If Jesus was not a King, in any real sense of the word, the notion that He was born in the city of David must have been a fancy of those who supposed Him to possess that honour. There is no need of argument to prove that the two beliefs stand or fall together. The attempt to sustain the credit of the place when that which gives it all its fitness is gone must be a futile one. Therefore, I conceive that modern critics may reckon upon an easy triumph over those who hold the language and adopt the mode of thinking which prevails among us.

If we separate the Saviour from the King, or use that last title in some metaphorical sense—even though we suppose it may acquire a real sense in some future age—we must not be surprised if other men draw the natural inference from such premises; if, the substance of the evangelical message having disappeared, they say that its accidents cannot remain. I apprehend it is better on all accounts that Nazareth should receive the honour heretofore bestowed on Bethlehem, unless we confess the reason for which it was bestowed. We shall sink into a poor rabbinical habit of mind if we ground our opinion that Jesus was the Christ upon the concurrence of his birthplace with some supposed prediction. St. John has taught us, in his seventh chapter, to what that slavish feeling about the letter of a prophecy leads, when its purpose has been overlooked. The officers who were sent by the chief priests to take Jesus, came back without Him, saying, '*Never man spake like this man.*' The Pharisees could not listen to such poor evidence; '*Out of Galilee ariseth no prophet,*' was an all satisfactory reason why they should not listen to Him who was called a Galilean. Jesus Himself never appealed to His birth at Bethlehem as any proof of His mission. Those who would not receive Him for what He did and for what He was, could not have received Him if the proofs of His descent from David had been ever so overwhelming.

A mere legend, doubtless, this account of the journey to Bethlehem, and the birth at Bethlehem, must be, if Jesus were *not* the Person whom the preachers of the Gospel proclaimed Him to be, if He were *not* the King whose appearing fulfilled the expectation of previous ages and explained their history. And yet, even readers who have wholly cast off the notion that He was this, must, I

think, discover something curiously simple, curiously
unlike the style of ordinary legends, in such a record as
this :—

*'And it came to pass in those days, that there went out a
decree from Cæsar Augustus, that all the world should be
taxed. (And this taxing was first made when Cyrenius was
governor of Syria.) And all went to be taxed, every one into
his own city. And Joseph also went up from Galilee, out of
the city of Nazareth, into Judæa, unto the city of David,
which is called Bethlehem ; (because he was of the house and
lineage of David :) To be taxed with Mary his espoused wife,
being great with child. And so it was, that, while they were
there, the days were accomplished that she should be delivered.
And she brought forth her firstborn son, and wrapped him in
swaddling clothes, and laid him in a manger : because there
was no room for them in the inn.'*

There is no grand reason, you see, given why Mary and
Joseph should go to Judæa. The angel who is said to have
announced the coming birth does not appear again to tell
them that they must travel, since otherwise the Son of
David will not be connected with His ancestral dwelling-
place. They go because every one else is going. A decree
of the Cæsar obliges the man to register himself in the
village, whatever it is, to which he belongs. It may be
an awkward contrivance—as a modern writer says it is
—to make the conception of royalty fit with the facts.
Assuredly the critic, or any ingenious man in this day,
could have invented a much better tale. And if forgers
of that day had, as he supposes, an unlimited command of
supernatural incidents, these poor peasants might have
been transported by any kind of celestial machinery to the
spot in which they were required to be. Nor can we doubt

that a Frenchman now, or an Oriental then, would have
introduced such an event with becoming pomp. If it was
part of the scheme that the birth should be humble, he
would have taken pains that we should observe that part
of it. There would have been starts of surprise, exclama-
tions at the stooping of the Highest of all to the lowest
place. Here is nothing of the kind. Events, the belief
of which has affected all the art and speculation of the
most civilized nations in the modern world, are recorded
in fewer words, with less effort, than an ordinary historian, or the writer of a newspaper, would deem suitable
to the account of the most trivial transaction. Such
marvellous associations have clung for centuries to these
verses, that it is hard to realize how absolutely naked they
are of all ornament. We are obliged to read them again
and again to assure ourselves that they really do set forth
what we call the great miracle of the world.

If, on the other hand, the mind of the Evangelist was
possessed by the conviction that he was not recording a
miracle which had interrupted the course of history, and
deranged the order of human life, but was telling of a
divine act which explained the course of history and
restored the order of human life, one can very well account
for his calmness ; if that conviction was a true one, we
might account for the impression which his brief sentences
have made on later ages. That the poll tax of the first
Emperors should be the instrument of bringing forth the
King before whom the Cæsars were to bow, would then
seem one of those incidents in the drama of the universe
which discover a God who is not suddenly interfering to
untie knots that are too difficult for human hands, but
who is directing all the course of the action, from the

beginning to the catastrophe; not crushing the wills of the persons in the drama, but leading them on, by methods which we cannot see or conjecture, to fill their places in it. And the birth in the manger would be felt, not as an embellishment of the narrative, but as a part of the revelation. The King, who proves His title and His divinity by stooping to the lowest condition of His subjects, is brought into direct contrast with him who had risen by intrigues, proscriptions, and the overthrow of an ancient order, to be hailed as the Deliverer and highest God of the earth.

(2) Taking the first words in this sense, Christendom has adopted that which follows as the true commentary upon them.

'*And there were in the same country shepherds abiding in the field, keeping watch over their flock by night. And lo, the angel of the Lord came upon them, and the glory of the Lord shone round about them : and they were sore afraid. And the angel said unto them, Fear not : for, behold, I bring you good tidings of great joy, which shall be to all people. For unto you is born this day in the city of David a Saviour, which is Christ the Lord. And this shall be a sign unto you; Ye shall find the babe wrapped in swaddling clothes, lying in a manger. And suddenly there was with the angel a multitude of the heavenly host praising God, and saying, Glory to God in the highest, and on earth peace, good will toward men. And it came to pass, as the angels were gone away from them into heaven, the shepherds said one to another, Let us now go even unto Bethlehem, and see this thing which is come to pass, which the Lord hath made known unto us. And they came with haste, and found Mary, and Joseph, and the babe lying in a manger. And when they had*

seen it, they made known abroad the saying which was told
them concerning this child.   And all they that heard it won-
dered at those things which were told them by the shepherds.
But Mary kept all these things, and pondered them in her
heart.'

The question concerning these Gospels is frequently set
before us in this way.   Are we to go on believing in a
supernatural record, when we might reduce it to nature
and common sense by leaving out certain incidents which
have been thrown in to give it greater effect?   Why, for
instance, not regard this old story of the shepherds, however much beauty there may be in it, however much it may
have taken hold of human hearts, as merely one of the
Arcadian stories which are to be found in other countries
of the world as well as Judæa; all having, no doubt, a
certain value; all, in some degree, serving to refine and
adorn human nature?

My answer is this.   The supernatural did, as you say,
cleave to all the stories of the ancient world.   To rob
them of their supernatural element is to destroy them.
And no part of these stories is so striking, or has had so
much influence over men, as that which speaks of higher
beings descending to hold intercourse with the lower, to
teach them and to do them good.   These stories bear a
witness to the hearts of men everywhere of that which
they need, in One whom they can reverence and trust, be
He ever so far above them.   It is a witness also that,
without beings above them whom they *could* reverence
and trust, their lives must be poor and dreary.   It is
equally true, that men at a certain time began to think,
'We have invented these stories for ourselves; we have,
in fact, created our gods.'   This conviction had spread

widely, had penetrated deeply in the days of Augustus Cæsar. It was expressed or muttered by philosophers; it was *felt* by the priests who were performing the services of the gods, and labouring to uphold their reputation. And at last comes the result of the opinion. A man— a general of armies, is recognised as the real King of kings and Lord of lords. The gods are under the protection of the Emperors. There you have the supernatural in one of its senses: a divine machinery grounded on a human foundation, upholding a human tyranny. I demand, Is there any other sense of the supernatural? Is there *that* sense of it which all those legends you speak of betoken? If that is merely an imagination, this Roman Empire is the exposure of the imagination. It adopts all the old fictions of the world into itself; it uses them all in its own service. You do not lose the supernatural, you have it everywhere, conscious of its own falsehood, always begetting fresh falsehoods. If that other sense pointed to a truth, has the truth come forth? Has the Divine shown itself to be not the mere invention of humanity, but the ground of humanity? Take the instance before us. Suppose we could have, not Arcadian shepherds, but Jewish shepherds, men of the people, with all their feelings, and sufferings, and ignorance. Suppose it were announced to them that a King was actually born in the city of David, who was not to mix with them for a few hours or days, but who was to establish *Glory to God in the highest, peace on earth, good will to men;* that is to say, who was to be exactly the reverse of the human divinity. Suppose this; you would have exactly what has been the belief of Christendom, what vindicates and purifies the dreams of heathens. Shall we not be flooded with legends, with

legends serving to support an unnatural tyranny by supernatural help, if we let this belief go ? If we hold it fast,
if we enter into it much more thoroughly than we have
ever entered into it, may we not banish the legends, and
shake the tyranny ?

II. The songs of Zacharias and of Mary exhibited a
contrast between the old world and the new, on which
I supposed that St. Luke would especially like to dwell.
The story of our Lord's circumcision and of the purification
of the Virgin, which is found only in this Gospel, has,
I conceive, a similar import.

'*And when eight days were accomplished for the circum-
cising of the child, his name was called Jesus, which was so
named of the angel before he was conceived in the womb.
And when the days of her purification according to the law
of Moses were accomplished, they brought him to Jerusalem,
to present him to the Lord : (As it is written in the law of
the Lord, Every male that openeth the womb shall be called
holy to the Lord:) And to offer a sacrifice according to that
which is said in the law of the Lord, A pair of turtle-doves,
or two young pigeons.*'

Here is a punctual compliance with all the terms and
conditions of the Law. It is assumed by the other Evangelists : it is carefully noted by St. Luke. That which is
to be superseded must be first observed. He that is to be
the King of men must be first shown to be a true Israelite.
He is declared to be holy to the Lord by the same rite
which declared the son of every Jewish mother to be
holy to the Lord. And this mother undergoes the same
purification which was appointed for every other mother.
Most carefully are we taught that neither child or mother
claims our reverence by taking an *exceptional* position.

Both *fulfil* that which others have done and been imperfectly. So the verses which follow acquire their full force. '*And, behold, there was a man in Jerusalem, whose name was Simeon ; and the same man was just and devout, waiting for the consolation of Israel : and the Holy Ghost was upon him. And it was revealed unto him by the Holy Ghost, that he should not see death before he had seen the Lord's Christ. And he came by the Spirit into the temple : and when the parents brought in the child Jesus, to do for him after the custom of the law, then took he him up in his arms, and blessed God, and said, Lord, now lettest thou thy servant depart in peace, according to thy word : for mine eyes have seen thy salvation. Which thou hast prepared before the face of all people ; A light to lighten the Gentiles, and the glory of thy people Israel. And Joseph and his mother marvelled at those things which were spoken of him.*'

Had there been the least exemption from the Law claimed for Jesus, the old doctor of the Law would not have seen in Him the Christ for whom he had been waiting. He had been longing for one who should Himself obey the Law, and enable all who honoured it to obey it. The King who should keep the Law in its spirit—the King who should impart a Spirit to His subjects that they might keep it—the King who should be shown not to be only the King of Israel but the King of men—this was He whom the heart of Simeon had recognised while reading the Prophets ; this was He whom he had learnt must come in great humility, if He was to be the consolation of all who were suffering and hoping.

The *Nunc Dimittis*, like the song of Zacharias and the song of Mary, has become a part of our worship. We hear it and join in it without much recollection of the

D

occasion upon which it was spoken. But that occasion gives it all its force as a living commentary on the New Testament; that makes it so beautiful and calm a vesper hymn. It is this occasion which teaches us how the Lord's Christ is manifested to any human being; how only an inward illumination can make the sacred letters intelligible even to those who study them most faithfully. It tells us that all Law and Prophecy are nothing till a Person is seen through them, till the shout of a king is heard amidst the thunders of Sinai, and the low wailings of the seer. It tells us how impossible it was that those thunders should really be recognised as the voice of the Lord God, merciful and gracious, slow to anger and of great mercy, till He was revealed in One who delighted to do the Will of God; how impossible it was that those prophetical wailings could be satisfied till One appeared who was the Light of the Gentiles as well as the Glory of Israel. Hard it was for an old Hillel doctor not to think that the glory of Israel must involve the darkness and downfall of the Gentiles. Through this Infant the truth flashed upon him that there must be a reconciliation of both; that He was the Reconciler. He would accomplish the meaning of circumcision. He would bestow that purification which the Jew and the Gentile needed equally, by which both might rise to be men. At the same time there is in all prophecy a bitter mixed with the sweet, a sorrow which the joy cannot quench. Simeon has known too much of himself, too much of his countrymen, not to perceive that one who should work out the Redemption he looked for would stir the heart of the nation to its depths, would bring out all its fierceness and evil as well as its good. ' *Behold, this child is set for the fall and rising again of many in Israel; and for a sign which shall be spoken against.'* And then turning to the mother, who is musing on these sayings, he says, ' *Yea, a sword shall pierce through thy own soul also, that the thoughts of many hearts may be revealed.'* Wonderful words, deeper than he could fathom even when his inspiration was fullest and brightest; deeper than we can fathom; words which fulfilled themselves in that day and have been fulfilling themselves in every day since.

The figure of the widow of fourscore years who departed not from the Temple, but served God with fasting and prayer day and night, as she comes at that moment and gives thanks, completes the picture of the circumcision, and combines—as in the Church they always have been and always must be combined—the man and the woman in the same retrospection and the same hope.

III. I can say nothing to you on the third subject—the appearance of the boy of twelve years old in the Temple—which has not been said with a life and power that no words save those of Scripture can reach, in a picture with which most of you will be familiar. The blessing of such earnest studies is that they bring a person before us, and remind us that it is with Christ as a Person, not with any discourses concerning Him, that we have to do. The Artist, too, has felt the transition from the old world to the new, to which the Evangelist points so often. Behind that house made with hands, one is coming forth which is eternal in the heavens; a Father's House in the fullest sense. Behind the weary interpreters of the Law is coming forth that Interpreter who is as yet only hearing and asking questions, but such questions as reveal to those who tried to answer them, secrets in themselves

and in the Divine mind which they had only dreamed
of, or never dreamed of before. He is still the boy ; not
restless in that state, not grasping at any of the rights
and faculties of manhood ; but on His gaze an abyss of
light is opening, and He makes even those around Him
feel a little of the awe which possesses Him. He is the
boy ready to obey those who are set over Him upon earth,
but who must be ever in communion with a Father,
different from any parent who asserts a claim over Him
below.

There the story closes. When it opens again it is to
tell us how that Father was preparing men for the manifestation of His Son ; how He did declare Him by this
name. I shall not anticipate that great subject. I only
desire to remind you that till this veil is withdrawn,
till the voice is heard in the Baptism, we are only in
the vestibule of the Temple. How grand the vestibule
is, how suitable it is to that which lies beyond it, I
have wished to show you. But the Annunciation, with
all its awe and its tenderness, the songs of Mary and
Zacharias and Simeon, though they have wrought themselves into the life of the wisest and the humblest people
on the earth for 1800 years, even the birth in the manger,
even the songs of the angels, even the looks and the
questionings of the Divine boy among the doctors, are but
the preludes to the Gospel of the Son in whom the Father
was well pleased, to His baptism with the Spirit and with
fire.

LECTURE IV.

THE KINGDOM OF HEAVEN AT HAND.

St. Luke III. 15, 16.

And as the people were in expectation, and all men mused in their hearts of John, whether he were the Christ, or not ; John answered, saying unto them all, I indeed baptize you with water ; but one mightier than I cometh, the latchet of whose shoes I am not worthy to unloose: he shall baptize you with the Holy Ghost and with fire.

In the homage of the infant John to the infant Jesus, painters have striven to express the contrast between them. The Evangelists present this contrast to us quite differently. St. Luke indicated it in his narrative of the two births ; the full declaration of it is in the words I have just read to you. They correspond almost literally with some which you will find in the third chapter of St. Matthew. They are in substance adapted by St. Mark in his opening chapter. I do not complain of the painters for departing from the text of Scripture, and adopting traditions which had become part of the oral teaching of Christendom. Every great picture has helped to elevate these traditions, to bring out their moral significance, to suggest the study of the books which have been darkened by them. Other influences have been, and are

more pernicious, than any which have proceeded from
artists ; but their works, especially when they have been
of a soft and sentimental character, have contributed to a
result which they could not foresee. Together with the
acts of devotion which have been directed to the sacred
heart of Jesus, with the society which has profaned that
name, with all the books and discourses of Romanists or of
Protestants which have separated it from the Christ, they
have led us to think that the difference between the
Baptist and Him whose shoes he was not worthy to stoop
down and unloose, was the difference between a certain
rough human excellence and a certain transcendent super-
human grace and sweetness. The Lord Jesus is set before
us not exactly as a Divine Person, not exactly as a human
person. Some qualities, which we suppose to be divine, are
mixed confusedly with some which we suppose to be
human. There is a certain amount of awe awakened by
the first—an awe which interferes with sympathy. There is
a certain amount of sympathy awakened by the last—a
sympathy which diminishes the awe. We feel such a state
of mind to be one that we cannot retain ; we accept one of
two alternatives. The image which we had tried to bring
near us recedes into an immeasurable distance ; we are
afraid to think of it ; practically, we dismiss it from our
minds. Or else it is stripped of all that made it wonderful
and adorable to our childhood. It shrinks into the form of
one whose acts we can easily measure and interpret, to
whom we attribute whatever of moral excellence does
not too much throw our own into the shade, to whom
we at last impute an untruthfulness which we acknowledge would be disgraceful in any teacher of our century.
Very painful it is to describe this habit of thinking

simply and distinctly. But it must be described, because it is a prevalent one, and is likely to be more prevalent; because we who preach the Gospel are in a very great degree answerable for it; because it should teach us to consider our ways and to repent of much for which we have given ourselves credit. If it does produce that repentance in us, we may be led back to the direct statements of the Evangelists, and through them to the belief which is contained in our Creeds; the belief not in a half-God and half-man, but in One who is very God, and therefore very Man; the perfect image of the Father, and for that reason the image after which we are created. What healthiness and freedom of mind, what deliverance from mawkishness and superstition, what a standard of morality for ourselves, what mercy to others, we should gain if we did heartily receive that old faith, I think we none of us know, though God may make our children know it. We and they may have to learn another lesson first; that there is a path to the most grovelling and the most antiquated forms of superstition and idolatry—to the most utter confusion of truth and falsehood—through those attempts to divide Jesus from the King and the Son of God, which many regard as the greatest achievements of modern refinement and discrimination.

You will see at once that the language of the text leads us to consider John as a messenger of God, great only in that character, great only as he acknowledges his calling and girds himself to the fulfilment of it. You will see that they lead us to think, not of some man born in Bethlehem, or in Nazareth, but of the Christ, the anointed of God, who was to bestow the Spirit with which He was anointed, upon men. Who this Christ was, no Evangelist

tells us that John the Baptist guessed. St. John introduces Him, saying in direct words that he did *not* know. He knew what the office of the Christ was ; what his was not. He could prepare the way for Him, by preaching the baptism of repentance for the remission of sins. That baptism, not John's wisdom, was to manifest the Christ to Israel.

Of this preparation for the Son of God, St. Matthew and St. Mark speak nearly in the same terms as St. Luke. Both quote a passage from the 40th chapter of Isaiah, as being fulfilled in John; St. Luke quotes more than the others. Now the question is often asked, Did Isaiah mean John the Baptist by *the voice crying in the wilderness ?* or if not, were his words distorted by the Evangelists from their right and natural signification ? Are they making a forced application of an old sentence ? I have answered the question in another case. John the Baptist, though a contemporary of Jesus, and even a kinsman of His mother, did not know Him as the Christ, if he knew Him at all. But he had a clear apprehension of what the Christ must be. This was the illumination of a prophet, this was that which had been given at sundry times and in divers manners to the prophets before him. The vision dawned upon them gradually, of one who must be the perfect King of others, who must be the perfect image of God. *When* He should be declared to men, the older prophets could not say ; *how* He should be declared to men they learnt by degrees through their own trials and the trials of their land ; they could announce the tidings as they were needed. But they were sure that if He were to be fully manifested in the ages to come, He was living then ; that He was manifesting Himself through imperfect

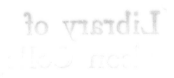

men, kings, priests, or prophets; that He was manifesting Himself through the judgments upon them when
they failed of their duty. And Isaiah knew in himself, knew in his countrymen, what hindered the per-
ception of this true King, what kept men from confessing
Him, and expecting a fuller discovery of Him. Some
were self-exalted, some were desponding of the Divine
goodness, some were finding the path of life very tor-
tuous and intricate, some were finding it very painful
to the feet. They could not understand how God could
have devised such ways for creatures whom He loved.
What must one do who should come in the name of
the Lord to prepare for a revelation of Him? He must
show that God was bringing down hills and exalting the
valleys, was making straight the crooked ways, was making
the rough ways smooth. He must show it by more than
words. He must have a message to all manner of people,
which all manner of people should feel to be a divine one,
and which each should feel was adapted to him and his
troubles. ' *The glory of the Lord*'—this is the portion of
the passage which the other Evangelists have omitted and
which St. Luke has preserved, ' *The glory of the Lord shall
be revealed, and all flesh shall see it together.*' How that
was to be, how all flesh could bear such an unveiling,
the prophet might not know. But this and nothing less
than this could answer to his sense of the deep necessity
of his race, and of the Divine purpose towards it. So far
the vision is clear and full as to the nature of the message, but it contains no limitations of space or time, no
intimation of one more than another who should accomplish it. Would it not be right to say that *every* prophet
must in his own time and in his own place act in conformity

with this divine announcement? There could be no account
of his functions so vivid and so accurate.

There is, however, one point in the description which
appears to be more local. ' *The voice is heard crying in the
wilderness.*' How often this incident would be repeated,
how often the preacher who spoke to people concerning
their God, would be literally as well as morally a speaker
in the wilderness, it is needless to inquire. The divine
impulse which led John to choose it as his appointed
place will not have been less divine, less inward, if it
gathered strength from the study of this very passage;
whether it did or not, there was something entirely fitting
in the place to the mind and object of the speaker. And so
without the least debating about the amount of foresight
which Isaiah possessed, without the least caring whether
he intended this application or not, the Evangelist could
say, ' Here is, in the strictest, completest sense, the *fulfilment* of the prophet's sense. He who knows the end from
the beginning, and has ordained words for our use, must
mean us to connect these words with this event, to interpret
them by it, and it by them.'

And surely, if by any act or by any speech, valleys
could be exalted, hills could be made low, crooked ways
could be made straight, rough ways smooth, the preaching
of the baptism of repentance for the remission of sins was
that act and that speech. All the children of Abraham,
without exception—the religious Pharisee and the harlot,
the most wise Sadducee and the most ignorant handicrafts-
man, the proudest Jewish patriot and the publican who was
profiting by the Roman tribute—were addressed as God's
people, were told that He was calling them to repent of
sins which separated them from Him, were all alike assured,

by a significant token, that He sent away their sins. What a universal message, yet what an individual message! It meant nothing till it found the particular man with his own particular burthen pressing upon his conscience. Then it said to him, ' He who knows of that burthen, He who knows how it came to thee, invites thee to cast it off. Thou mayest confess it. Thou mayest be delivered from it. Thou mayest go forth a free man.' Had the Pharisee anything to confess? Perhaps not; he was satisfied; he was better and holier than others. In that superiority and holiness he must abide. If that was all he wanted he might enjoy it. And then assuredly he would not see the salvation of God, for he would have nothing to be saved from. If he *did* confess that his self-glorification had kept him from God, that it was a great sin, a heavy burthen, it would be taken from him ; *the hill would be made low*. Had the harlot anything to confess? She might think she had nothing; she had fallen into that miserable condition through circumstances, through the faults of others, she could not charge it against herself. Then the burthen must still be borne. But if she confessed it, she might be set as free from her load as the Pharisee from his ; she, like him, might see the salvation of God. *The valley would be exalted.* Did the Sadducee see anything at all strange or crooked in his own course, or in the course of the world? Perhaps not, perhaps he had a theory which would account for everything; he wanted no straighter way than that which he was in. But if he did, if he found that his wit was at fault, if he owned himself a fool, that confession might bring him to see what he had supposed was a mere fantasy. He might see the salvation of God, and so his blessing would be

like that of the ignorant man whom he despised. He,
bewailing his ignorance, confessing that he could see in
what path he was to walk, might have *the crooked way made
straight.* And the weariness and despondency of those
who complained of weariness and despondency, might be
taken away by Him who bids His creatures be of a good
heart. *Their rough way might be made smooth.*

Thus, the message had all the qualities which prophetic
message could have. It bore witness of its origin from
One who knew what is in man. It appealed to all equally.
It appealed to each man by himself. It went home to that
in each which wanted remission and purification. It did
its work. It was at once levelling and exalting. St. Matthew and St. Mark are so busy with their main subject,
'*Prepare the way of the Lord,*' that they can think of no
other. For St. Luke, whose mind is occupied with the Gospel
to the Gentiles—to all mankind—the clause '*All flesh shall
see the salvation of God,*' was very important; it blended
itself with the previous sentence; he could not divide them.

But if the message 'Repent, and turn to God, who
puts away sins, who sets the conscience free,' is a blessed
message, what are we to say of this '*Then said he to the
multitude that came forth to be baptized of him, O generation of vipers, who hath warned you to flee from the wrath to
come ?*' They are certainly very unlike the previous words.
And yet the same man must have uttered them both.
Their resemblance is inward and essential; the opposition
is on the surface. Every prophet who had asked the
children of Abraham to turn to the God of their fathers
had asked them to turn from an idolatry and a slavery
which were destroying them. Every prophet had said
that idolatry and slavery would infallibly bring down

curses upon their land. In the form of invasion from some enemy, above all from the great Babylonian Empire, they would experience the misery of having sold their hearts to vain things, of having trusted in that which would give them no courage to resist, or fortitude to bear. Their horses and chariots would not save them from those who had a far greater multitude of chariots and horses. When these were their confidence they must feel their own pettiness; the enemy would laugh them to scorn. About the poor divided, sect-ridden, money-worshipping Jews of John's age the clouds were gathering close and thick. An empire mightier than any Chaldean Empire was trampling upon them—might in a little time extinguish them. The thought of this coming wrath was pressing intensely upon the mind of the preacher. This was the issue to which the pride of the Pharisees and the Sadducees was leading! This was the horror which the whole country would have to bear because the sins of its rulers had infected every part of it! In St. Matthew the speech of John is directed expressly to the opposing sects who were to be the ruin of the commonwealth. St. Luke speaks as if it had been addressed to the people at large. Both rulers and people were, no doubt, warned of that which would affect both. Rulers and people were asked alike to cast away the abominations which were bringing on the catastrophe. And of rulers and people it was equally true that if they merely came to the baptism because they were afraid of a wrath to come, they would remain a generation of vipers; that if they came to be delivered from sins which oppressed them, they would have the poison taken out of them—they would receive remission of their sins.

Therefore he bade them one and all bring forth fruits
worthy of that repentance which they had professed.
God wished to tear out their sins by the roots. He
was not striking at some forms of evil, but at the great
mother sin; at their trust in themselves, at their distrust
of Him. These had been the causes of all misery to
their forefathers; these were the causes of their misery.
They were saying to themselves, ' *We have Abraham to
our father.*' They were boasting of their difference from
other people. Cunningest, vilest form of infidelity!
Denial of the God of Abraham, under pretence of honour
to Abraham! Let them know that God was able of those
stones—of what seemed the hardest, most impenetrable
materials—to raise up children to Abraham.

If the message of John, as delivered by St. Luke, is
more general in its call and in its warnings than that
which we read elsewhere, it is also more minute and
definite. It is St. Luke who tells us that the soldiers, the
publicans, and the people at large asked John what they
should do—what fruits of repentance he demanded of
them; and that his answers in each case referred to their
ordinary duties and temptations. They were not to forsake their work that they might serve God more punctually
and faithfully,—that would be a distrust and denial of
Him. They were to serve Him *in* their work; they were
to avoid those things which they knew were inconsistent
with fidelity to it; they were to do the acts of simple
kindliness and good neighbourhood which belonged to
their position, and which came in their way. The
preacher in the wilderness, whose raiment was of camel's
hair, and whose meat was locusts and wild honey,
attached no worth to such costume or such food. They

were suitable to him; he recommended them to no one
else.   Soldiers and tax-gatherers were to be soldiers and
tax-gatherers still.

And then follow the words I have taken for my text.   I
have spoken to you already of their main import.   They
announced One who would be endowed with a divine
Spirit, and who would impart that Spirit.   They declared
this to be the distinction between Him and John, between
Him and all other prophets.   He who was not able to bestow this gift was not the King and Deliverer their fathers
had looked for.   He was not the King and Deliverer who
could raise them out of their low estate, or who could
confer any rights or blessings on mankind.

Strange is it to think of the contrasts which men have
drawn between John and Jesus, as if the first were merely
a severe preacher, and the last were all tolerance and pity;
and then to read this description.   '*Whose fan is in his
hand, and he will throughly purge his floor, and will gather
the wheat into the garner, but will burn up the chaff with fire
unquenchable.*'   Yet was it not such an one as this that
the people of Palestine wanted; one who could look into
the heart of their society, into the heart of each man, and
burn up its evils, and burn up *his* evils?   One who could
kindle a new and divine life within them?   Would anything less than this divine fire, than this divine Spirit,
have sufficed for their renovation?   My friends, will anything less than this divine fire, this divine Spirit, suffice
for our renovation?   Will it avail us to talk of the meek
and lowly Jesus?   Do we not know that we may talk of
Him, and think ourselves much better for talking of Him,
and may boast of our superiority to people who do not
know Him, till all meekness and gentleness depart from

us—till we become like the Jews, who said, ' *We have
Abraham to our father ?*' Will any soft, sentimental faith
purge out the sectarianism and the money-worship from our
English nation, from our English church ?   Must there not
be One with a fan in His hand, to accomplish for us what
no outward baptism, no preaching of repentance, has been
able to accomplish ? Is there such an One ? I think there
is, for I accept this as a true sentence. ' *Now when the people
were baptized, it came to pass, that Jesus also being baptized
and praying, the heaven was opened, and the Holy Ghost
descended in a bodily shape like a dove upon him, and a voice
came from heaven, which said, Thou art my beloved Son ; in
thee am I well pleased.*'

Here I find the commencement of that Kingdom of
Heaven which John declared to be at hand. Here is
the revelation of a Name which had been implied in
every revelation, but which had never yet been spoken.
He who is and was and is to come, is never forgotten ;
but *the Father* is discovered in the Baptism. The Word
who said, ' *Let there be light, and there was light,*' is never
lost sight of.   But this Baptism declares *a Son* who is to
do nothing of Himself, who is to show forth the will
whence all blessing and restoration proceed.   And the
Baptism reveals the *Spirit,* not as moving on the face
of the waters, but as possessing the whole heart and
mind of a man, as directing the thought and purposes of
a man, as uniting the highest rule with the most perfect obedience.   All that follows is the living exposition
of Christ's baptism.

LECTURE V.

THE TEMPTATION OF THE KING.

St. Luke IV. 13.

And when the devil had ended all his temptation, he departed from him for a season.

THE story of the Baptism of Jesus is followed, in this Gospel, by a genealogy ascending to Adam. He who has been declared to be the Son of God, we are reminded is emphatically the Son of Man. He is connected not merely with the family of Abraham, though His descent is traced through that. He is marked out as the Head of the race. If the ordinary succession from father to son has been interrupted, in His case, to assert a higher principle, to denote the express relation of the Lord of man to God, that succession has not been dishonoured. It has acquired a new sacredness from the interruption. Each birth into this world has a dignity which it must want, if the message at the Baptism was a fiction. If you dwell on this use of the genealogy, and compare it with the words of St. Paul, which must have been so familiar to St. Luke, respecting the first and the second Adam, you will not, I think, be disposed to occupy yourselves with minute questions about special links which may appear or may be wanting in the series. The discovery that there are difficulties in it which we cannot explain, has, I doubt

E

not, been of great use, in forcing us to seek more for the sense and purpose of the Divine narratives. Whilst we are slaves to the letter, as I shall often have occasion to show you in these lectures, the force of the letter escapes us; we continually pass over or pervert the plainest and broadest statements. To emancipate us from this slavery, to make us honest students of God's Revelations, to give us some adequate feeling of their grandeur, He may use many methods. That of confounding our ingenuity, and of obliging us to see inconsistencies which we cannot account for, is perhaps the one which humbles us most, and therefore for which we have most cause to be thankful. At all events, I have no solutions to offer of any difficulties which have been raised about this list of names; if I had, I hope I should not trouble you with them, knowing that you are busy men, and have not time for trifles.

It is quite otherwise with the next passage in this record. That, I believe, you need ask no leisure to understand. Work—the commonest work—will interpret it better than leisure. You have tests by which you can try what I say of the Temptation. I trust you will apply those tests strictly, that I may not fritter away, by any theories of mine, what you and all people require for the practice of every day.

'*And Jesus, being full of the Holy Ghost, returned from Jordan, and was led by the Spirit into the wilderness, being forty days tempted of the devil. And in those days he did eat nothing: and when they were ended, he afterward hungered. And the devil said unto him, If thou be the Son of God, command this stone that it be made bread. And Jesus answered him, saying, It is written, That man shall not live by bread alone, but by every word of God. And the devil, taking him up into an high mountain, shewed unto him all the kingdoms of the world in a moment of time. And the devil said unto him, All this power will I give thee, and the glory of them : for that is delivered unto me ; and to whomsoever I will I give it. If thou, therefore, wilt worship me, all shall be thine. And Jesus answered, and said unto him, Get thee behind me, Satan ; for it is written, Thou shalt worship the Lord thy God, and him only shalt thou serve. And he brought him to Jerusalem, and set him on a pinnacle of the temple, and said unto him, If thou be the Son of God cast thyself down from hence ; for it is written, He shall give his angels charge over thee, to keep thee : and in their hands they shall bear thee up, lest at any time thou dash thy foot against a stone. And Jesus answering, said unto him, It is said, Thou shalt not tempt the Lord thy God. And when the devil had ended all the temptation, he departed from him for a season.'*

What ! is this a part of the Gospel which I dare to claim as belonging to the business of life, as appealing to the sympathies and consciences of human beings ? Is not this just one of those supernatural additions which mingle so strangely with the common history, and which all who are trying to extricate that common history from its environment, instantly cast aside ? No doubt. The Temptation is treated by a number of those who accept, no less than by most of those who reject, the Evangelical narrative, as standing outside of it—as having, perhaps a doctrinal, perhaps a traditional value, but as altogether distinct from the records of our Lord's journeys and of His moral teaching. This separation I cannot make. I can understand no part of the subsequent history, if I omit the scene in the wilderness. All appears to me incoherent and fantastical. The Gospel loses its interest for me as a commentary on my own life and the life of my fellow-creatures. Perhaps I ought to receive it because it is written, but why it should have been written, what it has to do with us, I cannot discover. It is this preliminary struggle of the Spirit of God with the spirit of evil which shows me what our Lord's struggle was with the Jewish people, what is the struggle of every nation and age, what is going on in every one of us.

And this has been the conviction of different periods—of those periods which have been most energetic, and have left the deepest marks of their energy on the world's history; this has been the conviction of those men who have fought the stoutest battles, and done most for mankind. You may expect me to begin with warning you not to think of the Temptation as Dante and the men in the middle ages thought of it, or as Luther and the men at the time of the Reformation thought of it, or as Milton and the Puritans thought of it. I shall do no such thing. I believe they all thought of it imperfectly; that they impaired the beauty of the clear, sharply-chiselled marble, by colouring borrowed from their own fancy and the fancy of their times. But they have shown with what intense reality this record has come to them in the most terrible moments of their existence. If they have seen it through a mist, it has not created the mist; it has done more than all other lights to dispel the mist. Truth and falsehood, good and evil, have stood out before them in their unchangeable opposition; not as abstractions engaged in a shadow-fight, but as powers of life and death grappling in that fight on which the condition of the universe and of each person in it depends. We may learn something from each teacher

which the other could not tell us. Their mistakes may
warn us of those into which we are likely to fall. If God
gives us grace to enter heart and hand into the conflict
which He has appointed for us and our time, we shall read
this passage of St. Luke more simply than those read it
who have gone before us.

(1) He was led by the *Spirit*. That is the characteristic of the acts of the Son in all we read from this
time onwards. He has been baptized with His Father's
Spirit. He is guided by that Spirit whithersoever He goes.
He does not choose for Himself whether He shall be
in the city or the wilderness. Here is the secret of His
power. He is governed, and so exercises the highest
and most perfect government. It is a mystery surely, the
deepest of mysteries ; but if we reflect upon it, a light will
be thrown upon the mysteries of our life—upon that which
makes our acts harmonious—a light that you will find
nowhere else.

(2) The wilderness into which He went ' was haunted,
according to popular belief, by demons.' So speaks the
author of a recent ' Life of Jesus.' We surely do not want
the authority of a learned man to endorse so very probable
a statement. No doubt, popular belief filled Jewish deserts,
as it fills all deserts, with demons. The curious fact is,
that this being the case, the Evangelists, who are supposed
to have been the victims of all popular beliefs, do not
suggest the thought of demons in this desert. They say
much of demons elsewhere ; *what* they say, I hope to consider next Sunday. That which they speak of here is far
more serious and awful.

(3) Being forty days tempted of the *devil*. The difference
is all important. We are not in the region of dark forms

which haunt particular spots.   We have been brought into
the *spiritual* region.   That is to say, we have been brought
out of the region of *things* into the region of *persons ;* out
of the region of mere outsides and shapes into the region of
living powers.   The accuser, the slanderer, strikes at the
very being of Him to whom he speaks.   The desert may be
the place of the encounter.   It is a suitable place, because
creatures of flesh and blood being out of the way, we know
that the encounter itself is between spirits.

(4) ' *In those days he did eat nothing, and when they
were ended he afterwards hungered.'*   Another exhaustion of
outward circumstances.   The taste, the appetite, has been
continually represented as the cause of evil.   Take away
the motives which speak to the flesh, reduce that to nothingness—and then ?   Then, say the Evangelists, the power of the
tempter may be felt as it was not felt before.   Hunger may
be his instrument quite as much as food.   Reason and
experience would say so.   The Bible accords with them.
It bears witness against the widely-spread, the ever-recur-
ring, heresy which makes the animal nature the source of
wrong; against the innumerable practical deductions which
have been drawn from that heresy by those who have in
terms rejected it.   But that is not all.   Men are hungry
who do not deny themselves food for any purpose of mortification.   Is it nothing for them to know that their
anguish has been felt by the Son of Man—the King of
Men ?   Is there no Gospel in that announcement ?   Has it
not been felt as a Gospel by thousands ?   When we believe
more in One who took our nature, and less in One who
came to save select individuals out of the condition of their
race, may it not reach millions ?

(5) ' *And the devil said unto him, If thou be the Son of God,*

command this stone to be made bread.' Now we begin to
perceive the principle of the Temptation, its real force.
A stone may serve as the instrument of solicitation; the
natural craving for food may be all that is spoken to; but
this is the speech: '*If* thou be the Son of God.' 'The
' words at thy baptism cannot be true, if thou art not able
' to exercise this power for the relief of thy own necessities.'
He must do something of Himself and for Himself. What
is His name worth otherwise ?

(6) His name is worth this :—'*It is written, man shall not
live by bread alone, but by every word of God.'* I claim the
words because they are written of man. I claim the state
of man. I am one with men. There is the King; and
the King is the Son. He can depend upon the Word of
God. He can trust that for Himself, and for those with
whom He has identified Himself.

(7) A King ideally, perhaps. But actually is the world
His ? Is it His Father's ? '*And the devil taking him up
into an high mountain, showed unto him all the kingdoms of
the world in a moment of time. And the devil said unto
him, All this power will I give thee, and the glory of them,
for that is delivered to me, and to whomsoever I will I give it.
If thou, therefore, wilt worship me, all shall be thine.'* 'How
' was He taken to the mountain ? Did He see with His eyes,
' or only with His mind?' My friends, I know these questions
occur to us all. They have occurred to me. And I can
only find this answer to them :—I am reading of a temptation presented by a spirit to a spirit. If Christ saw all
those kingdoms with His bodily eye, still it must have
been His spirit which took in the prospect, which took in
the force of the Scripture words. That is what concerns
me—concerns me infinitely. The devil is reported to have

said something which seems to me most plausible. All
appearances in that time confirmed his words. The most
religious men in times since have thought that he spoke
truly. They have said that the kingdoms of the world and
the glory of them are his. And I fancy they have rendered
him no little worship because they have said so. They have
had a reserved homage for his enemy; but they have supposed he had a title to actual homage in virtue of that great
inheritance. If it is his, I am sure I shall worship him;
so far as I have accounted it his, I am sure I have worshipped him. I want then to know if there is one whom
I can trust who declared that it was not his, who would
not do him service. I read these words :—

(8) *'Get thee behind me, Satan, for it is written, Thou shalt
worship the Lord thy God, and him only shalt thou serve.'*
Is that true ? Did One in human flesh indeed say,
' Adversary, get thee behind me. All these things are
' the Creator's, not thine. All these things are His who
' redeemed His people out of bondage, not thine. He
' told the Israelites He was the Lord their God. I take
' my place as an Israelite. I call Him the Lord my God.
' I vindicate that name for myself, for them. I confess
' Him to be the Lord, Him only.' Is not that the word
of a Man, of *the* Man ? Is it not the word of a Son ? Is
it not a Gospel to us all ?

(9) *'And he brought him to Jerusalem, and set him on
a pinnacle of the temple, and said unto him, If thou be the
Son of God, cast thyself down from hence: for it is written,
He shall give his angels charge over thee, to keep thee: and
in their hands they shall bear thee up, lest at any time thou
dash thy foot against a stone. And Jesus answering said
unto him, It is said, Thou shalt not tempt the Lord thy God.'*

I need not discuss the question in this case, how He was
brought to Jerusalem, how He was set on a pinnacle of
the temple. I should say the temptation was the most
real that could be. He was actually tempted to try
whether God would not bear him up if He cast Himself
down. He was actually tempted by a text of Scripture to
give that proof of His Sonship and of His Father's faithfulness. Whatever were His circumstances, that thought
was presented to His spirit by the evil spirit. And so
we know that He was tempted like as we are. In all
varieties of circumstances this thought is presented to us.
Every man hears, at some time or other, a voice whispering
to him, ' Go out of the place in which you are put. Do
something extraordinary. Do something *wrong*. See
whether God will not help you. Can you not depend
upon His promise that He will? Is Scripture false that
He will ?' How many of those false steps, how many of
those first wrong acts which have made a second, a third,
a fourth necessary, have proceeded from this calculation!
Whence came that voice? I accept this story. I believe
that it is the voice of *the* tempter, the enemy of me, the
enemy of man, he who is seeking to make us distrust our
Father in heaven, he who is seeking to divide us from
Him. And therefore, I want to know if the argument
from Scripture has been answered, and how we may treat
that and the like arguments. Hear and consider this :
' *And Jesus answering said, Thou shalt not tempt the Lord
thy God.*' The Son of God once more claims the right
to obey a commandment—the right to trust and to depend. Once more He claims that right for us. We
may abide where we are placed, for our Father has
placed us there. If He was not the Lord our God, we

might make experiments on that which He would do for
us supposing we broke His law.   Because He is, we may
submit to it, and rejoice in it.

My friends, this story has pleaded its own cause for
eighteen centuries with those who are fighting a battle.
I do not think it can be accepted as true—in any important sense of the word *true*—by any others.   They
may maintain its canonical authority, they may insist that
it cannot be rejected without peril to their theory of the
infallibility of the Bible; but though they will defend it
against objectors, and for others, ·it will not signify anything to themselves.   If it did, they would not despair of
its coming with a demonstration of the Spirit and of power
to any objector—to any man.   They would set little value
on any demonstration but that.   In this sense it is, I think,
a most beautiful introduction to the rest of the Gospel.
May a man trust the word of God to supply him with
bread?   Are the kingdoms of the world the devil's, or
do they belong to the Lord our God?   Which is a man to
worship?   May a man trust God?   May he tempt God?
These questions were debated between the Spirit of Jesus
and the spirit of falsehood in the wilderness.   These were
the questions which He was to debate in synagogues and
in the streets, in Galilee and in Jerusalem.   The Son of
God was in all His acts and words to glorify His Father
and deny Himself—in all His acts and words to vindicate
for those whom He was not ashamed to call His brethren
the right to call His Father their Father.   He was to
manifest the Spirit of trust, of obedience, of love, of
peace, in opposition to the spirit of self-will, of division,
of hatred.

(11) We are told, that '*when the devil had ended all his*

temptation, he departed from him for a season.' Such
seasons of rest, of freedom from doubt, of joyful confidence,
are, I suppose, vouchsafed to the soldiers of Christ after
periods of terrible conflict, as they were to the chief
Captain. But the inward battle was to prepare Him, as
well as them, for battles in the world. The enemy in the
wilderness must be encountered there. We read :—

   *' And Jesus returned in the power of the Spirit into
Galilee : and there went out a fame of him through all the
region round about. And he taught in their synagogues,
being glorified of all. And he came to Nazareth, where he
had been brought up : and, as his custom was, he went into
the synagogue on the sabbath day, and stood up for to read.
And there was delivered unto him the book of the prophet
Esaias. And when he had opened the book, he found the
place where it was written, The Spirit of the Lord is upon
me, because he hath anointed me to preach the gospel to the
poor; he hath sent me to heal the brokenhearted, to preach
deliverance to the captives, and recovering of sight to the blind,
to set at liberty them that are bruised, to preach the acceptable
year of the Lord. And he closed the book, and he gave it
again to the minister, and sat down. And the eyes of all
them that were in the synagogue were fastened on him. And
he began to say unto them, This day is this scripture fulfilled
in your ears. And all bare him witness, and wondered at
the gracious words which proceeded out of his mouth. And
they said, Is not this Joseph's son ? And he said unto them,
Ye will surely say. unto me this proverb, Physician, heal thyself : whatsoever we have heard done in Capernaum, do also
here in thy country. And he said, Verily I say unto you,
No prophet is accepted in his own country. But I tell you
of a truth, many widows were in Israel in the days of Elias,*

when the heaven was shut up three years and six months, when great famine was throughout all the land; but unto none of them was Elias sent, save unto Sarepta, a city of Sidon, unto a woman that was a widow. And many lepers were in Israel in the time of Eliseus the prophet; and none of them was cleansed, saving Naaman the Syrian. And all they in the synagogue, when they heard these things, were filled with wrath, and rose up, and thrust him out of the city, and led him unto the brow of the hill whereon their city was built, that they might cast him down headlong. But he passing through the midst of them went his way, and came down to Capernaum, a city of Galilee, and taught them on the sabbath days.'

(12) It is in the power of the Spirit that He went into the desert; it is in the power of the Spirit that He goes into Galilee. It is of the Spirit which is upon Him that He speaks to the Nazarenes. The story of His visit to their synagogue occurs only in St. Luke. It is consistent with all that we have read in His Gospel hitherto. It prepares us for what we are to read hereafter. The writer of the Acts of the Gospel must tell us of a kingdom which conquers by spiritual might. He must tell us of a kingdom which is to set captives free. And he must warn us that the news of such a kingdom, uttered through Prophets, through Apostles, through the Son of Man, will be rejected precisely because it does address itself to spirits, and brings spiritual evidence of its reality. 'Is not this the carpenter's son?' 'Are not his sisters all with us?' will be one form—one chief form—of the arguments by which its claims are resisted. They are those which have especial weight among the kinsmen and neighbours of the Prophet or the King.

Among them, He has the first keen taste of the bitterness of the work which is to carry such blessings, which testifies of such love. The acceptable year, the divine jubilee, must be inaugurated by the effort of the subjects of the King to cast Him headlong from the brow of the hill on which their city was built.

LECTURE VI.

St. Luke IV. 33, 34.

And in the synagogue there was a man which had a spirit of an unclean devil, and cried out with a loud voice, saying, Let us alone ; what have we to do with thee, thou Jesus of Nazareth ? art thou come to destroy us ? I know thee who thou art ; the Holy One of God.

THE superstition which connects demons with a wilderness has been used, as I told you last Sunday, to explain our Lord's temptation. I showed you that the explanation had nothing to do with the story which is given us by the Evangelists. They speak of no demons in the desert. They describe the encounter of the spirit of Christ with the spirit of evil; the test of their veracity lies in the experience of human beings in cities as much as deserts, in one period as much as another.

But the subject of demons is, as I intimated, one which comes before us in the Gospels, as soon as our Lord enters upon His ministry. Not in deserts, but in places of concourse, in the synagogues, we hear of them. We cannot evade them. Casting out the demons is connected with all our Lord's acts of power. It takes precedence of all His other acts. If we follow the order of the Evangelists, we must not first inquire into the nature of His signs generally and then treat of these as having a peculiar and exceptional character. We must begin with them. If we can arrive at any light respecting them, we may hope that that light will guide us in the investigation of the purpose and character of His ordinary work.

Certainly there is no title which Christians so habitually claim for Jesus, as that of Redeemer. When we cease to acknowledge Him as a Redeemer, we cease to care for Him at all: His Gospel becomes no Gospel. We listen to any other tidings with more interest and more hope.

But if the New Testament is the history of a Redeemer and a redemption, how shall the Redeemer manifest Himself; what is there to be redeemed? The Evangelist assumes that the spirit of man has fallen into bondage; that if this be not delivered from bondage, *he* himself will remain in it; that if this *is* delivered from bondage, then highest of all must be the Deliverer. One who is above the man must speak to him, must awaken him, must stretch out help to him; he must answer the voice, he must obey the signal, he must grasp the help. It must be unseen aid, spiritual aid, through whatever audible voice or visible hands it is afforded. Such is the principle of the whole book. In every different stage of the revelation it is the same. A Divine Ruler discovers Himself to the creature which is formed to know and recognise its ruler; trust in that ruler is the act of recognition, is the mightiest, and yet the humblest, exercise of the subject's energy.

But is this a general abstract doctrine? Are we to talk of a redemption—a human redemption—and not to see any individual instances of it, any illustrations of the principle and the power? If Jesus was, as modern critics

say, an idealist, one who had a certain dream of benefiting
his countrymen and the human race, but had not power to
benefit them, it is reasonable to be content with fine words,
with what is described as a " delicious morality." His acts
we must account for as those writers account for them.
He must have been subject to accesses of gross delusion;
when He had deluded Himself, He will have practised on the
credulity of those who surrounded Him.   That is one view
of His life; supposing we do not adopt it, we ought to be
consistent in maintaining the other. Supposing we call Jesus
a Redeemer, we are bound to expect that He would give
some tokens of redeeming power.   We are bound severely
to question those who record His acts, whether He did, and
if He did what those tokens were.   If the Evangelists can
tell us of no such tokens, they are mocking us; if the
tokens are not such as concern human beings, they are not
tokens for us.

The Evangelists at least make a distinct answer to these
demands, whether it is a satisfactory one or not.   They fix
our minds upon people who, like this man at Capernaum,
had a spirit of an unclean demon.   What kind of person can
this have been?   I can only gather what he was from the
hints which are given me here and in corresponding passages of the Gospels.   He had evidently no command of
himself.   His words were not his own; his thoughts were
not his own.   His words were foul and fierce; his thoughts
were foul and fierce.   You ask if these were phenomena
peculiar to Galilee, peculiar to that age?   I cannot imagine
that they were.   I think we all know that they were not.
The language which I have used is that which we should
naturally adopt to describe cases which most of us have
seen.   They may take various shapes, but surely they are

to be found everywhere; the report of them is to be heard
in every time. And in every place and in every time this
calamity has been felt as in the deepest sense the sub-
version of the human being; the most awful, the most un-
utterable fall which any creature can suffer—a fall which
no *involuntary* creature can suffer. If there could be a
deliverance of a spirit from this abyss, that would be a
sign, indeed, of the presence of One who was above the
man, and who knew what was in the man; that would
be a pledge of the overthrow of man's oppressors, such
as could not be afforded in any other way conceivable
by us.

The form of speech which I have used at once brings
us to the part of the subject from which we often shrink.
Has man oppressors? That is not a question which we
ask the Evangelist: we ask facts; we ask the experience
and language of every people under heaven. The beautiful
things which God has given a man oppress him. All the
powers of nature oppress him. He is oppressed by his
fellows; he is oppressed by himself. Is that the last word
we have to speak? How then do you account for those
cases to which I have just referred? How do you account
for that desire in men to shake off a power which they
declare that they cannot shake off? Does this power
dwell in some visible thing? Is it not an invisible influence? Does it address itself to the senses? or to the
reason, to the will—to that which the senses and all the
energies of the body should obey? You know that this
influence, this power—call it by any name you like—is
actually felt and confessed. Well, this from which the
man needs to be delivered that he may be a rational, willing being, and may do the behests of his Creator, is here

F

called 'an unclean spirit.' Is that a vague term? Certainly not more vague than our term 'power' or 'influence.' On the whole, rather more definite; perhaps more nearly representing the facts of the case. For that which speaks to the spirit of man must, one would suppose, be spiritual; that which controls him must have some affinity with him. But was not the old world tormented by superstitions about demons? Was not the sense of their dominion a main cause of some of its coarsest, most material, superstitions? I cannot doubt it for a moment; and therefore I require this as a necessary token of the true King of Men, that He should reclaim men from the service of such demons, that He should assert His own fellowship with the victims, that He should adopt them as children of His Father. I can think of no redemption which is more wonderful than this—and also more practical—more completely overthrowing the charms and enchantments by which human creatures, in that day, tried to buy off what they felt a real, however inexplicable, tyranny; more fatal to the pretensions of all who should play and trifle with the great diseases of humanity in the times to come.

It is exactly in this form that St. Luke represents the deliverance which was effected for the man in the synagogue. I cannot change his words without weakening them. The unclean spirit confesses One who is mightier than itself; the Holy One, the Son of God. That Holy One, that Son of God vindicates the poor helpless slave as His; bids his tyrant depart. The words sound strange, I know. I am coward enough to cast about for some way of avoiding the strangeness. I cannot find it. Let us fly from superstitions, says the critic. I long to do so.

For I am in the midst of them.   We do not hear less of
spirits, less of spiritual communications, in this day than in
former days.   They do not assume less vulgar or less frivolous shapes.   I do not perceive that cultivated men, even
that scientific men, can point out a deliverance from such
superstitions to their fellows ; not a few succumb to the
superstitions themselves.   This language is very prevalent,
' How little we know! there may be some communications
' with the unseen world ; who can tell ? if there are, why not
' these as well as any others.'   My friends, an old Hebrew
said, 3000 years ago, ' *I have hated them which hold of super-*
stitious vanities, but my trust is in the Lord God.'   He held
no parley with superstitions; he loathed them ; they were
all connected in his mind with visible idolatry, with a
religion of distrust.   He believed in the invisible God.   He
trusted in the righteous and unchangeable God : so he rose
out of them.   I believe we shall rise out of our delusions,
if we can say to every man, ' There is a communication with
' the unseen world.   The Son of God has established it for
' ever in Himself.   *Therefore* thou art not the servant of
' demons or spirits of the air.   *Therefore* thou art not to
' play tricks with that which should be to thee awful, won-
' derful, blessed.   Seek fellowship with the unseen in Him
' who is the Head of both worlds.   Leave other roads to those
' who do not own the glory of man, his relation to God.'

It seems to me, then, most reasonable, not only for the
sake of anything which may have been peculiar to that
time, but for the sake of every time, that the Evangelist
should give these victories over demons a prominent place
in the history of Redemption.   The impression produced
in the synagogue of Capernaum is the simplest testimony
to the nature of such a sign.   ' *What a word is this,*' they

said. There was the sense of One who did not charm
away evils by a look or a touch. The calm divine energy
with which He declared that the Kingdom of God was
indeed among men—that God's power was manifesting
itself as of old, in breaking fetters, in setting the captives
free—this came forth in the command that the unclean
spirit should depart. The evil spirit was not the man's
lord. The kingdoms of the world and the glory of them
were not his. Holiness was mightier.

II. The emancipation of man's spirit from these tyrants
is then the first and highest manifestation of the Divine
King. Were their bodies indifferent to Him ? Did
He care nothing for the plagues and torments which
vexed them ? *'And he arose out of the synagogue, and
entered into Simon's house. And Simon's wife's mother was
taken with a great fever ; and they besought him for her.
And he stood over her, and rebuked the fever : and it left
her ; and immediately she arose and ministered unto them.'*

The accomplished author of that 'Life of Jesus' to
which I have referred before, made a curious mistake in
associating the Gospel exorcism with the wilderness. *That*
is said to have been performed in public places, in the
synagogues to which the Jews most resorted. But this
writer draws our attention to an important point in the
history of our Lord's acts of healing. He says that they
are, strangely enough, said to have taken place in private,
when there were very few to examine or report them.
Very strange indeed that circumstance must seem both
to him and to those who most differ with him—the
collectors of Christian evidences who suppose that these
wonders were chiefly done to confute deniers, and convince the crowd. But if Jesus was indeed a Redeemer—

if these acts were acts of Redemption—we may understand that they were done for the sake of those who
had need of the Redemption. We may believe that the
King cared for His subjects, for the lowest and meanest
of them, and did not care to use certain of them as
examples of what He was *not* doing for the rest. Which
kind of proceeding would be most like Him whom we read
of in these books? The narrative of such manifestations
of secret grace, known chiefly to those who were blessed by
them, has little force as an argument. But it has told all
generations of a King reigning then and ever. Such evidence
would have been wanting if these acts had been devised to
make an impression upon bystanders.

This subject will come before us again next Sunday;
but there is in this chapter a linking together of incidents
which I cannot overlook. The passage from the synagogue
to the house of Simon, illustrates the change from the
public to the private revelation of the Kingdom of Heaven;
as the cure of the fever succeeds the casting out of the
spirit. Finally, that we may not fancy any partiality
to have been shown to a disciple, that we may not suppose the King ever to lose sight of the people, we read
these words:—'*Now when the sun was setting, all they
that had any sick with divers diseases brought them unto
him; and he laid his hands on every one of them, and
healed them. And devils also came out of many, crying
out, and saying, Thou art Christ, the son of God. And
he rebuking them suffered them not to speak: for they knew
that he was Christ. And when it was day he departed and
went into a desert place: and the people sought him, and
came unto him, and stayed him, that he should not depart
from them. And he said unto them, I must preach the king-*

*dom of God to other cities also: for therefore am I sent. And
he preached in the synagogues of Galilee.'*

You may have asked yourselves sometimes in the course
of this sermon, 'But if this is so, may there not have been
exorcisms in later days?' I trust so indeed. If the King who
was declared then lives now, I cannot conceive how He can
ever cease to put forth this power, or we to be the better for
it. 'But were not exorcisms in the middle ages—are they
not now, associated with fraud and priestcraft?' Then certainly there is the mightiest need that *that* spirit should
be cast out. The spirit of religious trickery, of priestly
imposture, is the most unclean, the most devilish of all.
And it is a spirit which the force of laws, the sanctions
of civil judges, cannot reach. It goes beneath laws; it
makes the judges impotent, or corrupts them. It flourishes
wherever the belief of a present Spirit of Truth has
lost its power. It never can be shattered by a scep-
ticism which supposes anything to be possible because
it holds nothing to be true. In the presence of a
testimony to a real Kingdom of Heaven, it trembles and
grows pale. When Christ baptizes the nations with
His fire, every mask which the spirit of lies has put
on must be consumed. That will be the great final
exorcism. But let each for himself long and pray that
the evil spirits which have had dominion over him may
be cast out now. Let us ask that we may become exor-
cists ourselves. For is not every true and loving man
and woman an exorcist? Is not every one who will
yield himself to be Christ's servant, permitted to deliver
his brother from some spirit which has enslaved him?
Have not the weakest compelled dark spirits to cry out that
there is a Holy One of God from whose light they must fly?

LECTURE VII.

POWERS AND SIGNS OF THE KINGDOM OF HEAVEN.

St. Luke V. 6.

And when they had this done, they inclosed a great multitude of fishes: and their net brake.

THIS chapter records a series of those acts which the Evangelists describe as signs or powers of the Kingdom of Heaven, which we commonly speak of as miracles or portents. Before we can know whether their title or ours is the best—which, at least, answers best to the narratives themselves—we should examine those narratives one by one.

(1) The first is known as the story of 'the miraculous draught of fishes.' I do not suppose any of us can be quite satisfied with this account of it. St. Luke brings an actual scene before us. There are two fishing-boats standing by the lake of Gennesareth. The fishermen are gone out of them, and are washing their nets. Jesus is on the shore. The people are pressing upon Him to hear the word of God. He enters one of the boats, and desires Simon, the owner of it, to thrust it a little way from the land. He sits down and speaks to the people from the boat. Then He says, '*Launch out into the deep, and let down your nets for a draught.*' Simon Peter says, '*Master, we have toiled all*

night, and caught nothing ; nevertheless, at thy word, I will
let down the net. And when they had this done, they inclosed
a great multitude of fishes, and their net brake. And they
beckoned to their partners in the other ship, that they should
come and help them. And they came and filled both the ships,
so that they began to sink.'

'This,' you exclaim, 'was a miracle ; a startling event;
'a break in the ordinary laws of the universe. Some One
'was in that ship who could do what had never been done
'before.'   I do not think that was Simon Peter's feeling, if
he did what Luke says he did. *'He fell at Jesus' knees,*
saying, Depart from me, for I am a sinful man, O Lord.'
He feels that the Person who has caused that net to be
filled with the fishes is not One who is there for the first
time.   He is his judge, his lawgiver; One who knows what
is in him ; One before whom he trembles. The Power which
had enabled him in other days to fulfil his craft, who had
made his craft successful, is there.   He stands revealed
to him.   The sense of a Divine Presence which was
not of that moment, but of all moments, is awakened in
the heart of the poor Galilæan. He who has been speaking
the word of God out of the ship—He who has been
bearing witness of a Kingdom of God that is near them all—
He who has been calling them to repent because that kingdom is at hand—He has given this sign and proof of His
dominion.   He rules the lake, but oh, more wonderful
power! He rules the *man* who has been plying his trade on
the lake. That man is face to face with his Lord.   And
then is heard the sentence so reviving, and yet so awful :—
'Fear not ; from henceforth thou shalt catch men.'   'I *am*
'that Lord whom thou takest me to be.   I have been with
'thee in thy common work.   I am going to send thee forth

' on a higher work. Thou art to declare to men that gracious
' kingdom over their business, over their bodies, over their
' spirits, which I have awakened thee, by this token, to
' confess.'

In this instance I think the Evangelist justifies his own
nomenclature. He proves that it is far simpler, far more
significant, far more distinct, far more comprehensive, than
that which we have substituted for it. The fisherman who
would have merely stared at a prodigy, who would have
derived from it a transitory reverence for a certain human
person, is awed, humbled, raised to another level by this
indication of a Divine oversight of his work and of him.
The draught of fishes becomes an education for him. It
becomes an education for every fisherman, for every crafts-
man of every kind, in after days. It converts every failure
and every success in his ordinary business into a sign
which he may turn to his profit and to the strengthening
of his faith. It becomes an evidence of the Gospel indeed
—an evidence that it is from Him and concerning Him
who is the same yesterday, to-day, and for ever.

(2) The next narrative refers to a leper. I shall read it
to you, often as you have heard it. The manner of relating
these stories has to do with the nature and substance of
them. By changing them a little, and clothing them in
modern phraseology, we can easily make them appear just
like the reports of portents in the writers who give us
most of such reports. If we take them as they stand,
the contrast, I think, must strike all.

' *And it came to pass, when he was in a certain city,
behold a man full of leprosy :* who seeing Jesus fell on his
*face, and besought him, saying, Lord, if thou wilt, thou canst
make me clean. And he put forth his hand, and touched*

*him, saying, I will : be thou clean. And immediately the
leprosy departed from him. And he charged him to tell no
man : but go and shew thyself to the priest, and offer for
thy cleansing, according as Moses commanded, for a testimony unto them.'*

Now consider these facts. The law regarding leprosy
formed one of the longest and most elaborate chapters in
the code of the Israelite. He believed that the Lord God
had cared to preserve him and his people from the peril of
this disease ; that He had appointed the priests to watch
over those who had been overtaken by it ; that He had
taught them the signs of its approach, the proofs that it
had become dangerous, the rules for excluding the infected
man from the congregation and from the society of his
fellow citizens, the time when he might safely mix with
them again. A man undergoing the penalties which this
law had prescribed approaches Christ as One whom he
may dare to approach, notwithstanding its decrees; he
expresses his confidence that He can do for him what
none else can do. Here is an occasion for claiming that
kind of power which sets all ordinary laws at defiance.
He does respond to the petition of the leper in the most
direct, the most authoritative manner :—'*I will ; be thou
clean.*' But this exercise of will, instead of overreaching
law, pays the greatest homage to it. The man is to go and
show himself to the priest. He is to give evidence that he
is inwardly healed by the outward tokens which the law
has ordained. He is to offer the gifts which accompanied
those cures that had taken place by the slowest, most
customary process. And he is not to proclaim aloud that
which has been done to him. He is to be silently thankful
for it. Does not the Evangelist in this case vindicate most

strikingly his own mode of considering our Lord's acts? Is there one of the characteristics of the doer of strange irregular wonders here? Are we not reminded at every step of Him who said, that He did not come to destroy the law, but to fulfil it? that He came to do His Father's will? Was He not fulfilling the law by restoring the ordinary health, about which it had been so solicitous? Was He not doing His Father's will by banishing the diseases which had interrupted the order of His Creation?

Before I pass to the next miracle, I must call your attention for a moment to the fifteenth and sixteenth verses, in their relation to each other. In spite of His command the fame of Him spreads abroad : *multitudes come together to hear and to be healed of their diseases.* He retires into the wilderness and prays. Those words, ' *I will, be thou clean,*' did not then import an assertion of independence. He had disclaimed that when the Devil had tempted Him to show what He could do by making stones bread and by casting Himself from the pinnacle of the Temple. His will was still the trusting, dependent, praying will. It was mighty to heal and restore, because it was in entire harmony with the will of Him from whom He came.

That reflection will be the best possible preparation for the story of the palsied man.

(3) *And it came to pass on a certain day, as he was teaching, that there were Pharisees and doctors of the law sitting by, which were come out of every town of Galilee and Judea and Jerusalem: and the power of the Lord was present to heal them. And behold, men brought in a bed a man which was taken with a palsy ; and they sought means to bring him in, and to lay him before him. And when they could not find by what way they might bring him in because of the*

multitude, they went upon the housetop, and let him down through the tiling with his couch into the midst before Jesus. And when he saw their faith, he said unto him, Man, thy sins are forgiven thee. And the scribes and the Pharisees began to reason, saying, Who is this which speaketh blasphemies ? Who can forgive sins, but God alone ? And when Jesus perceived their thoughts, he answering said unto them, What reason ye in your hearts ? Whether is it easier to say, Thy sins be forgiven thee ; or to say, Rise up and walk ? But that ye may know that the Son of Man hath power upon earth to forgive sins, he said unto the sick of the palsy, I say unto thee, Arise, take up thy bed, and go into thine house. And immediately he rose up before them and took up that whereon he lay, and departed to his own house, glorifying God.'

Here we are not, as in the last case, occupied chiefly with the sufferer himself. There is a crowd about Jesus ; among them are those who are observing and criticizing His acts. The palsied man is brought unexpectedly among them. His friends are desiring a cure for him. The Phari- sees and doctors are watching what the Teacher, to whom such powers are ascribed, will say or do. What He says is altogether different from the anticipation of the friends —altogether startling and shocking to the learned men. *Man, thy sins be forgiven thee.* What sins ? Who knew that he had committed any, or that they were troubling him ? Those words must have been addressed to the man himself, to the conscience within him ; if they met nothing there, they were wasted. If they did meet something there, they came from One who knew what was in man, who could tell what this particular man needed, who was in direct communication with the secrets of his heart.

This would be a sign of the Kingdom of Heaven, the sign
of that dominion over human beings, of that fellowship
with human spirits, which our Lord was announcing in all
His discourses.   Accordingly it is this speech which pro-
vokes the indignation of the scribes.   Who is this that
speaketh blasphemies ?   Who can forgive sins, but God
alone ?   The whole question between Him and them was
gathered up into these words : ‘ Is there a Son of Man ?
‘ Is there One who unites man to God ?   Is there One in
‘ whom God is seeking man—seeking to reconcile man to
‘ Himself ? ’   The Scribes believed there was no such Person.
They thought there was a God, a very terrible God, who
might, perhaps, be induced to forgive the sins of some who
could find out the right method of influencing Him.   And
this forgiveness, what was it ?   Not the removal of a curse
which was crushing the spirit and separating it from goodness and truth, but simply the escape from a certain
amount of punishment which it had been decreed should
be the recompense for a certain amount of evil doing.
Forgiveness in any real sense—in any sense which it bears
in the mind of a true father among men, who wins back
his child to his home, and puts away out of his thoughts
that which has set them at war—this the scribe did not
recognise.   And therefore he could not practically recognise
it in his relations with his fellow-men.   Forgiveness
towards them meant only the allowing them to escape
punishment.   Was, then, the act of enabling the palsied
man to rise and walk an exceptional act of power, done to
show how Christ had broken through the laws of the
universe ?   According to the Evangelist, it was the vindi-
cation of an eternal law of the universe, of a principle in
which all human beings, throughout all generations, would

be interested. '*That ye may know that the Son of Man hath power on earth to forgive sins, he said to the sick of the palsy, Arise, and go into thine house.*' That they may know there is a Ruler over their spirits and over their bodies— a giver of peace and life to both ; that they may understand He is bringing them a message of reconciliation and forgiveness from His Father; that He is Himself the bond of this reconciliation and forgiveness ; therefore is this man made a sound creature again. A grand Gospel to humanity, if that is so; a deliverance from all the plots and contrivances for purchasing forgiveness of sins which men have devised, and which have been welcomed by sin-sick consciences, not for their relief but for the increase of their torment. And I will add, my friends, a warning to ourselves, whenever we are tempted to use the formula, ' *Who is this that speaketh blasphemies ?* ' It was used, so the Evangelists tell us, by the most approved doctors of the day against the Son of Man. It was used to condemn the thought that He really expresses the will of His Father towards men. It was used as an excuse for putting Him to death. Let us have an intense dread of blasphemy ; but let us keep these things in recollection when we are in haste to charge any brother with it.

In treating these different works of our Lord as manifestations of an abiding invisible power, which is never exerted irregularly, which is always exerted by a Father for the well-being of His children, I have had only to recover those exact New Testament expressions which we have carelessly or wilfully deserted for others far feebler, it seems to me, and suggesting often an opposite sense. But I am also vindicating the common faith of simple people ; that which has been continually making itself heard above our noisy arguments. These stories of the draught of the fishes, of the leper, of the palsied man, have been appropriated to their own use by people of every age and country in various circumstances and extremities. They have broken through all opinions and traditions which said that these were peculiar events from which no precedent could be drawn, and which had nothing corresponding to them in ordinary human experience. A true and divine instinct—the instinct of workers and sufferers—has perceived in all these instances the signs of a Son of Man, the witnesses of His presence with them just as much as with those who were gathered about the boats on the lake of Gennesareth, or were met in the room the tiling of which was broken to let down the bed.

(4) The next words will illustrate my meaning. '*And after these things he went forth, and saw a publican, named Levi, sitting at the receipt of custom : and he said unto him, Follow me. And he left all, rose up, and followed him.*' How does our Liturgy treat this event ? '*O Almighty God,*' we thus pray in the Collect for the 21st September, '*who by thy blessed Son didst call Matthew from the receipt of custom to be an Apostle and Evangelist ; Grant us grace to forsake all covetous desires, and inordinate love of riches, and to follow the same thy Son Jesus Christ, who liveth and reigneth with thee and the Holy Ghost, one God, world without end.*' This is not, in the cant language sometimes adopted by preachers—a language curiously combining vulgarity with profaneness—*improving* the story of Levi or Matthew to our use. It is grounded on the assumption that the Lord of Matthew is our Lord ; that the Lord who called Matthew is calling us ; that we have the same

temptations as he had ; that by trust in that Lord we can resist them as he did. The principle applies in all cases. He showed forth to Matthew the power which He exerts regularly and habitually over human wills, just as He showed forth to the leper and the palsied the power which He exerts regularly and habitually over human bodies.

(5) It will scarcely be questioned that in the next paragraph He announced an unchanging law of His kingdom. The new disciple invited Him to a feast. He ate and drank with publicans and sinners. The Scribes and Pharisees murmured. ' *They that are whole,*' He said, '*need not a physician ; but they that are sick. I came not to call the righteous, but sinners to repentance.*' The objection belongs to all times ; for the Pharisaic temper reappears in all. It can coin new phrases, and seem to discard—even contemptuously to discard—old ones. But essentially it never changes. And the answer to its arguments is equally unchangeable. None can be invented which is so complete as this, which is not involved in this. There is none which is so cutting and so comprehensive.

(6) We want some name, if we could find one, to gather up these different lessons ; to tell us what that Person was who wielded all these different powers. Before we finish the chapter the name is uttered. The doubt had arisen why our Lord's disciples did not fast like those of John and of the Pharisees. The answer is, *The* BRIDEGROOM *is with them.* That expression contains all that we have been learning, or trying to learn, from the records of our Lord's work on earth. The Bridegroom of Humanity had come forth. He was entering into its sorrows and joys, taking upon Himself all its burdens, that He might purify it, and exalt it, and give it a share of His glory. The

children of the Bridechamber, those who were told of the great marriage, and were to bear the tidings of it to all kindreds and people, could not fast while they had the discovery of His presence.   There might come times, very dark times, when He would seem to be hidden from them, and from the universe.   They would have reason for fasting in those days.   But even in those days they would be reminded by outward changes in their discipline and mode of life, that what former ages looked for had come to pass; that He who revealed God by His sympathy with man had appeared.   His appearing would be the consummation of an old age, the beginning of a new.   The vestures of the old time would not be suitable for that which was at hand; it must have a vesture of its own.   The old vessels would not be adapted to the new wine; it would require vessels of its own.   Is the coming Kingdom then to trample upon the past?   Is it not that eternal Kingdom in which the past and the present and the future are united?   Is not *this* the Kingdom which Christ declared by His words and His deeds?   Is it not of this Kingdom that we have been made heirs?   Oh that God may teach us what our inheritance is, that He may enable us fully to enter upon it!

G

LECTURE VIII.

THE LORD OF THE SABBATH.

St. Luke VI. 5.

And he said unto them, That the Son of man is Lord also of the sabbath.

THERE is one topic which each of the four Evangelists dwells upon; it would not be easy to say which dwells upon it most emphatically. That topic is the Sabbath Day. Evidently they regard our Lord's words respecting it as illustrating the whole course of His teaching and of His life. His difference with the Pharisees respecting it was not an external superficial difference. It did not concern certain cases which might be taken out of a general rule. It was radical and essential. If they were right in their maxims respecting the Sabbath, He was utterly wrong; He was a subverter of God's law, a blasphemer of His name. If He was right, they were not carrying a true principle to excess. Their principle was false. And it infected their whole conduct; it compelled them to reject the Son of Man; to deny that a Son of Man could be the Son of God.

There can be no doubt that this issue was involved in these controversies. All the Evangelists force it upon us. Read the report of the transactions which are recorded in this chapter as it is given in the twelfth chapter of St. Matthew,

in the second and third chapters of St. Mark ; read above
all the fifth chapter and the ninth chapter of St. John ;
and you will feel, I am sure, that the battle was, in the
judgment of the narrators, one of life and of death. So
St. Luke tells us in the eleventh verse of this chapter,
'*And they were filled with madness; and communed one
with another what they might do to Jesus.*' On the other
hand, St. Mark records that when Jesus healed the man
with the withered hand, '*He looked round about them with
anger, being grieved for the hardness of their hearts.*' There
is no sentence exactly like that in all the gospels. Remember that Christ's anger was caused by the objections
which were raised against Him for breaking the Sabbath,
and then consider whether the whole subject must not demand the most serious attention which we can give to it.
The particular errors of the Pharisees may not be ours.
The particular acts which Christ justified against them
may not be acts with which we should find fault. But if
it is a question of eternal truth, and of rebellion against
that truth, we may be sure that the circumstances of our
times will illustrate both the one and the other as much as
the circumstances of that time.

The words which I have chosen are the words upon
which the whole controversy turns. The Pharisees stood
upon what seemed to them impregnable ground. 'God
'has given us a law. By that law He has established an
'institution. He has allowed us six days in which we
'may do our own works. He has claimed one day for
'Himself. On that day He has commanded us to abstain
'from our works. On that day our services are due ex-
'pressly and exclusively to Him.' It was thus that they
translated the words, '*Remember the sabbath day, to keep it*

*holy. Six days shalt thou labour, and do all thy work :
but the seventh day is the sabbath of the Lord thy God :
in it thou shalt not do any work, thou, nor thy son, nor
thy daughter, thy manservant, nor thy maidservant, nor thy
cattle, nor the stranger that is within thy gates.'* Was it
not a most plausible interpretation ? Will it not occur to
some of us that there could not be any other ? We might
say so if another had not been given ; if that other did
not form a substantive part of the law itself; if that other
was not the divine interpretation ; if that other did not,
in letter and in spirit, contradict the interpretation of
the scribes. *‘ For in six days the Lord made heaven and
earth, the sea, and all that in them is, and rested the
seventh day ; wherefore the Lord blessed the Sabbath day, and
hallowed it.'* What difference did these words make ?
They declared (1) that work was divine as well as rest.
They declared (2) that work was appointed for man by
God just as rest was appointed for man by God. They
declared (3) that human work was the image of God's
work, as human rest was the image of God's rest. They
said to the Israelite, (4) The Sabbath day is the Sabbath of
the Lord thy God, because He desires the manservant and
the maidservant and the stranger in the gates to rest as
well as to work; in other words, not to be excluded from
any part of His blessedness. Set one of these statements
against the other. Contemplate them in all possible lights,
and see whether there can be two so utterly and absolutely
contrasted in their meaning and in their effect. But yet
observe how very naturally, how very easily, this amazing
contrast may be obliterated ; how confidently the words,
‘ It is the sabbath of the Lord thy God,' might be appealed to
as establishing the doctrine that God insisted upon that day

for His use; how certainly this doctrine would drive out every other when men had made a God after their likeness —had supposed that He was as self-seeking as they were.

No doubt there had been many divine precautions against this abuse. In the book of Deuteronomy another sentence is substituted for the one respecting the six days of creation and the seventh day. '*And remember that thou wast a servant in the land of Egypt, and that the Lord thy God brought thee out thence through a mighty hand and by a stretched out arm: therefore the Lord thy God commanded thee to keep the sabbath day.* Here the redemption of the Israelite from a hard and cruel bondage to taskmasters who cared nothing for those upon whom they inflicted it, is directly connected with the institution. It is not only a sign to him that he is made in the image of the Creator; it is a sign that the Creator is, what He is proclaimed to be in the preamble to the commandments, the Deliverer. The Sabbath, so said the Divine lawgiver, is a witness of my will to make the nation and all the members of it free, to break off a yoke from their necks. The Pharisee simply reversed the maxim of his sacred books. He converted the Sabbath into a sign of bondage. A taskmaster more cruel and powerful than Pharaoh had imposed it under tremendous penalties upon His subjects. And it was therefore esteemed a great gift and mercy that for six days they might be exempt from the service of such a taskmaster. On those they might be their own masters or have the comfort of being only under the dominion of earthly masters. This had become—there can be no doubt of it—the Pharisaic habit of mind. The Lord God, said that school, has enjoined upon us certain services, which must be punctually rendered. It is at our peril that we neglect them. The Sabbath day stands foremost in the list of obligations. It enters into the commandments themselves. Other duties may be desirable. We may gain many rewards by performing them. But this belongs to the whole land. This must be enforced upon every Israelite.

I. The question how it should be enforced, of course introduced a multitude of regulations, refinements, inevitable yet dishonest indulgences. There might be debates without end about what was to be tolerated and what was to be prohibited; debates most tormenting and at the same time most enervating to the conscience, drawing the man at every step further from the service of the Lord God. Who could break this yoke? It was far more galling, far more destructive of the true Jewish life, far more fatal to the true Jewish worship, than the government of the Romans. Can we wonder that the Christ, who came to set at liberty them that were bound, should at the very commencement of His ministry and throughout it wage war with this form of oppression?

The first case recorded in this chapter brings out one of the Pharisaical rules for keeping the Sabbath day. His disciples are walking through the cornfields. As they walk they pluck the ears of corn and rub them in their hands. They are asked how they can do that which is unlawful on the Sabbath day. The answer comes in the form of an example from their own history. '*Have ye not read so much as this, what David did, when himself was an hungred and they that were with him; how he went into the house of God, and did take and eat the shewbread, and gave also to them that were with him; which it is not lawful to eat but for the priests alone.*' To be confronted by an act of David was startling to the worshippers of precedent. The precedent too had a wide application. The institution of the shewbread had a purpose. One who knew its purpose could dare to break through any mere formalities relating to the observance of it. The hunger of David's soldiers was a more sacred thing, in David's judgment, than a rule about the priests. Did he not show that he was a man after God's own heart by acting as if it were ? Did not the Pharisees show that they were not men after God's own heart, by putting the institution of the Sabbath between man and God, when it was intended by God for man ? The Sabbath, Jesus says in another gospel, was made for man, not man for the Sabbath. Here He affirms the same doctrine as broadly in the words, ' *The Son of man is Lord also of the sabbath.*' We must not alter this expression, or substitute for it any seeming equivalent of our own. He does not say, ' I, being the Lord of all, the Son ' of God, can do what I like ; I can make laws bend to my ' pleasure.' He says the very contrary of this. He says, ' I ' am *the Son of Man*, and as such—in that character—I ' claim the Sabbath as mine. I claim it for man. So ' doing, I am not destroying the fourth commandment, but ' fulfilling it. I am asserting in act that relation between ' God and man which it asserts in letters. I, the Son of ' Man, am claiming the Sabbath day as a divine ordinance ' for the deliverance of men, for the protection of men. I ' say that if it is used *against* men, as a mere arbitrary rule ' which they are to observe, its purpose is frustrated ; it is ' turned from a blessing into a curse.'

We might have thought the complaint against rubbing the ears of corn a harmless folly—the superstitious exaggeration of a right feeling. He who knew what was in

man perceived that it involved a direct denial of the very
letter and sense of the commandment—an inhumanity
which was sure to discover itself in other and more palpable forms. We have great reason to be thankful that
the record of this walk through the cornfields has been
preserved. If we had merely heard that Christ healed on
the Sabbath day, it might have been said, ' No doubt
' He made an exception for these cases. He authorized
' them on the Sabbath day by His example. But He cer-
' tainly would not have sanctioned any indifferent acts, offen-
' sive to the religious feelings of His countrymen, which
' might have been avoided by a little vigilance. He would
' not have been displeased at any rules which enjoined the
' more rigid and careful observance of the holy day.' He
did, directly, solemnly, with all the weight of His authority, denounce one of these rules. He treated it as incompatible with any right apprehension of the divine law—
with the freedom claimed by the true servants of God—
with the confession of the Son of Man as Lord of the Sabbath day.

II. The next case, that of the withered hand, may show us
why He dealt so severely with the other objection. ' *It
came to pass also on another sabbath, that he entered into the
synagogue and taught : and there was a man whose right hand
was withered.   And the scribes and Pharisees watched him,
whether he would heal on the sabbath day ; that they might
find an accusation against him.   But he knew their thoughts,
and said to the man which had the withered hand, Rise up,
and stand forth in the midst.   And he arose and stood forth.
Then said Jesus unto them, I will ask you one thing ; Is it
lawful on the sabbath days to do good, or to do evil ? to save
life, or to destroy it ?   And looking round about upon them*

all, he said unto the man, Stretch forth thy hand. And he did so : and his hand was restored whole as the other.'

The Pharisees are looking with keen hungry eyes upon one whom they have marked as their victim. To cherish these feelings, to be plotting murder, was not in their judgment at all unsabbatical. Their reverence for the law of God led them, so they believed, into this state of mind. Then comes forth the command to the sick man, to arise ; the life-giving power which restores his body to its proper orderly state. Here is surely a sign of the Kingdom of Heaven ; a sign of its nature ; a sign that it was the fulfilment of the Law. And then the searching question follows, ' Which is lawful—which is in conformity with the law of ' God—with the law of the day of rest—the exercise of the ' killing power, or of the renovating power ? Am I keeping ' the Sabbath, or are you ?' No inquiry could be more exasperating. It must either have brought them to the feet of the Son of Man, or have led them to commune among themselves how best they could accomplish their design of putting Him to death. St. Luke recurs to this subject in his thirteenth and fourteenth chapters. I shall speak of those passages when they come before us in their order. They exhibit the Pharisaical character in another aspect ; they belong to a later stage in the divine history. Meantime there are some very deep lessons—lessons, it seems to me, specially needful for our times—which lie in the verses I have already considered.

III. (1) The first is this. Many say ' The Sabbath is an ' essentially divine institution. It rests on a divine com- ' mandment ; therefore it is of universal obligation.' Many say, ' It is a national institution. It belonged to the Jews. ' If we adopt it, we do so out of deference to an old

'tradition or to our experience of its advantages, not to
'God's appointment.'

There is much in each of these statements which commends itself to the conscience of Christian men. There is
something in each of them which their conscience, I think,
rejects. In the best state of our minds we cling most
to divine commands. To appeal from man's decrees to the
judgment of the Righteous God is an elevation and emancipation of the spirit. Those who have been crushed under
the opinions of their own age, under the traditions of
other ages, under the burden of some dogmatist who practically or theoretically claims infallibility, feel the infinite
blessing, the absolute necessity, of turning to the everlasting God ; if He has not spoken, if He does not speak
still as He spoke of old, they cannot breathe ; they have
no hope.

The Sabbath is a strong instance. See how it seizes the
very principles on which the universe stands ! How it
connects work and rest with the nature of God, with the
nature of man ! How it harmonises the ideas of a resting
God and a working God, which all mythologies, all philo-
sophies, have rent in twain ! How it associates these ideas
with the common life of the vulgarest people ! How it
claims the highest blessings for the poorest man ! Is there
not divinity here ? Can this be the device of imperial or
priestly legislators ? Can it be meant only for one period
or one people ?

And yet who can deny that the Sabbath *was* an institution for a certain people ; that traces of the week are very
faintly discoverable among any nations except the Jews,
or those who have learnt from them ; that great teachers
of the Church denounced the Jewish sabbatising ; that

Jesus came to unite the nations, and that every struggle of the Jews to maintain their exclusiveness was in fact a struggle against Him?

If we suppose that He came to establish that Kingdom of Heaven for which the Law and Prophets were a preparation, and that we are living under this Kingdom, there is no contradiction in these opinions. We are then not more out of the range of the divine commandments than the men of old. The voice of God is speaking more directly to those who are born after the Incarnation than to those who were born before it. Therefore we have a right to claim this order of the week—the day of rest, and the days of work—as a revelation of God—a revelation of His purpose in creating the world, of His purpose towards the race which He has created in His image. We have a right to tell all men, ' It is no longer confined to one nation. ' It is a sign to you.' And by speaking so, we protest in the name of God Himself—of the God of Abraham, and Isaac, and Jacob—against the tyranny of those who would abuse the Sabbath day as the Pharisees abused it. We say, ' The words to which you appeal are your refutation. ' Because the commandment is holy and permanent, all ' efforts to make the Sabbath a bondage are acts of treason ' against the King whom we obey.'

(2) Again, it is often said, ' There is a distinction be-' tween moral principles and positive institutions. The ' first are unchangeable, the latter are transitory. This ' distinction must be applied to the commandments, for it ' is grounded in the nature of things. The law concerning ' the Sabbath must have a different worth from the laws ' against murder and adultery.'

It is said on the other side, ' How can you draw a

' line between God's own precepts !   How can you deter-
' mine which is entitled to the greatest weight !   Give up
' all or accept all.   Do not let your distinctions overrule
' His wisdom.'   Here, again, there is that in our consciences
which responds to each of these arguments—that which
rebels against each.   And again, I think it is the Gospel
of the Kingdom of Heaven which vindicates the truth
of both, and removes the confusion which is mingled with
both.

The Gospel not only asserts in terms, but makes us
feel practically, the truth of the difference between mere
decrees which may be suitable for one time, unsuitable for
another, and the eternal principles which belong to the
nature of God and His relations with man.   The distinction of the moral and the positive is brought out with a
fulness and practical strength in the New Testament which
the mere verbal divisions of schoolmen, however useful,
cannot approach.

But an institution may be a discovery of the nature of
God, a discovery of His permanent relation to man, even
more than any precept can be.   I have tried to show you
that the institution of the day of rest and of the days of work
is such a discovery.   The law against murder reveals the
care of God for life ; the law against adultery reveals the
care of God for the marriage bond.   We *perceive* the morality
of these laws in the benefit which they confer on men, in
the mischief which comes from the violation of them.
But when Christ draws forth their meaning, their essential morality, it is found that they point to a likeness
in loving-kindness, in purity of heart, between the child
on earth and the Father in Heaven.   *This* likeness is
set forth in the institution which the fourth command-

ment speaks of. It has, therefore, besides the practical benefits which are its test, as they are the test of the other commandments, an inward moral significance. That is expressed in the reason given for the Sabbath. And the failure to perceive that moral significance was the cause of all the Pharisaical scrupulosity—all the Pharisaical cruelty. We need not, then, divide the commandments, or set up our judgments of their respective value, in order to maintain this fundamental distinction of the positive and the moral. We shall realize it in the effort to keep them. We shall find that when we forget it we do *not* keep them. We substitute our own maxims for them. We subvert them.

(3) The last remark leads me to notice another conflict of opinions by which many are perplexed. ' You cannot ' refer to the Ten Commandments,' it is said on one side, ' as the authority for your Sabbath. If you adhere to them ' you must follow them strictly. But you keep the first ' day, not the seventh. For that change you must urge some ' Church or State authority, or some long custom. Prac- ' tically, therefore, that Church or State authority, or that ' long custom, is the warrant for the day, not the words ' spoken on Sinai.' It is said in answer, ' The principle ' of the institution is best preserved by the commemo- ' ration of the day on which Christ rose. Therefore we ' may claim for that day all the sacredness which be- ' longed to the other day. We may learn the conduct which ' is fitting on the first day from the conduct which was ' fitting on the seventh.'

I recognise a justice—and I think the consciences of Englishmen generally recognise a justice—in these opposing statements. And I seek the reconciliation of them where

I sought the reconciliation of the others. If the Law was leading on to a Kingdom of God—if in that only is the fulfilment of the Law—we may expect to find some sign of the transition from one to the other; some witness of an imperfection in that which was awaiting the full discovery of its own meaning. We have such a sign in the change of this day. This change has affected the order of life in the most civilized nations of the globe. You cannot account for it by any words of Apostles, by any regulations of Emperors, by any votes of Councils. You are obliged to give these a force which they do not possess; to put a violent strain upon sentences or hints of sentences; after all, to assume a divine purpose as indicated or implied in them which must have given them their efficiency. If you believed in a Kingdom of God—if you thought that the New Testament was the declaration of such a Kingdom —you would have no difficulty in saying, ' I confess here ' the divine government working in the course of human life ' and history, as it works in the course of Nature, silently, ' unobtrusively, through agents known or unknown; but ' accomplishing its purpose, making it manifest in due ' time, fashioning human wills by no sudden effort into ' conformity with it.'

And therefore I entirely accord with those who plead the reason and principle of the fourth commandment as explaining the transgression of its letter. I see in that fact, as they do, the clearest witness of its divine origin, and of its divine preservation. But then if they take up that ground, I must ask them to maintain it consistently. Having once appealed to the reason of the commandment, they must not fall back upon the notion that it is the arbitrary institution of an arbitrary Being who

commands without a reason, and would have us obey without a reason. I cannot appeal to the New Testament as a
justification of the first day without accepting all the lessons
and warnings of the New Testament respecting the seventh
day. Those lessons and warnings are written with sunbeams on its pages. They cannot belong to one time only ;
they must be meant for all times. They cannot furnish
us with an excuse for casting stones at the Pharisees, or
judging the Pharisees. They must strike at a Pharisaic
temper, which is our temptation as much as it was the
temptation of those who lived under the old covenant.
Close to the real Sabbath, the divine Sabbath which carries
a message to menservants and maidservants of the watch-
fulness of their Father in Heaven over them, of His desire
that they should enter into the rest of which His creation
speaks, and should take their places as free sons and
daughters in His household—lies the spurious Sabbath,
which speaks not of a Father but of an oppressor, which
shuts out the calmness and beauty of the creation, which
substitutes the condition of the slave for that of the adopted
child. Beside that Sabbath of which the Son of Man is
the Lord, which testifies of His life-giving acts for His
suffering brethren, lies the inhuman Sabbath of the rulers
of the synagogue—the Sabbath which leads men to regard
the six days as the blessed days, because they are *not*
God's days. Yes ; every good gift of the good God is
dogged by some counterfeit, often undistinguishable from
it in its outward shape ; eternally opposed to it in its
inward spirit. No man has a right to say to his brother,
' Thou art keeping the evil Sabbath, and not the good.'
Every one may say, and ought to say, ' Son of Man, Lord of
' the Sabbath, teach me to choose the good and to hate the

'evil; to delight in the one which will bind me more
'closely to Thee and to Thy Father, and to those whose
'nature Thou hast taken. Teach me to eschew the one
'which led men of my flesh and blood to trample on Thy
'flock, to deny Thy Father, to plot Thy death.'

LECTURE IX.

ST. LUKE VI. 13.

And when it was day he called unto him his disciples; and out of them he chose twelve, whom also he named Apostles.

WE are keeping to-day the festival of him whom we call the last of the Apostles. The passage at which we have arrived in St. Luke concerns the calling of the twelve Apostles. I shall not, therefore, interrupt the order of my discourses that I may speak of St. John. We may discover what he was by considering what the function of an Apostle was. His words and acts may in turn be the greatest helps in explaining that function to us.

(1) The words, 'when it was day,' recall the preceding verse : ' *It came to pass in those days, that he went out into a mountain to pray, and continued all night in prayer to God.*' I have spoken already of the prayers of Christ in connexion with His works. When the work most expressed His authority, when the healing act was preceded by an ' *I will*,' He was still renouncing all independence. *Every* prayer is a renunciation of independence. *Every* prayer says, ' We can do nothing without Thee.' As *His* prayer were the essentially true prayers, they must have had this meaning perfectly, without any reservation. St. John's Gospel is here, as elsewhere, the interpreter of that which

H

is implied in the others. It is he who repeats to us those words of Christ, ' *The Son can do nothing of himself, but what he seeth the Father do: for what things soever he doeth, these also doeth the Son likewise.*'

How necessary is this recollection, if we would understand the calling and choice of the Apostles, we shall see presently. I would remark here, that when we describe Jesus as *the Messiah*, we mean that He was the Apostle of God. That title the writer of the Epistle to the Hebrews gives Him in a very memorable passage : ' *Wherefore, holy brethren, partakers of the heavenly calling, consider the Apostle and High Priest of our profession, Christ Jesus ; who was faithful to him that appointed him, as also Moses was faithful in all his house.*' He goes on : For ' *Moses verily was faithful in all his house, as a servant . . . but Christ, as a son over his own house.*' The faithfulness and obedience of the son is not less than the faithfulness and obedience of the servant—but greater. The filial submission is the perfect submission ; the servant's is only a foretaste of it, an aspiration after it. And if we follow the Creed we shall remember, that the Son of God did not *acquire* obedience by taking upon Him our nature. Obedience was His divine nature. He endowed ours with it. He showed forth in human life, under the pressure of human temptations, that loving surrender of His whole being to His Father, wherein consisted His eternal delight.

(2) That night in which He was not alone, because the Father was with Him, prepared Him to come down amidst the disciples whom He had gathered about Him. *He* had gathered them ; they knew it. Each of them had heard a voice, more or less distinctly, bidding him come. Each had yielded to One who, he felt, had a right to command

him. The disciples had not picked out a leader from the
number that were then offering themselves to their choice.
They had not said, 'We prefer this Nazarene Teacher to
'that Pharisee who has come out of Judæa, to that
'Herodian, to that Sadducee.' They had not said, 'We
prefer Him to that insurgent chief who is saying that he
'has a commission to overthrow the Romans and restore
'the kingdom of David.' None of these fishermen would
have used that language. They had been drawn to this
Person. Why He has brought them together, what they
are to do, they cannot yet tell. They are following a
Master. He will show them in due time what work He
intends for them. And now He takes twelve out of their
number. Are these to be the special servants of the
King? Are they in time to fight for Him? Are they to
have the chief offices in His palace? He does not say.
But He calls them Apostles. They are to be *sent forth*.
That is clear, whatever else is hidden. Where they are
to go, what they are to speak, what acts are to accompany
the speech—on these points He will not surely leave them
ignorant. But at first their separation from the rest of
those who followed Christ—what it signified, what kind
of eminence or dignity it conferred upon them—will have
occupied them chiefly.

(3) Clearly they *were* distinguished from the other
members of the little flock. What had caused the difference? Did He merely like them better than the rest?
Had they merited some greater honour at His hands?
Had He discovered some peculiar capacity in them?
All such questions would occur to these poor fishermen;
would occur to them not less because they were poor
fishermen. They are human thoughts—thoughts that do

not belong to one class of men more than another. With them would of course come such as these : 'We twelve ' cannot be all alike in His estimation. His choice must ' be the reward of desert. Some of us must have higher ' merits than the rest. When all is arranged, when He ' can finally apportion His dignities, which of us will ' be the greatest ?' We do not imagine the existence of these jealousies. They are carefully reported to us by the Evangelists. No effort is made to disguise the unsuitableness of the times at which they broke out. St. Luke will tell us that the Last Supper was one of these. And it is St. John who tells us that, at that Last Supper, Jesus took a towel and girded Himself, and stooped down and washed His Apostles' feet, and said unto them, 'What I have ' done ye know not now, but shall know hereafter. As I ' have washed your feet, so are ye *to wash one another's feet.*' It is St. John who tells us that at that Supper Jesus said, ' *Ye have not chosen me, but I have chosen you, and ordained you, that ye should go and bring forth fruit, and that your fruit should remain : that whatsoever ye shall ask of the Father in my name, he may give it you.*' Here are the opposing explanations of the nature and grounds of the Apostolical calling. Meditate on them carefully. Meditate on them to-day especially. We have been told recently that St. John spent the last years of his stay on earth in putting together accounts of his Master's doings, for the express purpose of exalting himself above the other Apostles, of proving himself to be the favourite of Jesus, of confounding the earlier Evangelists who had not gratified his vanity sufficiently. I need not tell you, that the man who could do this must have been of all who ever dwelt on this earth the basest and the falsest. Every year of his long pilgrimage this horrible conceit must have been ripening in him; every year it must have been making him capable of profounder dissimulation and treachery. Christendom has been for eighteen centuries drawing lessons from him concerning love and truth. Dying men and women have been sustained by his lessons. Churches have felt them to be stinging reproofs of their untruth and selfishness. And these have all proceeded from a man who surrendered himself to a habit of mind which we should pronounce execrable in any neighbour, or in any fictitious character; whose language must have been most hypocritical when it was most elevated. Those who can believe this may believe it. The supposition makes a more tremendous demand on my credulity than all the miracles which have ever been palmed on the world since it was created. But I do not allude to such a calumny for its own sake. I allude to it because I wish you to see how very natural such an hypothesis is, if we assume the Apostle to have been merely following the bent of his own inclinations. He might have sunk to this deep moral degradation. Any of the Apostles might have sunk into it. Judas actually fell into it. The self-exalting, covetous spirit which was working in all, became master of him. He gave himself up to it. He betrayed his Master—not so foully as St. John would have betrayed Him, if he had acted as these critics say that he acted—but so that all mankind have regarded him with trembling and horror. The other Apostles learnt that the Son of God was manifested that this devil might be cast out of them. They learnt that, as the Father had sent Him forth, so they were sent forth to bear witness by word and deed that love is mightier than selfishness; that Christ revealed

His Father as the unselfish Being, as the Author and
Example of all sacrifice; that Christ chose them from no
partial affection, but as witnesses of His Truth and
Love to all mankind. And the one who was nearest to
Him, and received most of His love into his heart, was
the one whom He called to show forth most fully the
love with which He loved the Universe in giving Himself
for it.

(4) The number which our Lord fixed upon for His
Apostles of course reminded them of the tribes into which
their nation was divided. They could not suppose that
He had adopted that number carelessly, or without reference to their history. In their early work, there was much
to confirm this impression. They were not to enter into
any village of the Gentiles or of the Samaritans. They
were to preach to the lost sheep of the house of Israel of
the kingdom which Israelites had been so long expecting.
Was it different in after times? St. Peter felt—so St. Luke
tells us in his other treatise—that the place of Judas must
be supplied before the promise that they should receive
power from on high to testify of their Lord's resurrection
could be fulfilled. When the door of the Kingdom of
Heaven was opened to the Gentiles, the charm of the
number might seem to be dissolved. St. Paul and St.
Barnabas were called Apostles. St. Paul in terms asserted
the title against those who would have denied it to him.
No one vindicated his right to it more practically. No
one so distinctly perceived what was involved in the
command, '*Go ye, and preach the gospel to every creature.*'
If any formality about the difference between twelve or
thirteen or fourteen stood in the way of such an object, it
was to be treated with contempt. Wisdom would be justi-

fied in breaking through its own rules. The principle
of the shewbread would be applicable in another case.
What is given for men must not be used against men. If
St. Paul had not declared with vehemence that one called by
Christ in heaven was as really an Apostle as those whom
He called upon earth, the message of the Apostles of the
circumcision would have been enfeebled, not less than his
own. It would not have been the testimony to an actual
kingdom, to a living Christ.

Nevertheless, when we read the Epistle of St. James,
and observe to whom it is addressed; when we read the
Epistle of St. Peter to those who were dispersed through
the different provinces of the Roman and Parthian empires;
above all, when we read the book from which our second
lesson has been taken this morning, and compare it with
the few records that remain to us of St. John's life; we
must feel that the twelve tribes of Israel had still a
mighty significance for the world, and that the relation
of the twelve Apostles to them had been deeply, inefface-
ably impressed upon the minds of those Apostles. The
twelve tribes represented to St. John the sealed witnesses
of God upon earth. It was when he had contemplated
these most earnestly, that he became aware of the truth
that a '*multitude, which no man could number, of all
nations, and kindreds, and people, and tongues, stood before
the throne, and before the Lamb, clothed with white robes, and
palms in their hands; and cried with a loud voice, saying,
Salvation to our God which sitteth upon the throne, and unto
the Lamb.*' And so, in his last chapter but one, we read:
'*And he carried me away in the spirit to a great and high
mountain, and shewed me that great city, the holy Jerusalem,
descending out of heaven from God, having the glory of God:*

*and her light was like unto a stone most precious, even like
a jasper stone, clear as crystal ; and had a wall great and
high, and had twelve gates, and at the gates twelve angels,
and names written thereon, which are the names of the twelve
tribes of the children of Israel. . . . And the wall of the city
had twelve foundations, and in them the names of the* TWELVE
APOSTLES OF THE LAMB.'

I believe this vision was presented to the mind of the
prophet when the old Jerusalem had disappeared or was
about to disappear. If it vanished from the earth, only
leaving the Roman Empire, its conqueror, to exult in its
ruin, an Apostle would have groaned over such a contradiction of all the divine promises. He believed that
its overthrow was the fulfilment of the divine promises,
that it would be the revelation of that kingdom whereof
the twelve tribes had borne witness by their original constitution, by their strange preservation, by their incapacity
to maintain their unity, by their passionate eagerness to
assert it ; that kingdom of which the twelve Apostles had
borne witness, declaring its unity to stand not in any
fleshly election, but in the union of God with man, of
the Father with the Son. Such a kingdom could not be
shaken by any earthquake. It could not be limited by
any measures of time and space. Death could not divide
the members of it from each other. It would exist from
generation to generation in its living Head—the conqueror
of death. Its nature might be misunderstood, its principles might be set at nought, by those who were adopted
into it. But it would go on manifesting itself more and
more, till all its enemies were put under Christ's feet. Yet
in its full manifestation, in its most perfect glory, its
ancient walls would only look clearer, brighter, firmer.

The names of the twelve tribes of Israel, and of the twelve
Apostles of the Lamb would be visible in the city which
needed no temple, and no sun to lighten it.

(5) St. John's day has tempted me to connect these passages from the Apocalypse with that simple narrative which
we read in the chapter from St. Luke. But I do not think
I could have illustrated that narrative better from any
other source. For the more we remember that the Apostles
were Jews, that they were sent forth as Jews to bless all the
families of the earth, the better we shall understand their
institution, in its growth, in its completion ; the less we
shall wonder when we hear of a final Apostle—of one who
tarried till the Lord came. To a very respectable and very
earnest body of men in our day it has been a great offence
that the Apostolical order should have ceased in the
Church. They are sure that it must have been removed
as the punishment of some great sin; they are sure that,
however long we have been without it, there must be a
restoration of it. If it had the especial fitness which
I have supposed to the Jewish economy—if the whole
formation of it denoted it as a Jewish order—if it existed
to tell Jews of a Kingdom of Heaven, for which their
national institutions had been preparing, and which would
be revealed as they expired ; one can understand why there
should be an Apostle to announce this consummation, and
why there should be no other to take his place. He saw
the night torches go out ; he saw the Sun rising. He
needed no successor to bear his name. He left the world
with the assurance that the kingdoms of the world were
the kingdoms of God and His Christ, and that they would
be shown to be so. The old forms would be changed ;
there would be new bottles prepared for the new wine ;

but the law and the prophets would not perish; the Old
Testament and the New would live on; the walls of the
city would still have the names of the twelve tribes; the
deeper foundations of the city would still have the names
of the twelve Apostles of the Lamb.

(6) But while I cannot see why we should wish the
order of God's universe altered, or any return to one which
has done its work and passed away, I do feel that we have
a heavier sin to confess than the sin of being no longer
directed by a body of twelve Apostles. It is the sin of
pretending to believe the message of the twelve Apostles,
and not really believing it; the sin of supposing that they
were divine and inspired men, and yet that they pre-
varicated when they said that a Kingdom of Heaven was at
hand, and that it would actually be revealed in their day;
the sin of keeping Christmas Day, and of not owning
that God has indeed given His only begotten Son to take
our nature upon Him, that we, being regenerated and
made His children by adoption and grace, might daily
be renewed by His Holy Spirit. If we believed that
this union and reconciliation of heaven and earth had
taken place—if we held that our baptism into the name
of the Father, and the Son, and the Holy Ghost was not a
delusion—we should also believe that the sacred writer
was sincere in saying, '*Ye are not come unto the mount
that might be touched, and that burned with fire, nor unto
blackness, and darkness, and tempest. . . . But ye are come
unto mount Sion, and unto the city of the living God, the
heavenly Jerusalem, and to an innumerable company of
angels, to the general assembly and church of the firstborn,
which are written in heaven, and to God the Judge of
all . . . and to Jesus the mediator of the new covenant,*

*and to the blood of sprinkling, which speaketh better things
than that of Abel.'* The tidings of this city of God
were those which the Apostles carried first to their own
nation, then to the different tribes of the earth. A
Christendom rose to the sound; a modern world appeared
out of the ruins of the ancient world. We have ceased to
believe in such a city. There were Apostles, inspired men,
1800 years ago. We spell out with difficulty some of their
words, and call them divine. We fancy that there has
been a feeble transmission of their authority from generation to generation among ourselves. And people in other
lands tell us that except we own an Apostle who was
crucified on a Roman hill as the head of the Universal
Church, we can never know who our Father in heaven
is ; we can never really be one family in His Son ; we can
never really be baptized by His Spirit.

To all these doctrines I would oppose the doctrine of
that Apostle whom we remember to-day. If we have not
yet learnt to regard him as a self-seeking, self-glorifying
deceiver, let us accept the other—I believe the only other
—alternative. Let us recognise him as the teacher through
whom those bright beams of light were shed upon the
Church, which illumined it in the hour when the old
world was passing away with a great noise, which shall be
shed upon it again when its divisions, and hatreds, and
falsehoods are bringing back the darkness and chaos out
of which it arose.

'*Many other signs,*' he says in his Gospel, '*truly did
Jesus in the presence of his disciples, which are not written
in this book : but these are written that ye might believe
that Jesus is the Christ, the Son of God, and that
believing ye might have life through his name.*' Thus he

defines the office and work of an Evangelist, the end of
all Scripture ; not to fix our thoughts upon the letters of
a book, but to direct us to that Son who died, and rose,
and liveth for evermore.

'That which was from the beginning,' so he writes in his
Epistle, *'that which we have heard, which we have seen with
our eyes, which we have looked upon, and our hands have
handled, of the Word of life ; (for the life was manifested,
and we have seen it, and bear witness, and shew unto you
that eternal life, which was with the Father, and was manifested unto us ;) that which we have seen and heard declare
we unto you . . . and truly our fellowship is with the Father,
and with his Son Jesus Christ. . . . This then is the message
which we have heard of him, and declare unto you, that
God is light, and in him is no darkness at all. If we
say that we have fellowship with him, and walk in darkness, we lie, and do not the truth : but if we walk in the
light, as he is in the light, we have fellowship one with
another, and the blood of Jesus Christ his Son cleanseth us
from all sin.'* There is the theology, there is the morality
of an Apostle ; a theology and a morality, as I think, fresh
and young for all times, striking at the root of *our* denials
and *our* self-deceptions, showing us why we cannot believe
in ourselves, or our notions, and theories ; showing us in
whom we may believe, who is able to deliver us from all
our darkness and enmities, who is able to bring us into
His perfect light and love.

And if we pass from the Gospel and the Epistle to
that book which is rightly called the Revelation, or unveiling of Jesus Christ, we find the old Apostle, the last
of the Apostles, telling of Him which is, and which was,
and which is to come ; of the seven spirits before His

throne; of Jesus Christ the faithful witness, the first
begotten from the dead, the Prince of all the kings of
the earth.   He is telling us of the kingdom under which
we are living, of the Name with which we are sealed.
He looks back to the past, claiming his own kinsmen after
the flesh, his own beloved nation of Israel, as heirs of
promises which must be fulfilled.   He looks onward to
the future, claiming all nations as intended to walk in the
divine light, to bring their treasures into the divine city.
In that city may be found the names not of one but of all
the Apostles.   For all testified of the truth which St. Peter
declared in express words, ' *Wherefore also it is contained*
in the scripture, Behold, I lay in Sion a chief corner stone,
elect, and precious : and he that believeth on HIM *shall not*
be confounded.'

LECTURE X.

THE SUBJECTS AND LAWS OF THE KINGDOM.

St. Luke VI. 20.

And he lifted up his eyes on his disciples, and said, Blessed be ye poor, for yours is the kingdom of God.

So begins a discourse which has often been said to contain a code of very high morality for those who forsake the low level of the crowd, and aim at a specially elevated standard of excellence. The previous sentence explains to whom the discourse was addressed. '*And he came down with them, and stood in the plain, and the company of his disciples, and a great multitude of people out of all Judea and Jerusalem, and from the sea-coast of Tyre and Sidon, which came to hear him, and to be healed of their diseases.*' Those were the people who heard Christ say : '*Blessed are ye poor, for yours is the kingdom of heaven.*'

(1) We are wont to mitigate the force of this sentence by referring to the one in St. Matthew's Gospel, which most resembles it. For 'poor' we say, the other Evangelist gives us 'poor in spirit.' Is not that the sense in which we must understand the words here? I am most thankful for the expression in St. Matthew, and am quite willing to use it for the illustration of the discourse in which it occurs. We may find it a great help hereafter in understanding St. Luke. But I must take *his* language as it

stands. He says that our Lord lifted up His eyes on a miscellaneous crowd. He cannot have expected that crowd to introduce any spiritual qualification into the words, 'Yours is the Kingdom of Heaven.' What, then, did those words import ? Might they be addressed to a multitude similarly composed in London ?

It seems to me, my friends, that the answer to these questions must depend entirely upon the meaning which we attach to the phrase, *Kingdom of Heaven.* How important that phrase is for the understanding of the Gospels we have seen already. The Kingdom of Heaven is the subject of the Gospel. The acts of Christ in healing the sick and casting out devils were signs of the Kingdom of Heaven. The Apostles were the ministers of the Kingdom of Heaven. They had just been selected out of a body of fishermen and tax-gatherers, that they might go and preach the Kingdom of Heaven—whilst their Master was upon earth, to their own countrymen, when He had left the earth, to all nations. And now, with these Apostles so chosen, He comes down to some table-land upon the mountain, and He says to the poor—the actual poor—about Him, 'Yours is the Kingdom of Heaven.' Suppose those words were limited to the disciples who were close to Him —suppose, even, they were limited to the twelve. Still we know upon their own authority that the twelve were not yet poor in spirit ; that they were continually giving evidence of being proud in spirit, the best as well as the worst of them. In what sense, then, was theirs the Kingdom of Heaven ?

Surely, in this very simple and direct sense. Our Lord had come to tell them who was governing them—under whose authority they were living. Who had they fancied

was governing them? One who regarded the rich with
affection; who had bestowed great advantages upon *them*;
who had given *them* an earnest here of what He might do for
them hereafter. It was most natural for poor men to put this
interpretation upon that which they saw, and that which
they felt. It was difficult for them to find any other interpretation. It was not *more* difficult for the people who dwelt
about the coasts of Tyre and Sidon than for the people who
dwell in the courts and alleys of London. The difficulty
is the same precisely in kind. The degree of it must be
greater on some accounts for the dwellers in a crowded
modern city than for those who breathed the fresh air of
Galilee. The difficulty was not diminished for the latter
(I mean for the Galileans) by anything which they heard
from their religious teachers. It was enormously increased.
God was said to demand of these poor people religious services which they could not render; an amount of knowledge about His law which they could not possess. His
prizes and blessings here and hereafter were said to
be contingent upon their performing these services—
upon their having that knowledge. Whichever way they
turned—to their present condition—to the forefathers, to
whose errors or sins they must in great part attribute that
condition—to the future, in which they must expect the
full fruit of the misery and evil into which they had fallen
—all looked equally dark and hopeless.

Startling indeed, then, were the tidings, ' *Yours is the
Kingdom of Heaven.*' Most startling, when they were
translated into these, ' You have a Father in Heaven who
' is seeking after you, watching over you, whom you may
' trust entirely. He ruled over your forefathers. He pro-
' mised that He would show forth his dominion fully and

' perfectly in the generations to come. I am come to tell
' you of Him; to tell you how He rules over you, and how
' you may be in very deed His subjects. I am come that
' you and your children may be citizens in God's own city;
' that the Lord God Himself may reign over you.' I cannot
render the phrase into any equivalents that are simpler,
more obvious, than these. And if they were true, must
they not have been true for all that crowd, for every thief
and harlot in it? Was not this the very message of John,
delivered by Him who could not only call to repentance
but give repentance?

(2) 'Yes,' it may be answered—'That might be so, if
' the language only declared to the poor that there was a
' Heavenly Father who cared for them *no less* than He
' cared for the rich; but the sentences which follow give
' them a positive advantage: it would appear as if the
' blessing on the poor involved a curse on the rich. What
' other force can you put on such sentences as these? "*Blessed
' are ye that hunger now, for ye shall be filled. Blessed are
' ye that weep now, for ye shall laugh. But woe unto you
' that are rich, for ye have received your consolation. Woe
' unto you that are full, for ye shall hunger. Woe unto
' you that laugh now, for ye shall mourn and weep."*'

Language so explicit as this cannot be evaded. And I
hold it is greatly for the interest of all of us who are leading easy and comfortable lives in the world, that it should
not be evaded. If any amount of riches, greater or smaller,
does give us consolation, it is well for us to understand
that there is a woe upon those riches. They were not
meant to give consolation; we were not meant to find it
in them. If any laughter of ours does make us incapable
of weeping, incapable of entering into the sorrow of the

I

world in which we are dwelling, we ought to feel that
there is misery and death in that laughter. Our Lord
does not speak against laughter; He sets it forth as a
blessing. He does denounce all that laughter which is an
exultation in our own prosperity, and in the calamities of
others. He does promise that those who are indulging
that sort of laughter shall weep. I use the word *promise*
advisedly. It is a promise, not a threatening; or, if you
please, a threat which contains a promise. It is the proof
that we are under a Kingdom of Heaven; that God does
not allow such laughter to go on; that He stops it; that
He gives the blessing of sorrow in place of it. And thus
all alike are taught that they are under this fatherly
government. All are shown that the Father in Heaven is
aware of the discipline which they need, and will apportion it. All may be brought to take their places with
their brethren in this Kingdom. All may be taught that
the common blessings—the blessings from which one cannot exclude another—are the highest blessings. All may
be brought to know that this one fact, that they have a
Father in Heaven, is worth all others. And so that poverty of
spirit, which is only another name for childlike dependence
upon One who is above us, and is all good, because we have
found we cannot depend upon ourselves, may be wrought
by Him with whom we have to do in poor and rich equally.
The heavenly treasures may be revealed to both which
moth and rust cannot corrupt—which thieves cannot break
through and steal.

(3) Thus far, assuredly, the tendency of this discourse of
our Lord's has been to level, not to exalt. The Kingdom
of Heaven has not been a prize for those who are unlike
their fellows, but for those who will take their stand by

them—who will set up no exclusive pretensions of their own. But what shall we say of this benediction ? '*Blessed are ye when men shall hate you, and when they shall separate you from their company, and shall reproach you, and shall cast out your name as evil, for the Son of Man's sake. Re-joice ye in that day, and leap for joy, for, behold, your reward is great in heaven: for in the like manner did their fathers unto the prophets.*' And again of this woe ? ' *Woe unto you, when all men shall speak well of you, for so did their fathers unto the false prophets.*' Is there not here a glorification of the little minority which is persecuted ; a denunciation of the majority which persecutes ?

The comment on the language is in the actual history. Why was St. Stephen, whom we have been remembering lately, cast out of the city of Jerusalem and stoned ? Because he was accused of breaking down the barriers which separated the chosen people from the surrounding nations. Why was the young man at whose feet the witnesses against Stephen laid down their clothes afterwards de-nounced in the same city as one who ought not to live ? Because he said that he was sent with a message of peace and reconciliation to the Gentiles. What was it that sus-tained and comforted Stephen in the hour when his coun-trymen were gnashing upon him with their teeth ? The sight of the Son of Man standing at the right hand of God ; the Saviour and King, not of him and his brother dis-ciples, but of mankind. What was St. Paul's deepest sor-row, and how was it that in the midst of that sorrow he could always rejoice ? His sorrow was that his kinsmen after the flesh were to be cut off, because they were enemies to God, and contrary to all men. His joy was in the thought that ' all Israel should be saved ;' that ' God had

I 2

' concluded all in unbelief that He might have mercy upon
' all.'   This, then, was the witness of the little band of the
persecuted, that God is the Father of all ; that His Kingdom is over all.   And the determination of that powerful
majority of persecutors was to keep the favour of God and
the Kingdom of Heaven to themselves.   Those of whom
all men speak well are those who flatter their exclusiveness ; who lead them to think that they are better than
others, and that they shall have mercies which are denied
to others.   The comfort of the persecuted, which the per-
secutor could not have, was the comfort of believing that
God would conquer all obstacles ; that the Son of Man, for
whose sake they loved not their lives, would be shown in
very deed to be King of kings and Lord of lords—all
human wills being subjected to His will.

(4) And so you perceive how the next precepts, which
we often read as if they were mere isolated maxims, are
connected with these blessings and these woes.   *But I
say unto you which hear'*—unto you, that is, whom I have
told that men shall separate you from their company, and
cast out your persons as evil,—*' Love your enemies ; do good
to them which persecute you.   Bless them that curse you, and
pray for them which despitefully use you.   And unto him
that smiteth thee on the one cheek offer also the other ; and
him that taketh away thy cloke forbid not to take thy coat
also.   Give to every man that asketh of thee ; and of him
that taketh away thy goods ask them not again.   And as ye
would that men should do to you, do ye also to them likewise.
For if ye love them which love you, what thank have ye ? for
sinners also love those that love them.   And if ye do good to
them which do good to you, what thank have ye ? for sinners
also do even the same.   And if ye lend to them of whom ye hope*

to receive, what thank have ye ? for sinners also lend to sin-
ners, to receive as much again.   But love ye your enemies,
and do good, and lend, hoping for nothing again.   And ye
shall be the children of the Highest : for he is kind unto the
unthankful and to the evil.   Be ye therefore merciful, as
your Father in heaven is merciful.'

In these passages is contained the sum of what we have
been used to call the peculiar Christian morality.   It is
supposed to be very admirable, but far too fine for common
use.   He who aims at following it is to be counted a high
saint.   He claims a state immensely above the ordinary
level of humanity.   He even discards the maxims by which
civil society is governed—those which the statesman considers necessary for his objects.   No doubt, it is said, this
transcendent doctrine has had a certain influence upon the
nations in which it is promulgated.   It has modified some
of the thoughts and feelings which are most adverse to it.
The beauty of it is confessed by many who never dream
of practising it.   There are some unbelievers who try to
practise it, and say, that if this part of Christianity could
be separated from its mysterious part, they could not
reverence it too highly.   But though this is true, we have
proofs, it is said, every day and hour, that this love to
enemies, this blessing them that curse, this turning the
one cheek to him who smites the other, is altogether contrary to the habits and tempers of the world.

My friends, the evidence goes much further than that.
We need not derive our proofs that the natural heart re-
volts against these precepts from what is called *the World.*
The records of the *Church* will furnish that demonstration
much more perfectly.   Hatred of those whom they have
counted their enemies,—this has been the too characteristic

sign of men who have called themselves Christ's servants
and soldiers.   Curses have been their favourite weapons.
No Church can bring that charge against another without
laying itself open to retaliation.   And it cannot be pleaded,
' Oh, there is a corrupt unbelieving leaven in every Christian society.'   The habit I speak of has come forth often
most flagrantly in those who were denouncing this leaven,
who were seeking to cast it out.   I am not saying that they
were not good men.   The case is all the stronger if they
were.   I am not saying that a genuine zeal for truth was
not at the root of their rage, and did not mingle with the
most outrageous acts of it.   Of all this, God will be the
Judge.   We are not wise to anticipate His decisions.   But
such facts, which are notorious, and are repeated in every
age and in every country, show the absurdity of the theory
that what our Lord lays down as the Laws of the Kingdom
of Heaven, are intended for the use of a particular class
of persons who aspire to outstrip their fellows, and win
higher prizes than the rest of mankind.   They lead us
to suspect that those who have aimed at such distinctions
and pursued such objects have not been able to submit to
His government—have assumed a position which was
essentially rebellious.   They lead us back to the levelling
sentence with which the discourse opens, and which must
be accepted as the key to the whole of it.   What business
has any citizen of a kingdom to talk of a certain standard
which is meant for him and not for all the subjects of it ?
What is that but adopting the maxim which the Roman
poet unfairly ascribed to the Greek hero, that ' laws were
not born for him ? '

How reasonable on the other hand—how perfectly consistent—is our Lord's language, if we suppose Him to be

revealing the laws under which God has constituted human beings, the laws which are the expression of His own Divine Nature, the laws which were perfectly fulfilled in His Son, the laws which His Spirit is seeking to write on all hearts! What signifies it to the reality of such laws that this or that man transgresses them; that he who transgresses them calls himself Churchman or Dissenter, Catholic or Protestant, believer or infidel? If they are true they must stand in spite of such transgressions; they will make their power manifest through such transgressions. There will be a witness on behalf of them, such as we see there is in all human consciences; there will be a resistance to them, such as we see there is, in all human wills. Our belief in their ultimate triumph over that which opposes them must depend on our belief in Him who is the Author of the Law. If we think that He is our Father in Heaven, and that His Law of Forgiveness has been fully accomplished in Christ, and that His Spirit is stronger than the Evil Spirit, every sign of the victory of Love over striving and hating wills must be a pledge how the battle is to terminate; *no* success of bitterness, and wrath, and malice, however it may shake our minds, can be anything but a proof that less than Almighty Love, less than a Divine Sacrifice, would have been unable to subdue such adversaries. But if we think this discourse to be the announcement of a refined ethical system, not the proclamation of a Kingdom of Heaven, as it professes to be, we may well complain how feeble and ineffective it is and must always be. We may say that its power can never be recognised beyond a circle of rare exceptional persons. And we may find that these rare exceptional persons are always supplied with a set of evasions, equivocations, and apologies, for violating every one of its principles, especially in those acts which they consider most religious and meritorious.

Those who confine this discourse to saints speedily contradict themselves. When they bring forth evidences of Christianity, or evidences of the influence of the Catholic Church, they appeal to the power which the Cross, with its proclamation of divine forgiveness to enemies, has exercised over the wild warring tribes that have fashioned modern Europe. They ask whether the conscience of those tribes, in the midst of all their bloody feuds and acts of personal vengeance, did not stoop to the authority of a Prince of Peace; whether it did not confess Him as King of kings and Lord of lords; whether it did not acknowledge those as especially His ministers who, in bodily weakness—in defiance of the physically strong —showed forth the loving-kindness which they said was His, and claimed the serf and the noble as alike His subjects and His brethren. The facts cannot be gainsaid. They are written in sunbeams on all the darkest pages of modern history. What do they prove? Surely that our Lord was not proclaiming a code which was at variance with civil order and obedience—a transcendental morality—but principles which were the foundation of civil order and obedience; principles which were to undermine and uproot the very evils which all national codes are endeavouring to counteract. The national code—the most exalted, the most divine code—can only forbid, only counteract. If it aspires to do more; if it strives to extirpate vices instead of to punish crimes; if it enjoins virtues instead of demanding simple submission to its decrees; it proves its own impotence. It is always asking for help to do that which it cannot do. It wants a power to make the obedience which it needs voluntary; to kindle the patriotism without which it will only be directed to a herd of animals, not a race of men. Wherever there has been voluntary obedience, wherever there has been a patriotism which has made men willing to die that their land might not be in the possession of strangers, there has been faith in an unseen Ruler; there has been a confidence that He wills men to be free. The Jewish history interprets other history. It shows what has been the source of law and freedom; what has been the destruction of both; what has been the preservation of both. This discourse, because it proclaims a more universal principle than the Jewish or national principle, is supposed to set that aside. I accept our Lord's words, 'I come not to destroy, but to fulfil,' as true in every case. He does not destroy the fundamental maxim, that God is the Author of the commandments. He fulfils it by proclaiming the *mind* of His Father in Heaven as the ground of all the acts of His children. He does not destroy one sacrifice which any patriot had made for his people's freedom. He fulfils it in His perfect sacrifice to God and for us. He does not destroy any one precept of duty to God or to our neighbour. He fulfils it by baptizing with His Spirit; by making duty to God the surrender of man's will to His Will which is working in us; that Will binding men to each other as members of the same body; that Will fighting with all the selfish impulses which tear us asunder. There is no opposition between the Kingdom of Heaven and any kingdom of earth, except what is produced by this selfishness, which is the enemy of both. If the civil ruler sanctions one law for the rich and one for the poor, he offends against the maxims of the Kingdom of Heaven: but then he also introduces a confusion into his own. If he prefers war to peace, gambling to honesty, bondage to freedom, and if he seeks religious sanctions to uphold him in these tastes, he offends against the maxims of the Kingdom of Heaven, and he is preparing ruin for his own state. If the ecclesiastic proclaims one law for the saint and another for the common man, he overthrows the common order and morality of nations; but he sins still more directly against the laws which Christ proclaimed on the Mount. If he sets up the priest against the magistrate, he disturbs the peace of civil communities; but he also exalts the priest into the place of God, and so commits treason against the Kingdom of Heaven. If he assume the office of a judge of His brethren, he may do much mischief on earth which the ruler on earth cannot hinder. But he falls under *this* sentence:—*'Judge not, and ye shall not be judged; condemn not, and ye shall not be condemned; forgive, and ye shall be forgiven.'*

These laws of the Kingdom of Heaven seem very hard to keep. See what hinders us from keeping them. It is not some incapacity. It is our determination to assume a place which is not ours. Each of us is continually setting up himself to be a God. Each is seizing the judgment throne of the universe. We know that it is so. And from this throne we must come down. We must confess that we are not gods; not able to pronounce on the condition of our fellows, needing forgiveness every day from our Father, and from each other, permitted to dispense what He sends us. The lesson is a simple one. Yet every other is contained in it. If we do, in very deed, come to the light, our deeds may be made manifest; if we ask to be judged—if we ask our Father in Heaven to make us His ministers and not His rivals—we shall be able to enter into the wonderful precept that follows (v. 38) : ' *Give, and it shall be given unto you ; good measure, pressed down and shaken together, and running over, shall men give into your bosom.   For with the same measure that ye mete withal it shall be measured to you again.*' They had been told before that they were ' *to do good and lend, hoping for nothing again.*' How is it that we are encouraged to hope here that if we *give it shall be given to us ?* The two passages explain each other ; experience confirms them both. *Only* the man who gives, hoping for nothing again, who gives freely without calculation out of the fulness of his heart, ever can find his love returned to him. He may win hatred as well as love ; but love does come in measures that he never could dream of.   We see it every day ; and every day, perhaps, we may be disappointed at finding some favours which we thought were well laid out bringing back no recompense. They were bestowed with the hope of something again.

Yes, friends ; most truly are these the unchangeable Laws of the Kingdom of Heaven. That which we measure is measured to us again ; selfishness for selfishness, love for love. It may not be clear to us now that it is so. We shall be sure of it one day—in that day which shall show Him who spoke this discourse to be indeed the King of kings and Lord of lords. For, as His next words tell us, this has been the great inversion of order : ' *The blind have been leading the blind ; the disciples have been setting themselves above their Master.*' We have been laying down our own maxims and codes of morality. Each one has been saying to his brother, ' *Brother, let me pull out the mote out of thine eye.*' We have had such a clear discernment of these motes ! And all the while none of us has

been aware of the beam in his own eye. And how can
any of us become aware of it; how can we escape the
charge of hypocrisy which our consciences own to be so
well deserved? Only if there is a King and Judge over
us who detects the beam; who makes us feel that it is
there; who Himself undertakes to cast it out. To that
point we must always return. We may boast of this
morality as something to glorify saints. We may call
it 'delicious,' as a modern French critic calls it. Only,
when it actually confronts us, as the word of a King
who is speaking to us, and convicting us of our depar-
tures from it—only then shall we discover that it is for
sinners, not saints; that it is terrible, not delicious. But
only then shall we know what the blessedness is of being
claimed as children of this Kingdom; only then shall
we begin to apprehend the glory of which we are inheritors. For we then shall understand that there is a
selfish evil nature in every man, let him call himself
Churchman or man of the world, believer or unbeliever,
which cannot bring forth good fruit—which is utterly
damnable; and that there is a Divine root of humanity,
a Son of Man, whence all the good in Churchman or man
of the world, in believer or unbeliever, springs—whence
nothing but good can spring. If we exalt ourselves upon
our privileges as Christians or saints, the King will say
to us, ' *Why call ye me Lord, and do not the things which
I say?*' If we submit to His Spirit we may bring forth
now the fruits of good works which are to His glory; we
may look for the day when every Law of His Kingdom
shall be fulfilled, when all shall know Him from the least
to the greatest. And Churches, in the sense of their own

nothingness, may seek after the foundation which God has laid, and which will endure the shock of all winds and waves. And Churches which rest upon their own decrees and traditions and holiness will be like the man '*who without a foundation built an house upon the earth, against which the stream did beat vehemently, and immediately i fell; and the ruin of that house was great.*'

LECTURE XI.

THE KING CALLING FORTH THE FAITH OF HIS SUBJECTS.

St. Luke VII. 50.

And he said to the woman, Thy faith hath saved thee.   Go in peace.

The Epiphany, or Manifestation of Christ to the wise men who came from the East, is the introduction to a number of Epiphanies or Manifestations which are commemorated in the Epistles and Gospels for these Sundays. All the acts of Christ upon earth—though there are other aspects of them to which our minds are directed at other seasons —may be most fittingly contemplated under this aspect. I shall, I think, be doing my best to illustrate the different topics which are brought before us in the 7th chapter of St. Luke, if I trace this thread through them all. I have chosen the last verse of the chapter as my text, not only for its own sake, but because it bears upon all the previous manifestations of which the Evangelist has been speaking.

They were addressed not to the eye but to the faith of those who received them. That is the characteristic of an Epiphany in the sense in which the Church uses it. The wise men have been asking the stars to tell them if there is any King of men, any one mightier over human hearts than the lights which shine in the firmament can be.

They are led to Bethlehem. They *see* only a child lying in a cradle. A glory within that child reveals itself not to their sight, but to their spirits. A circle of legends forms itself about this story. The glory becomes an outward, visible glory. The craving for wonders is gratified by imaginations of what these magicians may have been, and what must have convinced them that the King was there. The passages which we read on Wednesday from Isaiah and St. Paul drew away our thoughts from an incident to the universal principle which it illustrates and embodies. The Gospel of the Kingdom of Heaven to the nations can only be described as the arising and shining of a light upon the consciences and hearts of those who were sitting in darkness. God revealed to those consciences and hearts their true King. A Church rises up to bear witness of His Name and of His dominion to the human race.

(1) The first story which comes before us in this chapter is in direct connexion with the illumination to the Gentile sages. The hero of it, indeed, is not a sage. He is a simple Roman centurion ; one who had been bred in the camp ; one whose experiences had been all derived from the camp. '*He is a man under authority. He has soldiers under him. He says to one, Go, and he goeth ; to another, Come, and he cometh ; to his servant, Do this, and he doeth it.*' Very obvious facts these ; what could they be worth ? What could they have to do with his acknowledgment of Jesus as One who could heal his servant, even if He only spoke a word ? These simple lessons about obedience and authority—about the might of words spoken by a weak man in governing a number of strong men—had been of quite unspeakable worth to this Roman. They had been, in the strictest sense, a Divine education to

him. They had prepared him to believe that the highest power of all has nothing to do with force. They had led him practically, insensibly, through no arguments of religion or philosophy, to confess a Divine Word from whom a governing, restoring power might go forth. They had taught him to own such a Word as speaking in the lowly man whom he besought, through others, to heal his servant ; whom he did not think himself worthy to receive under his roof. Faithful to his vocation as a soldier, as the wise men were faithful to their vocation as students ; profiting by the Roman discipline, as they profited by their oriental discipline ; he was ready, as they were, for the manifestation of the Light which had risen upon the earth, let the outward medium through which it came to him seem ever so poor. And so it is written : ' *When Jesus heard these things, he marvelled at him, and turned him about, and said unto the people that followed Him, I say unto you, I have not found so great faith, no, not in Israel.*' He had found men in Israel who were astonished at the strangeness of His acts, who thought that He must be endued with rare and wonderful powers. He had not found any who, with the frankness and simplicity of this centurion, bowed before a power which had been exerted over him and his soldiers and his general ; before that Word of God who had been *always* enlightening, ruling, quickening. This faith—faith rising above the present and the visible—faith taking hold of the eternal—came forth in a Gentile who had not known the letter of Scripture, but who had been instructed by the Living Teacher—the source of all the wisdom which Scripture imparts.

(2) The raising of the child of the widow of Nain—which is the subject of the verses from the 11th to the 18th—is

the next of the manifestations that I desired to bring under
your notice. In what sense did this act reveal Christ's
nature and Christ's power? Undoubtedly the compassion
to the mother, which was expressed in His countenance,
would have brought to her the sense of a divine compassion
—thoroughly divine, and therefore thoroughly human—of
which she might have dreamed before, but which she had
never realized. I do not overlook that influence. I consider it all-important. The instinct which has fixed on
the collateral incidents of this story and of similar stories
in the Gospels, and has prized them above all the formal
arguments which apologists have built upon them, is a
true and holy instinct. Still I cannot help perceiving
another and deeper purpose in the minds of the Evangelists,
when they record so naturally, with so little effort and
pomp, the words of Christ to this young man, to the
daughter of Jairus, to His friend Lazarus. I find in those
words a clear and distinct proclamation that the man was
then as much within the Kingdom of the Son of Man—
within the reach of His voice—as while his breath dwelt
in his body, whilst his friends could look into his face, and
he could smile upon them. It is not to the eye or the ear
in us that Christ has spoken here. It is not the closing
of the eye or the ear which will hinder Him from manifesting Himself to any human spirit. That spirit can
understand Him, and respond to Him, at all times, and in
all places. If we would earnestly meditate on that truth
which the Evangelists so distinctly assert, these narratives
would be signs to us indeed. We should never dream of
limiting their meaning to that country or that generation.
We should close the eyes of those we have loved best on
earth in sure and certain hope that He who is the Resur-

K

rection and Life is calling them not to die but to arise
out of death. We should not have need to ask curiously,
however we may long to know, what is the condition of
those whose dust we commit to the dust. We know who
He is that came into the world to seek them—that He died
and rose again. Are they not in His hands? Will He
not deal righteously with them, so as to fulfil His Father's
divine purpose towards them? Can we not trust them to
His keeping? Are we afraid to say that He in His great
mercy has taken them to Himself? Have we been such
faithful stewards of our brothers' souls that we suppose
they would be safer if they were trusted any longer to us?

There is, I know, a notion in some of us that faith
ceases and sight begins for those who have fallen asleep.
A strange fancy, surely! Are we not learning slowly to
believe during our earthly pilgrimage? Is not our contest
with all the impressions which our senses make upon us?
Are we not practising—awkwardly, and as little children
—the use of our spirits? Is all this to be changed, and
are we to fall back into the condition out of which we have
been so painfully growing under God's gracious guidance?
Was this what St. Paul meant when he said that the
tongues and prophecies which belonged to the time of
our pupillage will pass away in the fulness of manhood,
and then added, ' *But now* ABIDETH *faith, hope, charity?* '
Did he not mean that these were the permanent and substantial blessings which would *not* pass away, which would
be ripest in the noblest condition that human creatures would
ever attain? And if *this faith* comes, as we are told, *by
hearing, and hearing by the Word of God*, am I not justified
in saying that the Divine Word manifested Himself to the
spirit of the young man who was on his bier at Nain, and

that his faith, just as much as the faith of the Roman centurion, confessed its rightful Lord?

(3) The next incident in the chapter is directly and obviously connected with faith. '*The disciples of John shewed him of all these things. And John calling unto him two of his disciples sent them to Jesus, saying, Art thou he that should come? or look we for another?*' The disciples came. '*And in that same hour he cured many of their infirmities and plagues, and of evil spirits; and unto many that were blind he gave sight. Then Jesus answering said unto them, Go your way, and tell John what things ye have seen and heard; how that the blind see, the lame walk, the lepers are cleansed, the deaf hear, the dead are raised, to the poor the Gospel is preached. And blessed is he, whosoever shall not be offended in me.*' *John*, as it is written, *did no miracle*. He bore witness of the Light which was about all men. He bade them turn to this Light. He gave the sign that the sins which had been brought home to their consciences by that Light, and which they had confessed, were put away. He said that One should come after him who would do what he could not do; who should baptize with the Holy Spirit and with fire. Was the Person who, as he heard, was performing so many cures, indeed this baptizer with the Spirit, as he had once supposed? Did not these miracles rather create a suspicion that He might *not* be completing John's mission; that He might *not* be bringing men to repentance; that He might only be one of the pretenders to rare powers, of which there had been many in all ages, and were many then? His disciples would tell him that Jesus and His disciples were wholly unlike them in their discipline and mode of behaviour. They might suggest the thought to him that

if Christ had such powers, it was wonderful they were not
used to deliver a great prophet out of the hands of Herod.
I apprehend many doubts, many contradictory impressions,
were struggling in his own mind—were unsettling the
minds of those to whom he had done good. Let them
go and see for themselves what this teacher was, and what
He was really doing. They are present at those acts which
make them suspicious. Are these acts done for display ?
Or are they parts of a Gospel to the poor ? Did they not
proclaim to them John's own message, ' The Kingdom of
Heaven is at hand ? ' Did they not show that there was
really such a Kingdom, that it was at work upon the
humblest Israelite, for the humblest Israelite ? The disciples of John saw and heard these things, But the seeing
and hearing were not of themselves convincing. John had
not taught them to set any store by mere appearances. He
had warned them against appearances. They might explain these miracles as the Pharisees did. Jesus might be
casting out demons by the help of Beelzebub, the prince
of the demons. Unless these acts spoke to their consciences—unless they were to them manifestations of a
divine Prince and Deliverer—the mere sight of them would
not convince the scholar—the report of them would have
no effect on the master. That report was accompanied with
a message which can have been clearly understood by none
but him who received it. *' Blessed is he whosoever shall not
be offended in me.'* It was a message to the heart of that
imprisoned prophet ; it has reached the hearts of a number
of imprisoned prophets, and of sufferers who had no claim
to be called prophets, in all periods : ' Thou criest bitterly,
' How long, oh Lord, how long ? When shall this oppres-
' sion which is on me and on Thy earth end ? When shall

'the Deliverer come? Cry, and cease not. But it is a
'blessing for thee, for every man, not to be offended while
'the waiting lasts. Take the signs which are given thee,
'that God's purposes are accomplishing themselves; that
'He is beating down the enemies of men—the enemies of
'their bodies, the enemies of their spirits. Believe that He
'who has begun the work will complete it. If the battle
'is long the victory shall come. Hold fast that faith. As
'you hold it fast you will know that you are one with all
'the seers of old who have fainted and been weary but
'whose strength has been renewed, with all to whom the
'Word of God has come in their hours of gloom, and who
'have been assured that His brightness will one day fill
'the whole earth.'

(4) The discourse respecting John which followed the
departure of the messengers refers, first, to the kind of
power which he exercised. He drew crowds into the
wilderness. By what attraction? There was nothing to
entice them in the sight of reeds shaking with the winds.
Had he the habits and acts of a prince? Or did they go
to him because they felt that he was a prophet—one not
speaking his own words—one with a message to them from
the Searcher of Hearts? That, then, was his power. He
called them to repent, and they felt God was calling them
to repent, and was showing them what they had to repent
of. Yes! John was a prophet, the most remarkable of
all the prophets, more than a prophet—the messenger
who told that the King of Heaven was Himself asserting
His dominion of men—that He was about to be manifested. Thus the power which addresses itself to the
conscience is magnified above all other powers—is shown
to be that which is widest as well as deepest in its operation.

But it is said, secondly, that though the messenger of the Kingdom of Heaven is greater than all that went before, the least in the Kingdom of Heaven is greater than he. The man, however insignificant in himself, however feeble his speech, who can say, 'The Father has redeemed men by His Son, has baptized men with His Spirit,' has a mightier responsibility, a larger knowledge, a greater power of calling men out of darkness to light than John had. Thirdly, He explains by whom such prophets as John are welcomed, by whom they are rejected. The people— the publicans and sinners—however bewildered in their impressions, however open to impositions—still justified the man who told them of a deliverance from burdens which actually oppressed them, from the evil which was close to them and which they could not shake off. But Pharisees and lawyers, satisfied with themselves, asked for no deliverance. The command of God to repent had for them no practical signification. Repentance was good for the wicked; how could it be needful for the righteous? And therefore He goes on to say, that people of this sort will find cause of complaint against all who disturbed their self-complacency, though the complaints might be of the most contradictory kind. The man who came with a leathern girdle about his loins would be in their eyes a morose madman. He who mixed with men, eating at their feasts, would be a '*gluttonous man and a winebibber, a friend of publicans and sinners. But wisdom,*' He adds, '*is justified of all her children.*' These opposite methods approve themselves to the consciences of those who are really craving for light and guidance. They meet the different wants of their minds at different periods. An inner harmony is recognised under their superficial disagreement. Here

then, as everywhere, our Lord appeals to a faith which
alone can receive what the hard dogmatist scorns. To
that He manifests Himself; to the faith which seeks a
divine refuge from the misery and torment of self-indulgence, self-will, self-glorification.

(5) So we come naturally and in order to the last and
most striking passage of this chapter. It is the story of
the sinful woman who came to the entrance of the house
of the Pharisee, Simon, in which Jesus had been sitting at
meat. The consistency of such a story with oriental
habits is attested by the writer who rejects most rigidly
all that he considers supernatural in the records of our
Lord's life. To me nothing seems more supernatural than
this story in which he discovers truth as well as grace.
Two figures are brought distinctly before us,—Simon,
wondering that Jesus should not be able to discern a
woman that is a sinner, certain that if He be a prophet,
He must have that power; the woman, thinking little of
the difference which separates her from all respectable
people, not afraid to approach Him who is most unlike
her, casting herself before Him, washing His feet with her
tears, and wiping them with the hair of her head. All
of us know the picture well. And all know the story
by which our Lord explained the coldness of the host,
the fervent devotion of the sinner. A creditor has two
debtors; one owes five-hundred pence, the other fifty. He
forgives both. Which of them loves him most? A light
had burst in upon the woman's conscience, discovering to
her an infinite evil. That same light had discovered an
infinite goodness. She must escape from the one. She
might escape to the other. She knew that she might.
She heard that same voice which bade the widow's son rise

out of his death calling her to rise out of her death. The Light had shone upon Simon also, but it had not penetrated far. It had shown him some little faults which might easily be corrected, which did not, in any serious sense, demand forgiveness. By various religious acts he might hope to avert the punishment of them. To cast them off—to cast off himself—he felt no necessity for that. And, therefore, according to the eternal law, each found what each sought. The woman could not be content with indulgence or with remission of penalty. She needed a remission of sins. There was One who could give her that. The words, 'Thy sins be forgiven thee,' had that sense for her. She rose up another person. She believed in a righteous almighty Friend. She might believe in Him always. Her faith had saved her from herself; she could go in peace. Here, then, was another Epiphany, the greatest of all; the Epiphany of the God in whom there is mercy that He may be feared, who seeks to bring men out of their falsehoods that they may be partakers of His truth. Thus it was to the faith of men in all cases that Christ revealed Himself on earth. To their faith He reveals Himself now. The faith to which He speaks is not one which will content itself with the letters of a book, or the authority of a priest. If it hears of a revelation in a book, it asks whether that book speaks of a living Person; if it hears of the authority of a priest, it asks whether he can tell of a living Person who knows what is in us, and who is able to send us away saved from ourselves, at peace with Him. If we substitute the book, or the priest, for the Son of Man, He will confound us in His final and perfect Epiphany.

LECTURE XII.

THE PARABLE OF THE KINGDOM OF HEAVEN.

St. Luke VIII. 9.

And his disciples asked him, saying, What might this parable be?

This chapter contains the first parable which St. Luke has reported. That parable may be called in one sense the parable of parables. St. Matthew and St. Mark both put it before the others; both connect it with a special explanation, and with the reason which our Lord gives for teaching by parables generally. Our thoughts are therefore naturally drawn to this subject, and I shall keep it before me throughout this lecture.

It would be a great mistake, however, to overlook the words with which this chapter opens if we wish to understand this method of instruction. '*And it came to pass afterward, that he went throughout every city and village, preaching and shewing the glad tidings of the kingdom of God: and the twelve were with him, and certain women, which had been healed of evil spirits and infirmities, Mary called Magdalene, out of whom went seven devils, and Joanna the wife of Chuza Herod's steward, and Susanna, and many others, which ministered unto him of their substance.*'

We have found this message, '*The kingdom of heaven is at hand,*' to be *the* message of the Gospels. It came to the

Jews as a message which they expected. It came as a
perplexing overthrow of their expectations. They wanted
a kingdom in which a Jewish emperor should crush the
nations as a Latin emperor did crush them. They were
told of a Son of David who was in the midst of them—
that Son of David spoke of God as His Father. It
was His Father's kingdom which He said was at hand.
Into that the poor in goods and the poor in spirit might
enter. It was, no doubt, a kingdom that was to come.
The glad tidings pointed to a future for those who were
on earth, to a future for those who should leave the earth.
But the kingdom was over those to whom our Lord and
His disciples preached. They might feel the powers of it.
Those powers had come forth to do them good.

The message of such a kingdom, I said, contradicted
some expectations which the people of Palestine were
cherishing. But it fulfilled a number of expectations.
The 107th Psalm, for instance, which must have been continually heard in their synagogues, sets forth the character
and acts of the Lord God of Israel. You will remember *how*
it sets forth that character and those acts. The dangers
of the man who goes down to the sea in ships, the blight
and mildew of the land, the commonest calamities which
men bring on themselves by their folly and wilfulness, are
recorded as occasions which 'show forth the goodness of
'the Lord, and His wonderful works to the children of
'men.' That is the Psalmist's phrase, *children of men*. They
are human pursuits, human troubles, human wrong-doings,
on which he dwells. The purpose and the dominion of
the Lord God who had brought their fathers out of the
house of bondage is shown .from generation to generation,
in breaking asunder the bonds of men generally, of those

especially who had transgressed His laws, and so had reduced themselves into misery.

The acts of Christ were manifestations to all who read and understood this Psalm and their other Scriptures, of Him in whom they had believed. If He were revealing Himself as the King of kings and Lord of lords, these ought to be the signs of His kingdom. The more humble the people were who felt the plagues—the more the plagues were the ordinary visitations of the children of men in all countries—the more these plagues were the effects of their own moral evils—the more would they be discoveries of such a kingdom, of such a Heavenly Father, as Christ was proclaiming. I do not care to inquire what the seven demons were which are said to have gone out of Mary Magdalene. Any one who has leisure for such speculations may amuse himself with them. I am content to believe that she was fast bound in misery and iron of some kind; I do not doubt that she had become, in some way, the slave in body and spirit of oppressors whom she could not shake off. I think that those who have felt their own spirits or bodies mastered and enchained by evil inclinations, tempers, habits which they could not overcome, have been right to look upon her as the type of their condition, whether or not they could tell exactly the nature of her tormentors. They have not been deceived in turning to the same Lord whom she and the Galilean women recognised as their friend and helper, to whom they ministered of their substance; not deceived in supposing that the virtue which went forth from Him to deliver Mary Magdalene was only a specimen of what is going forth from Him every day and hour for the relief of human woes.

I have no wish, therefore, to divide those *acts* which we call miracles, from those *words* which we call parables. They are as distinct as words must always be from acts. They are illustrations of the same divine dominion. They are parts of the glad tidings of the Kingdom of Heaven.

A writer, to whom I have several times alluded in these Lectures as the enemy of everything which assumes to be supernatural in our Lord's history, dwells with much earnestness and beauty on the natural character of His illustrations, upon the contrast between the life in them and the hard dogmatism or the artificial rhetoric of those who call themselves preachers of His Gospel. Such observations are of great worth, and should be laid earnestly to heart by us. If the supernatural means that which is *un*-natural—if it has any the least affinity with school notions and formulas—I am satisfied that it will never retain its hold on living men ; elaborate reasonings are not needed to expel it ; let in the fresh air upon it and it will drop to pieces like any other corpse. What I believe is, that Nature itself becomes such a corpse, a mere collection of dry bones or atoms, if there is not a breath from heaven, a higher spirit, to quicken it. That spirit I find in our Lord's parables. They are, indeed, most natural. That which is apt to become utterly flat and unmeaning in Nature they renovate by connecting it with the life of man, with the relations of God to man. The familiar things of earth which we have passed over in our search for the strange and rare start into significance, because they are associated with the Kingdom of Heaven. We understand how much we have to do with the world around us, because a light falls upon it from the world above us, and because we are assured of our relation to that. Every fact in nature becomes a fact of humanity, a fact of divinity. We have the solemnest protest from Him whom we believe to be the Creator of both worlds, against any disparagement of either and against any attempt to sunder them. There is a discovery to us of an unfathomable meaning and mystery in their union, a meaning and mystery to which the peasant has as much access as the doctor. The Kingdom of Heaven is shown to be at hand— to be presenting itself to the spirit of a man as the trees which his fathers planted as the firmament under which he walks present themselves to his eye.

Nowhere is there more of this revelation than in the parable of the sower. ' *What might this be ?* ' asked the disciples with some impatience. To what does it point? What does it tell us of the heavenly kingdom which Thou art making known to us? Before they had the answer, they surely had learnt something which it much concerned them to know. There might be a mystery *beneath* the sowing of the seed. But there was a mystery in *that*. They were dwelling amidst mysteries. Look what the sower in that field is about. What a simple business he is engaged in! Only scattering a few tiny seeds over the ground. How often you have watched him vacantly—how often you have been drawn away from the sight of him by any passing trifle, which seemed worthier of observation because it was extraordinary. But might not you think a little of those seeds; why they are cast there, what is likely to become of them? What, for instance, will happen to those which have dropped by the wayside? The birds already have got sight of them, in a few moments they will be gone. Will it fare the same with those which have fallen on the soil that is so near the rock? No, there

will be a promise in them, the blade will come up quickly.
But do not expect anything from it. When the sun is
strong it will wither. And that which is fallen among
briars or weeds; what of that? Both will grow up
together; the wheat will be choked; there will be no
produce. But think again of the process which the seed
will have to go through that does spring up and bear
fruit. How long it will remain under ground. When it
appears, how unlike it will be that which was put in.
Yet it will be the same. And it will come at the regular
season, according to a fixed order. And it will give bread
to the eater, fresh seed to the sower for the next year.

Here you have, assuredly, the very reverse of dogmatic
teaching. It is emphatically teaching about facts, about
common facts, about the facts of the outward world. It
awakens the mind of the hearer to observation and reflection. ' Is this so indeed? Have all these wonders been
' surrounding me and I knew them not? He has taught
' me to think of them. To *think* of them? And what are
' these thoughts? They have more to do with me than
' these seeds, though they have so much to do with me,
' though my whole existence would be so different if there
' was not this sowing, this growing, this reaping, this
' turning the corn into bread. Is there any one to command
' these thoughts? Can I know what the source of *them* is?
Can I know whence *I* came? who is Lord over *me?* Can
' any one tell me that?' One who has begun to ask these
questions has passed from the mysteries of the kingdom
of earth to the mysteries of the Kingdom of Heaven.
He is puzzled about them. He wants an interpreter of
them. This the disciples did. And to them came the
answer. ' *To you it is given to know the mysteries of the*

kingdom of God.' You, who want to learn what there is in you that answers to these processes in the ground ; who is directing these processes : what there is that answers to the seed which is sown in the ground ; who is the sower : you *can* learn, poor men, ignorant fishermen, as you are. But to others who do not care to know this, who are not feeling their need of one to sow and plough the soil which is in *them, all these things are in parables.* They see the images. They do not see that which the images represent. They hear all the messages which nature is bringing to them, all the thousand voices which are sounding through the world, but they do not understand.

I do not derive this explanation of our Lord's sentence from the commentators, to whom it has caused extreme perplexity, but from His own answer to the disciples respecting the Parable of the Sower. It was a likeness of the Kingdom of Heaven. Where, then, is this kingdom ? *' The seed is the word of God. Those by the wayside are they that hear ; then cometh the devil, and taketh away the word out* OF THEIR HEARTS, *lest they should believe and be saved.'* The heart of man then is the kingdom with which we are now occupied. The living powers and influences which act upon that ; who is directing the processes which go on in it ; these are the facts we require to be instructed in. We are not for a moment left in doubt what are the powers and influences, and who is exercising them. *Words* are to the man what *seeds* are to the ground. He whose word bade the earth appear, and bear seed and bring forth fruit, He whose word has been sustaining the life in the earth and in the seed, and has made it fruitful ever since, He by that word is speaking to us. By it He is cultivating the mind and heart of the creatures whom He has formed in

His image. And this creature—being formed in His image, having the divine faculty of Will—can reject, can receive that which is sown in it. The word may fall on the unretentive ear, from which the spirit of vanity will catch it quickly away; may be welcomed as mere pleasant or exciting news, not as a reforming principle and power— may soon therefore be thrown off through weariness, or cowardice, or disgust; may mix with the myriad cares which distract or with the pleasures which enervate the spirit, and be stifled by them; may penetrate into a will which has been prepared and purified for its entertainment, and so may appear at the appointed season in noble thoughts and deeds.

These verses have given occasion to a multitude of discourses. Preachers have delighted to dwell on the way-side hearers, and the hearers who listen for awhile and then fall away, and the hearers who are bewildered by the troubles and delights of earth, and the hearers who show tokens of a heavenly culture. So they explain their own ill or good success. Often, no doubt, their explanations call forth a witness and response in those to whom they are offered. Yet I wish we had adhered more closely to our Lord's explanation. I wish we had supposed the seed to be the Word of God, not the words which fall from our lips. There may be other causes besides the neglect, or shallowness, or occupation of our hearers which make *them* unproductive. We need to ask ourselves carefully *what* causes; whether there are no waysides, no stones, no thorns in *our* hearts which have destroyed their force in their passage through us to other men. The warning which our Lord gives applies at least as much to us as to you. His seeds may fall into your hearts through our ministry. But the Word who gives us power to hear, to think, to speak, is never far from any of us. If we darken His counsel, He will speak to you, and to us also, out of the whirlwind, or by that still small voice which makes its way to the heart when He is not felt to be in the whirlwind. It is of *this* Sower, of the Son of Man, of the eternal Word of God, that the parable bears witness. Woe to us if we contract and enfeeble it by our self-conceit. The message may come through any human voice ; through the parent, the wife, the child. It may rise out of the tombs from those who loved us, or from those whom we have wronged. It may reach us through the letters of a book, or through music, or through a picture. It may be brought to us by the glory of a sunset, or the darkness of a night. It may come by fervent expectations or by bitter disappointments, by calm joy or by intense anguish of body or soul. But the source is ever the same living Word of God. Every word that enters any man's heart is from Him. Every word that does not lie dead in a man's heart derives its quickening energy from Him.

And what if it does lie in vain? That question is suggested by the parable. Perhaps it is the one which comes most home to us. Often we stammer in answering it. We say, and say truly, that the grace of God is directed to the will of man; that it comes with no force like that which might move a stone ; that it can, therefore, be resisted. Such assertions are confirmed by our own experience, and the experience of all men. The parable obliges us to consider them. It obliges us to say, ' The fault is not in the sower, or in the seed, but in the soil.' If that were all, would not the conclusion be a despairing one ? Who is to rectify the soil? *The* soil ; *what* soil? Do

we not find in our own hearts all the obstructions which
we denounce in the most indifferent, the most unbelieving?
If so, we must ask, for our own sakes, 'Was it not
'promised of the Son of Man, that He should baptize
'with the Spirit? Does He merely sow the seed? Does
'He not also fit the ground to receive it, to entertain it, to
'return it, not as it was taken in, but in the richness and
'pregnancy which it owes to the divine rain and sunshine?'
Are we then to despair because Christ's word has been
ever so much checked by that which it has met with in
us? Is it not part of the revelation of the Kingdom of
Heaven, that the word shall accomplish at last that for
which it is sent; that if our wills be ever so untractable,
there are resources in the divine Will by which it can
subdue them to itself?

That lesson I derive from the words which follow in
obvious connexion with the parable. '*No man, when he
hath lighted a candle, covereth it with a vessel, or putteth it
under a bed ; but setteth it on a candlestick, that they which
enter in may see the light. For nothing is secret, that shall
not be made manifest ; neither anything hid, that shall not
be known and come abroad.*' I give these sentences the
most awful meaning that has ever been given them. I
believe them to say, that thoughts of good or evil will
not lie for ever in the recesses of the heart; that they
will come forth in acts which men will bless or curse.
And therefore the admonition in the next verse is a
searching one. '*Take heed therefore how ye hear : for
whosoever hath, to him shall be given ; and whosoever hath
not, from him shall be taken even that which he seemeth to
have.*' But we do not weaken this warning if we suppose
our Lord to say, 'God Himself has kindled a light within

' you. He wishes it to shine forth upon your fellows. His
' light can overcome the darkness which is opposed to it.
' Whilst, therefore, you are most careful to cherish all seeds
' of good—most afraid lest you should lose all that have
' been planted in you if you do not cultivate them—have
' confidence that His purpose will not be frustrated. Ask
' that, by the means which may seem to Him best, it may
' be brought to effect in you and in all men.'

It is, therefore, the might of the Divine Word as a living
and life-giving power which is the subject of the parable.
The sense of that might in the Evangelist's mind led him,
I conceive, to introduce in this place the story of Christ's
answer to His mother and brethen. *And it was told him
by certain which said, Thy mother and thy brethren stand
without, desiring to see thee. And he answered and said
unto them, My mother and my brethren are these which
hear the word of God, and do it.'* This is a striking, even
a startling, sentence. Like that spoken by our Lord in
the Temple in His twelfth year, it appears as if it were
inserted to warn the ages to come against any theories or
any acts of devotion which should put the earthly mother
between the Son of God and the Eternal Father, between
the Son of Man and those whose nature He had taken.
We cannot explain the harshness of the language till we
discover the permanent necessity of it. If we would assert
the Incarnation not as a tenet merely, but as a fact and
as a principle, Christ must teach us how to think of His
mother and of those who do His word.

I have spoken so recently of the signs of the Kingdom
of Heaven, that I have no excuse for dwelling on the
passage which follows. Still, I would have you read it
carefully, and meditate upon it, as a living illustration of

the calm dominion of the Son of Man over nature, and of His appeal to the faith of those who are in peril by sea or land. It commends itself to every sailor now, as much as to the disciples on the lake of Gennesareth. *'Now it came to pass on a certain day, that he went into a ship with his disciples: and he said unto them, Let us go over unto the other side of the lake. And they launched forth. But as they sailed he fell asleep: and there came down a storm of wind on the lake; and they were filled with water, and were in jeopardy. And they came to him, and awoke him, saying, Master, master, we perish. Then he arose, and rebuked the wind and the raging of the water: and they ceased, and there was a calm. And he said unto them, Where is your faith? And they being afraid wondered, saying one to another, What manner of man is this! for he commandeth even the winds and water, and they obey him.'*

The story of the demoniac and his exorcism, bears a similar witness to the King and Deliverer of the human spirit. On that subject, also, I have said all that I need to say. You will see how poorly and feebly I said it, and what the simplicity and grandeur of the testimony of the Evangelist is, if you will study the verses from the 26th to the 41st. Do they not tell of Him who preserves the sanity of the sane, no less than of Him who rescues those who have fallen into madness and despair?

The stories of the daughter of Jairus, and of the woman who had spent all her living on the physicians, neither could be healed of any, are intertwined. You cannot feel either to be a repetition of any you have heard before; each has its own incidents, its own scenery. For they are not artificial proofs of a mission; they are manifestations of a life, they are the acts of a Life-giver. Each sick woman finds herself in the poor creature who sought to touch the hem of Christ's garment. Every parent enters into the impatience of the ruler of the synagogue as the crowd stops the way to the bed on which the child is dying, hears the noise and the scoffs of the minstrels, wonders at the words, '*Maid, I say unto thee arise.*' That effect proceeds from no art in the writer. It is the witness of the human spirit that sickness and death cannot be the lords of us or of our children. There must be a mightier than they.

I do not think that these stories tempt us to forget our main subject. They rather lead us to feel how all events are parables of the Kingdom of Heaven. When we one day give thanks for a birth, when another day we are present at a marriage feast, when on the third we stand beside a grave, the thought arises in our minds, 'What a parable is this human existence; what can it mean?' He who was born, and went to the marriage feast, and died and rose again, has interpreted it. Birth is sacred, for *the* child has come into His world; marriage is sacred, for He unites hands and hearts; death is sacred, for them that sleep in Jesus shall God bring with Him.

LECTURE XIII.

THE GLORY AND HUMILIATION OF THE KING.

St. Luke IX. 26, 27.

For whosoever shall be ashamed of me and of my words, of him shall the Son of man be ashamed, when he shall come in his own glory, and in his Father's, and of the holy angels. But I tell you of a truth, there be some standing here, which shall not taste of death, till they see the kingdom of God.

In every one of the three Gospels which record the Transfiguration, these words, or words nearly identical with these, introduce the narrative of it. We should not forget them if we wish to know how the Evangelists regarded that event. But they are equally important for the illustration of every other passage in this chapter; how important they are for the life of each one of us—of each minister of Christ especially—may He enable us to consider.

We have seen how closely the Kingdom of God is connected in the New Testament with an Epiphany or manifestation of the divine glory in human weakness. The Son of Man in His cradle, the Son of Man in His baptism, the Son of Man in all His acts of healing power, was showing forth, through the veil of His flesh, His glory and His Father's, and the glory of the holy angels. He was showing that glory not to be destructive, but life-giving and restoring. What He says here is, that a time would

come when this glory, which was discovering itself here and
there to a few Galilean fishermen, or to a few poor lepers
and lunatics, would be revealed to the universe. Here on
earth there should be authentic proofs that this Kingdom
of God was mightier than all which opposed it. Some
were present who should not taste of death till they had
evidence of its triumph.

St. Luke certainly does not intimate to us, nor do any
of the Evangelists, that this promise was fulfilled in the
Transfiguration. That they represent as transitory. The
cloud was lifted for a moment to show what was behind it.
Then it descended again. But the voice which came out
of the cloud, 'This is my beloved Son,' was the same
that had been heard at the beginning. That did not
pass away; that was to be the hidden strength of the
Apostles while they were fulfilling their Master's commission here; that was to be their conscious strength
hereafter. If we go through the different incidents of
the chapter, we shall see how they were learning the
lesson; how difficult it was; how one side of it seemed
to clash with another; how necessary it was that they
should have glimpses and foretastes of the glory; how
necessary it was that they should be led to it through
ever fresh humiliation.

(1) The opening of their work as Apostles is grand. It
is spoken of in the first verse of this chapter. '*He gave
them power and authority over all devils, and to cure
diseases.*' I have told you that I am obliged to take the
language literally, that I cannot explain it away. I think
the whole Gospel is the news of a battle of the Spirit of
good against the spirits of evil, of man's Deliverer against
man's tormentors. These poor Galileans were to enter

into that battle, to bear arms in it. If they could not
contend with invisible foes, they had no work to do at all.
They had no weapons against visible oppressors. If these
are all that disturb the peace of men's minds or the health
of their bodies, the message which the Apostles carried
was, from first to last, a mockery; the power which that
message has exerted over mankind has been the power
of a lie. That there was no magic in them to encounter
diseases or death, their preaching proved. They preached
of the Kingdom of God. They declared that the God of
Abraham was delivering the children of Abraham from
plagues which tormented them. The Apostles were witnesses of His presence, of His care for those who had
most excuse for fancying that He had forgotten them or
that He hated them.

But along with these great powers were the tokens of
their poverty. They were to go forth taking nothing for
their journey, neither staves nor scrip, neither bread, neither
money; they were not to have two coats apiece. Visible
insignificance accompanied invisible energy. And yet
that invisible energy was not to make them in the least
independent of ordinary mortal support; it was not to
make them independent even of the persons to whom they
ministered. Those who received them would give them
what they needed; they were to trust their fellow-creatures
as well as God. But they were to abide in the house
into which they went at first, not seeking better entertainment elsewhere; if they were rejected in any city, they
were to bear witness, in the ordinary Jewish way, that a
divine blessing had been proclaimed and offered to its
inhabitants, and that they would not have the blessing.

(2) This message concerning a kingdom, and these exer-

cises of royal power to attest it, could not be indifferent
to the rulers who were reigning in Palestine as creatures
of the Roman Empire, by its appointment and authority.
Herod hears strange tidings of one who, as the people
suppose, may be a reappearance of John the Baptist lately
beheaded, who may be Elijah, who may be some other of
the prophets.   He is puzzled; all these opinions are possible; perhaps the supposed king may be less formidable
in actual presence than in a vague report.   Herod desires
to see Him.   The curiosity is not gratified at that time.
When the Apostles return from their mission, Jesus takes
them into a desert place, near the city which is called
Bethsaida.   Men who have been doing any unusual work
need retirement.   In the crowd these poor peasants might
have spoken of the great things they could do, how much
mightier they were than Herod.   Quietness with their
Master may restore the balance of their minds.

(3) Retirement is good, but not as a luxury.   The people
pursue Jesus; He speaks to them of the Kingdom of
Heaven.   He heals those that have need of healing.   Then
follows the story of His feeding the five thousand men
with the five loaves and fishes.   All four Evangelists
speak of it.   From St. John's narrative we discover that
this act made a kind of impression on the multitude which
the cures had not made.   They wished to take Jesus by
force and make Him a king.   They were reminded of the
manna which had fallen upon the Jewish camp.   This man
must have some power of dispensing gifts from heaven—
not upon one here and there but upon great bodies of men.
Was not this the Monarch they were looking for ?   St. Luke
does not report the discourse which took off the edge of
this admiration.   The message concerning One who could

give them better bread than the bread that perisheth, who would give His flesh for the life of the world, concerns the purpose of St. John's Gospel. It would have been out of place here. But St. Luke does relate a conversation with the disciples, which seems to have been suggested by the remarks of the people who had been eating of the loaves. Like the discourse reported by the other Evangelist, it raised and yet depressed their thoughts and hopes respecting His kingdom.

(4) '*And it came to pass as he was alone praying, his disciples were with him : and he asked them, saying, Whom say the people that I am ?*' They had heard the surmises which perplexed Herod, and which were common, no doubt, in Galilee. The spirit of some old prophet had passed into Him ; of which prophet, there were different opinions. '*He said unto them, But whom say ye that I am ? Peter answering said, The Christ of God.*'

'It is not the spirit of some prophet which has taken 'possession of Thee. It is the Spirit of God Himself. He 'has anointed Thee.' That is involved in the very name Christ, even if we do not join to it the words which St. Matthew ascribes to St. Peter, '*The Son of the living God.*' The fact that 'He had been praying,' which St. Luke gives us, may have added strength to the conviction. There may have been an illumination in the countenance at that moment which will have come to the fishermen with the force of a revelation. That it *was* a revelation—not an outward one, even if there were some sign which fixed and attracted the Apostle as the burning bush did the old lawgiver—our Lord Himself, according to St. Matthew, declared. '*Flesh and blood hath not revealed it unto thee, but my Father which is in heaven.*' The Spirit who is in

the Christ has taught thee of Him.   The Father has brought
thee to confess the Son.

(5) But then comes the other aspect, the reverse side, of
the discovery.   '*And he straitly charged them, and commanded them to tell no man that thing ; saying, The Son of
man must suffer many things, and be rejected of the elders
and chief priests and scribes, and be slain, and be raised the
third day.*'   The glory of the Christ, the Son of God, could
not be manifested in the most august words.   It could only
come forth in suffering.   Only the Cross could make it
known.   Only in enduring death and overcoming death
could He show what His oneness with God was ; only so
could it be shown what His oneness with men was.

(6) Here is the foundation of Christian theology, here
is the foundation of Christian morality.   My friends, a
frightful attempt has been made in our days to put asunder
what God has joined inseparably, eternally together.   It
has been said that the sacrifice of Christ to His Father
has nothing to do with our sacrifice of ourselves.   It has
been said that to bring the thoughts together is little short
of blasphemy.   But our Lord Himself brings them together
here and everywhere.   He makes His sacrifice the very
ground of all other sacrifices, the only power in which
they can be offered, that which alone interprets and blesses
them.   '*And he said to them all, If any man will come
after me, let him deny himself, and take up his cross daily,
and follow me.   For whosoever will save his life* (or his *soul*)
shall lose it : but whosoever will lose his life (or his *soul*)
for my sake, the same shall save it.'   The absolute giving
up of Himself—His life or soul—to His Father on the
Cross, is declared to be the consummate act of the Christ,
the Son of the living God.   And those who would follow

Him are told that they must do the same. They must not
seek to save their lives or souls. They must give them up to
Him. The Son of Man, not their own souls, must be the
object which they set before them if they would really
have His salvation.

A mighty paradox, surely! yet one which every day and
hour of human experience establishes as a fundamental
truth. The self-seeker must lose his heart, soul, all his
faculties, in that base pursuit. He who loses himself rises
to a higher life. You repeat the lesson continually. You
cannot help reverencing the man who gives himself for his
family, his country, his convictions. You cannot help
despising the man who gives up his family, his country,
his convictions, to save himself. You are sure the one
attains the blessings which he seems to abandon, that the
other abandons the blessing which he seems to attain.
Alas! alas! it has been supposed that in our religious
life the doctrine is reversed. There, it is said, we are to
be self-seekers. Everything is to give way to the object
of saving ourselves. Men even dare to plead our Lord's
authority in this very passage for that contradiction of His
example. They quote the question, ' *What is a man advan-
taged if he shall gain the whole world and lose himself, or
be cast away.*' They tear it from its context. They refuse
to read it by the light of the sentence which has immediately preceded. They deny what has just been solemnly
declared, that every man must lose himself who would be
saved. My friends! Christ does not set aside the verdict
which He has taught our consciences to give respecting
every instance of self-sacrifice. He ratifies it. He shows
the true principle of it. We are created to give up ourselves for the Son of Man, the Head and King of our race.

It is our privilege to lose in Him these miserable selves which have been our torments, which have always divided us from each other, which have always come between us and every high object. And therefore the words of my text have this blessed and this terrible signification. 'Whoso-'ever seeks something for himself, and not that salvation 'which I the Son of Man have revealed to mankind, shall 'not know what my glory is, the glory of the Father, the 'glory of His holy angels. But those who seek me shall, 'even before they die, have a vision of my Kingdom. They 'shall know that I am the Lord of the whole earth.'

(7) To sustain them in the expectation of this future revelation, to show them that the glory was real, although their eyes could not bear the sight of it, was surely a reason—if we might dare to assign a reason—for that vision upon Tabor, which so soon passed away. It is described in a few simple words. The anxiety of the Evangelists seems not to fix our minds upon it, but to show that it could not stay. He who said, '*It is good for us to be here, and let us make three tabernacles,*' '*knew not what he said.*' And yet the Transfiguration has lived on through ages, and has shed its light upon all ages. It has brought the past into union with the present. Moses and Elijah have been felt to be not dead forms, but living men, because the Son of God and the Son of Man lives. *The decease which he should accomplish at Jerusalem* has been owned as the bond of fellowship between those who walk the earth, and suffer in it, and those who are departed from it. In the light of that countenance *which was altered, of that raiment which was white and glistering,* all human coun-tenances have acquired a brightness, all common things have been transfigured. A glimpse of the divine beauty

has broken through the darkness, and has cheered the
humblest pilgrims. They have been unable to pierce the
gloom of their own destinies, perhaps to shake off the
coil of their own unbelief. But they have had a sense of
a Son of Man who was higher than they; who could see
further than they saw; who could unravel all threads;
who could discover beneath all that appeared most hopeless, the glory of Himself and His Father and the holy
angels.

(8) Greatly has this impression been deepened by the
story of the boy in epilepsy, which follows so immediately
upon the Tabor vision. The spirit which rent and tore him,
the crowd of spectators, the questioning of the scribes, the
impotency of the disciples, the agony of the father—
who would not hold these to be the most flagrant contrasts
to the brightness, stillness, awfulness of the scene above?
Thanks be to God! such contrasts form the harmony of the
Gospel. Thanks be to God, the ugliest facts are never in
that Gospel softened or kept out of sight, that there may
be more room for celestial contemplation. Thanks be to
God, those ugly facts are never, while that Gospel lasts,
able to conceal the divine love, but are penetrated by it,
are the means of discovering it to poor men. For we have
not here the picture of a lazy benevolence, looking down
from a serene region of enjoyment upon a world of
misery and wishing it well. We have the history of
a divine descent into the misery to wrestle with it, to
bring back the victims of it into the home of peace from
which they had wandered.

(9) '*And they were all amazed at the mighty power of
God. But, while they wondered every one at all things which
Jesus did, he said unto his disciples, Let these sayings sink*

*down into your ears: for the Son of man shall be delivered
into the hands of men.'* He whom they had seen in that
glory, He who had done these works at which they were
amazed, would be given up in weakness and helplessness
into the power of men, to be scorned and crucified. Was
it wonderful that *they understood not this saying, and it
was hid from them, that they perceived it not, and they
feared to ask him of that saying ?*

(10) They had something to learn before that saying could
become intelligible to them. *' Then there arose a reasoning among them, which of them should be greatest. And
Jesus, perceiving the thought of their heart, took a child,
and set him by him, and said unto them, Whosoever shall
receive this child in my name receiveth me : and whosoever
shall receive me receiveth him that sent me : for he that is
least among you all, the same shall be great.'* While the
dispute who should be the greatest went on among them,
they could not enter into the humiliation of the Son
of Man ; therefore they could not enter into His glory.
When they saw Him in every little child, they would
begin to have some apprehension of His royalty and
Divinity. But that they might receive Him and His
Father in the little child, they must cease to be proud
men.

LECTURE XIV.

THE ETERNAL LIFE OF THE KINGDOM OF HEAVEN.

St. Luke X. 25—28.

And, behold, a certain lawyer stood up, and tempted him, saying, Master, what shall I do to inherit eternal life? He said unto him, What is written in the law? how readest thou? And he answering said, Thou shalt love the Lord thy God with all thy heart, and with all thy soul, and with all thy strength, and with all thy mind; and thy neighbour as thyself. And he said unto him, Thou hast answered right: this do, and thou shalt live.

THERE is no one of the Apostles who dwells so much upon this commandment as St. John. He dwells upon it in that character. He does not speak of love to God or our neighbour as raising us above commandments. It is His commandment—*the* commandment—that we should love. In this commandment, he says, there is life; it carries with it the power of fulfilling it, because it proceeds from the Almighty Father—because it comes to us through Him who *has* fulfilled it.

(1) The passage which immediately follows that at which I paused last Sunday, tells us something of the discipline by which St. John was led to these conclusions. We fancy him of a particularly gentle tender nature. He is exhibited to us in the Gospels in quite another aspect. '*Master,*' he says, '*we saw one casting out devils in thy name, and we forbad him, because he followeth not with us.*' He had taken up the place of a fierce partisan of Christ. When

his Master had told them that they must receive little children in His Name if they received Him, there was a pricking in the Apostle's conscience. That sentence had nothing, apparently, to do with his prohibition. But it struck him that one was not quite in harmony with the other. Perhaps if they were to receive children in Christ's name, they need not have rebuked this man for using Christ's name. His suspicion was well founded. His Master's answer condemned that act of judgment, and a series of similar acts which should be done in the ages to come. '*Forbid him not; for he that is not against us is for us.*'

The son of Zebedee was not cured by this admonition. The next story exhibits him again as the fierce fanatical partisan, pleading, as fanatics in all times have pleaded, the precedents of Scripture for their own designs. St. Luke seems to mark the crisis as an important one. Jesus had steadfastly set His face to go to Jerusalem. He intimates that He was going there for the last time ; at least I know not what other signification we can put upon the singular expression, ' *When the time was come that he should be received up.*' It certainly seems as if all the discourses and acts which are recorded between this verse and the 28th verse of the nineteenth chapter, occurred in this journey to Jerusalem. Be that as it may, He was entering into a village of the Samaritans, and the inhabitants, seeing whither He was bound, refused to receive Him. Which, when ' *His disciples James and John saw, they said, Lord, wilt thou that we command fire to come down from heaven, and consume them, even as Elias did?* ' What could be a more venerable example ? What could be more applicable ? Had they not conversed with Moses and Elias on the mount of Transfiguration ? Had not Moses and Elias

M

done homage to their Master? Why might He not put
forth powers as great as theirs? Why not, indeed! And
what, then, *are* the great powers? John and James could
have no doubt. Powers of destruction, of course. To call
down fire upon a city, what can be so wonderful as that?
They thought so. Churchmen have thought so in all times
since. Very much they have grieved that they could not
do like Elijah. Very often they have tried, or feigned, to
do, exactly like him. Our Lord vindicated the real object
of those acts which were done in the old time, by showing
forth clearly and brightly what was the object of His acts.
The deeds of all Prophets, if they were ever so terrible,
were witnesses *against* destructive Gods, *for* the living
God, the Creator. His true Image, His perfect Son, came
not to destroy men's lives, but to save. So He did His
Father's will. Whoever has any other purpose than
that, be he Saint, Apostle, what he may, is not doing
God's will, but a will opposed to God's. By such lessons,
hard to be taken in, needing often to be repeated, very
humbling to his self-conceit, disagreeable to that nature
which we have flattered so much and which he does
not flatter at all, St. John was converted not into a
weak sentimental enemy of all that is strong and stern,
but into a resolute asserter of the doctrines, ' *Whosoever
hateth his brother is a murderer;*' ' *If a man say, I love
God, and hateth his brother, he is a liar.*'

(2) The verses which follow to the end of the chapter I
will not leave without notice, because it is more honest to
say that I do not clearly understand them. The first sentence
was evidently addressed to an over-confident disciple, who
had not counted the cost of his intention and needed to be
told what it might involve; the second, to one who was

finding plausible excuses for not doing what he yet thought he was bound to do ; the third, to one who was inclining to withdraw from a work on which he had already entered. So much we can easily perceive ; and if we believe that the same Searcher of hearts who discovered the false zeal or false excuses of those men is detecting ours, is bringing them home to our consciences, we shall draw the best possible lesson from the narrative. But I do not pretend to know the precise signification of the words, ' *Let the dead bury their dead.*' I am only sure that they did not mean anything which was at variance with the mind of Him who denounced the Pharisees for setting aside God's commandment, 'Honour thy father and mother,' by their tradition. I am only sure that those who attribute any such sense to our Lord's words are perverting the New Testament as the two Apostles perverted the Old, the example of the Son of Man as they perverted the example of Elijah.

(3) But there is one remark which is suggested by all these words of our Lord. He speaks to His disciples as one who has authority to tell them where they shall go, and what they shall do. He speaks as one who has called them to be the ministers in a divine kingdom ; only in that sense to be the preachers of a doctrine. I must speak to weariness of this characteristic of the Gospel history, because we are so apt to forget it, and because a long familiarity with the phrase, 'Kingdom of Heaven,' blinds us to its great significance. Give it the force it had in St. Luke's mind, and the passage which follows respecting the mission of the seventy, whom the Lord sent into every city and village whither He Himself should come, will all bear the impress of a royal discourse. The commands resemble those which were given to the Apostles.

St. Luke evidently dwells upon them not so much for
any peculiarities in the directions themselves, as because
they signified that there were other ministers besides the
twelve, who were ordained by Christ Himself to preach
the Kingdom of Heaven and to exercise the powers of it.
St. Luke looked upon the kingdom as at hand then, which
he was proclaiming as established in the ascended Lord.
He felt that his own office was good for nothing if he were
not as much sent forth by the Son of Man as any one of
the twelve.   He is speaking of One who would be the same
yesterday, to-day, and for ever ; of a kingdom which was
to have no end.   Whilst, then, he repeated these commands which were specially adapted to the wants of men
who were going only amidst the sheep of the House of
Israel ; he will have felt that the same voice, issuing commands as real, as binding, would go forth through all
lands ; that all who should presume to preach in Christ's
name in any time or country, must listen to that voice,
must try to learn from it the message which men were to
receive, and how the message should be delivered.

(4) Nor can I think that St. Luke anticipated any less
effect, or any different effect, from the proclamation in one
time than in another. There would be always those to whom
the news of a Kingdom of Heaven would be the best news
conceivable, just what they had been waiting and wanting
to hear.   There would be always those to whom it would
be indifferent or incredible.   There would be always those
who would refuse it, because they regarded the universe as
the subjects of that kingdom which Christ's Kingdom was
to overthrow. The Apostles and the seventy disciples were
to heal sickness and cast out evil spirits. They were to
act as deliverers ; they were to be witnesses of God as the

Deliverer from bodily sufferings, and from the worse evils, which degrade and destroy the spirit. The mind of the Jewish people—the mind of the Jewish rulers especially —was more and more beginning to regard God as the Destroyer, not as the Deliverer ; to think that bodily evils were signs of His disposition towards His creatures; to think that here and hereafter He would use these bodily calamities, not as instruments of raising them out of their moral and spiritual misery, but as instruments by which He would avenge it and perpetuate it.

This habit of belief, or unbelief, prevailed among men who counted it their highest glory to possess commandments, the first of which told them that they should worship no God but the Deliverer from bondage—to possess Scriptures which proclaimed Him in every line to be the God of Salvation.

I have just told you how our Lord rebuked those Apostles who would have called down fire from heaven to destroy a village of the Samaritans. How, then, are we to explain those denunciations of the cities of Galilee which occur in the midst of the charge to the seventy disciples ?—' *Woe unto thee, Chorazin! woe unto thee, Beth-saida! for if the mighty works had been done in Tyre and Sidon, which have been done in you, they had a great while ago repented, sitting in sackcloth and ashes. But it shall be more tolerable for Tyre and Sidon at the judgment, than for you. And thou, Capernaum, which art exalted to heaven, shalt be thrust down to hell. He that heareth you heareth me ; and he that despiseth you despiseth me ; and he that despiseth me despiseth him that sent me.*' How, I ask, are these words consistent with those—' *The Son of man is not come to destroy men's lives, but to save ?*' If the message of the seventy was, as the words of St. Luke show that it was, a message concerning a God who was not destroying men's lives but saving them,—and if the people of Chorazin and Bethsaida and Capernaum turned away from that message because they worshipped a God who was *not* a Saviour, but a Destroyer,—the fulfilment to the very letter of this prophecy would surely confirm, and not annul, the language which was addressed to John and James. They were sharing the evil notions of their countrymen; they would see whither those evil notions were leading a land which God had called out to be a blessing to all lands. It refused to be such a blessing; it had become a curse to all lands. It spoke of a God who wished to curse all lands. The judgment which it had anticipated for the rest of the world was coming upon it; the darkest, the most terrible judgment that can come upon any nation or city of men—the judgment of being permitted to have its own way; the judgment of being left to fight against the Will which is to do only good; the judgment of suffering the exclusion to which it has consigned all but itself. That judgment the cities of Palestine would have to undergo in a sense in which the corrupt heathen cities of Tyre and Sidon had not undergone it, and would not undergo it. Our Lord, who knew what was in man, testified that if Tyre and Sidon had heard what Chorazin and Bethsaida were hearing, they would have repented long ago. My friends, how many sentences which we have passed in our wisdom upon the heathen world, even upon the darkest parts of it, are reversed by that sentence! How many hopes are awakened by it, that even the worst inhabitants of that world shall hear the Voice which must sound through the whole creation—that they shall turn to it and live!

(5) '*And the seventy returned again with joy, saying, Lord, even the devils are subject unto us through thy name.*' A warrant for joy, surely, for those men, and for the successors of those men, in all times to come, if they see physical evil and moral evil giving way before the name of Christ—if they feel that even their weak words bear witness of Him that sent them, in whom all power dwells in earth and in heaven. But yet the sense of power—even of such power—is dangerous. It passes soon into the feeling, ' In Thy name *we* can do something ;' the delight in saving power soon mingles with the lust to use destructive power. '*Lord, the devils are subject to us,*' has meant, in the dialects of Christendom, ' Lord, we can excommunicate, we can consign men to evil 'spirits, as enemies of Thee.' Wherefore Jesus said to them, in the full foresight of the final triumph of good over evil, '*I beheld Satan as lightning fall from heaven.*' Then, because men were to be fellow-workers with Him in winning that triumph, because men in all different ages would receive strength from Him, in one way or another, to overcome the powers of nature and deliver the world from its tormentors, He added, '*Behold, I give unto you power to tread on serpents and scorpions, and over all the power of the enemy: and nothing shall by any means hurt you.*' But, He added, finally, '*Notwithstanding in this rejoice not, that the spirits are subject unto you ; but rather rejoice, because your names are written in heaven.*' An exhortation which cannot signify, as we sometimes take it to signify, ' Rejoice that you are secure of going to heaven, from which other people will be rejected.' Those who were sent to preach the Kingdom of Heaven would have felt such language utterly incongruous with their

mission. They must have understood Him to say, 'Re-
'joice that you are chosen to do a heavenly work, to be
'heralds of the Father in heaven to His children. Rejoice
'that you have your names in the roll of those who did
'in the generations of old, who shall in the generations
'to come, testify for light against darkness, for heaven
'against hell.'

(6) We cannot be mistaken about the nature of this joy,
for it is written, '*In that hour Jesus rejoiced in spirit, and
said, I thank thee, O Father, Lord of heaven and earth, that
thou hast hid these things from the wise and prudent, and
hast revealed them unto babes: even so, Father; for so it
seemed good in thy sight. All things are delivered to me of
my Father: and no man knoweth who the Son is, but the
Father; and who the Father is, but the Son, and he to whom
the Son will reveal him.*' This was the joy of Christ, the
joy of Him whom we call the Man of Sorrows—a joy
coming out at that moment in some unwonted radiance
of countenance, but really pervading His spirit at all
times, sustaining it in all anguish ; the joy of a Son in
doing a Father's will, in giving up His own ; the joy of
a Son in seeing that will revealing itself silently, gradually,
not to those who would boast of it as their own, but to the
ignorant and the feeble who would cast themselves upon it
to illumine in them that which was dark, to raise and
support that in them which was low ; that so God's ways
might be justified to the universe, that good and only
good might be shown to come from Him, men's works to be
good so far as they are His works.

(7) Most fitly do the words, which He spoke privately to
His disciples, follow that wonderful thanksgiving—'*Blessed
are the eyes which see the things that ye see : for I tell you, that*

many prophets and kings have desired to see those things which ye see, and have not seen them; and to hear those things which ye hear, and have not heard them.' The poor fishermen had that revelation of the Father which kings and prophets longed for. They had entered upon this great inheritance; they were to call other men, babes like themselves, to share in the inheritance.

(8) A lawyer came in to give them some help in understanding the nature and the worth of this inheritance. He stood up and tempted Christ, saying, *' Master, what shall I do to inherit eternal life?'* Eternal life! Yes, that must be the highest of all gifts. How could it be earned? What sacrifices could be costly enough to win it? Had not Jesus some special rules for obtaining it? No, apparently none. He refers the lawyer to his own books. What is written there? The student and interpreter of the Scriptures considers. Some very remarkable words occur to his mind in the Book of Deuteronomy, words about loving the Lord God with all the heart and soul and strength, words about loving one's neighbour as oneself. Perhaps those were the words in the Law which Jesus meant. Perhaps the lawyer had heard that He often referred to those words. Yes, the quotation was an apposite one. He had found out the way to eternal life. *' This do, and thou shalt live.'* Had he done this, then? The question was a painful one to the lawyer's conscience. There was a way out of it. The law did not define the neighbour—who is he?

(9) You know what story was the answer to this question. We call it the story of the Good Samaritan. We could not, perhaps, give it a better name. But why was the Samaritan good? Did his country give him some advantage over the Levite and the priest? Did his faith? Did

something specially blessed in his own individual nature? If his goodness could be referred to any one of these causes, he was no example to the Jew—the lawyer could not be fairly bidden to '*go and do likewise*.' No! But that commandment which the lawyer found in the Book of Deuteronomy—that law of loving the neighbour as himself—had been written in the heart of the Samaritan. He confessed that he was bound by it. Therefore he took account of the man who was by the wayside, though he had come from Jerusalem to Jericho, though he was of an alien and hostile race, though those of his own race did not esteem him their neighbour. Therefore he sat him upon his own beast; therefore he poured oil and wine into his wounds; therefore he took care of him. He made no pretence to exalted virtue; he did not ask for any reward. He did the things which a voice within him bade him do. He yielded to a law, but it was a law of love, a law of liberty, and in that law there was life.

The lesson is keen and pointed; it strikes its roots deeply; they spread themselves far. The Samaritan heretic obeys the divine law in its largest sense; the strict Jew breaks it in its most limited and narrow sense. But it *is* a law to one as much as the other. The notion of love or charity as a self-indulgence, as the mere following of a kindly impulse, is as foreign to the New Testament as to the Old. God commands, man only obeys; this is equally the doctrine of both. But from *what* God does the command come? How is it to be obeyed? Christ shows forth in Himself what the God is from whom the command comes—how it is to be obeyed. The Son does what the Father wills to be done. All the acts of the Son are acts of willing self-sacrifice—acts of service to mankind. These are the acts by which He pays homage to His Father, in which He reveals His Father. To be moulded into conformity with His will, to have the Spirit of the Father and the Son who alone can mould us—this is the blessing of all blessings. This is that which prophets and kings longed for. To have this gift is the privilege of all, for Christ has died and risen and ascended; to accept it and live under the law of love—this is what we shall find to be the true, the eternal life, when we have been stripped of all our own pretensions, when we are content to receive all things from the Son of Man. This life is not a reward for keeping the commandment. In keeping the commandment you will possess it, you will enjoy it. If we did love God with all our hearts and soul and strength and mind, if we did love our neighbour as ourselves, we should have the divine, perfect life, the life of the eternal God. We should want nothing more, we could have nothing more. Oh, my friends, let us think of this as we kneel at God's altar to-day. The infinite eternal charity of which the Epistle has spoken to us,* is all gathered up in the sacrifice which Christ made for the world. The eternal life is shown forth in His death. We are permitted, we are invited, to partake of that Sacrifice, to eat the flesh and blood. We are permitted then, we are invited, to lay hold of eternal life. We do lay hold of it if we obey those commandments which the Samaritan, who had so little of our light, obeyed when he treated his enemy, the Jew, as his brother. For then we confess that a God of charity rules us and rules the universe; then we ask Him to forgive us all our breaches of charity, and to fill us with His charity, since we have none of our own.

* On Quinquagesima Sunday.

LECTURE XV.

THE SPIRIT OF THE KING AND OF THE JEWISH RULERS.

St. Luke XI. 39, 40.

And the Lord said unto him, Now do ye Pharisees make clean the outside of the cup and the platter; but your inward part is full of ravening and wickedness. Ye fools, did not he that made that which is without make that which is within also?

THE last chapter closes with a simple domestic picture which has fixed itself on the heart of all Christian nations. Jesus in the house of Martha and Mary, served diligently by the one, listened to by the other—this story has been felt to be true for that time, true for all times. Such diversities of character, such impatience of the busy spirit against the thoughtful one, there must have been in the villages of Palestine, because they are to be found in the villages of England. And it has been felt that the love which binds together tempers so naturally at variance, which enables them to work together in their own ways, for the same end, must dwell in One above themselves. There must be a hidden guest in every family group, who appoints the special tastes of its members, who gives them a common centre; without such a guest the father, the mother, the brother, would only confuse them by their opposing counsels and hasty judgments.

The chapter which follows—that of which I am especially to speak this morning—ends with a very different feast from that with these women. Jesus is in the house of a Pharisee. He pours forth there one of those terrible denunciations of the Pharisaic mind and temper which have been thought so unlike His language to His disciples. Was all this burning wrath, it has been asked, working in Him who said, '*Love your enemies, pray for them that hate you and despitefully use you*'—in Him who had compassion upon the crowd that was hungry, and the woman that was a sinner?

I purposely bring together the story of Martha and Mary with these sentences of indignation, that you may feel the force of the contrast. Till we feel it, I do not think we can enter into the Revelation of the Son of Man and the Son of God. If in the voice of the Saviour we do not hear the voice of the Judge, we shall not confess Him to be indeed the Saviour. If in the voice of the Judge we do not hear the voice of the Saviour, we shall not confess Him to be indeed the Judge. We may divide these characters in our minds, clinging to the one, turning away from the other; but our delight in the first will prove to be a weak, maudlin, ineffectual one; our dread of the second will lead us to cherish all the habits of mind which are most alien from the mind of Christ, from His true gentleness.

If we follow the incidents of the eleventh chapter, I think you will see how this lesson rises out of them all.

(1) The disciples, we are told, on a certain occasion asked Jesus to teach them to pray, as John also taught his disciples. He does teach them. They may have wondered as they found that most of the petitions were not new. They had heard them from other lips. The hallowing of the Name, the coming of the Kingdom, the doing of the

Will, these prayers gathered up the strongest expressions
of the old Psalms, of the prayers with which they were
most familiar. To ask for bread enough for their daily
wants, this was surely nothing new. Could there be any
prayer in which the thought of forgiveness did not mingle
—any which was not a refuge from temptation—any which
was not a cry for deliverance from evil? Had they learnt
anything which they did not know before? Had Jesus
given them the help which John gave his disciples?

For twelve centuries this prayer has been used in this
land, in every church of it, in every corner of it. We have
repeated it several times this morning. Can we then
answer this question? Why is it the Lord's Prayer?
What is it that Jesus taught which only He could teach?

I should answer, my friends, our Lord taught His
disciples, and teaches us, precisely what makes this form
of words a prayer; precisely that which had made any
words that had ever been spoken in any age, in any
country, by any man, a prayer. When He bade them say,
'*Our Father*,' He explained the nature of prayer, the pos-
sibility of prayer, the necessity of prayer. If there had
not been in men the sense of a Father, the impulse to pray
would never have been awakened in them. The sky, the
sun, the earth, would not have created that impulse.
Because they had the yearnings of children, they could
turn to every object in creation in hopes of finding what
they wanted there. They could dream that He might be
in the grandest objects which they admired, or in the
meanest things which did them good. Every one who
left the world might be invoked, for he might know the
secret; it might be in the invisible region, if the visible did
not contain it. Against the worship of all these created

things the Jew had borne witness. For the worship of
One who created them all he had borne witness. His
negative protest was still vigorous and fierce. His positive
testimony was perishing. He worshipped a God who was
not in the sky, the sea, or the earth; who was *not* like
animals, or like human forms. What *was* He then? Just
or unjust? Light or dark? The Friend of man or the
Destroyer of men? The Jew hesitated; he could not tell.
And therefore, practically, he arrived at a very decisive
judgment. The God whom he worshipped *was* the Destroyer. He was the dark Fate that was plotting against
the peace and life of the Universe. He was the invisible
Power which Heathens had concealed from themselves
behind forms of nature and conceptions of art; which had
only now and then forced itself upon them in its full
terror; which they thought might possibly be propitiated
by costly sacrifices, or diverted from its deadly purpose
by the influence of the more benevolent divinities. Was it
the Name of such a Being as this that the Jews wished
to hallow? Was it *His* kingdom that they wished to
come? Was it *His* Will that they desired to be done?
Did He care to give any bread? Could He forgive? Was
not every temptation of His devising? Was not Evil that
which He desired and designed for His creatures? See,
then, how those words, "*Our Father*," endorsed and interpreted every hope that man had ever cherished, in the
Gentile world as well as the Jewish! See how they
scattered the horrible fictions of both! See how they
translated petitions which, in the mouths of Pharisees, were
imprecations upon mankind, and even upon themselves,
into entreaties for the greatest blessings that could come
upon both! For would not the real hallowing of a Father's

name, the coming of a Father's kingdom, the doing of a
Father's will, be a blessing to the Pharisee as well as the
Heathen, such as neither had ever dreamed of?

(2) In this light, then, we must read the words of our Lord
which follow respecting importunity in prayer. 'The man,'
he says, 'does not rise from his bed when his friend asks
'him for the three loaves for a neighbour who has come to
'see him; but if he persists in his entreaty, *he will rise
'and give him as many as he needeth.*' 'There,' it has been
said, 'you see how our Lord Himself encourages us to over-
'come the will of God by the urgency of our petitions!'
Does He so? Had He not just been teaching His disciples
to say, '*Thy will be done on earth as it is in heaven?*'
Do you suppose, when He told them to be importunate
with His Father and their Father, that He meant them to
imitate those worshippers who cried from morning to
noon, 'Oh, Baal, hear us!' and showed their earnestness
by cutting themselves with stones? To that importunity
the Bible says:—'*there was no answer, neither was there
any that regarded.*' Our Lord supports His counsel of
importunity by these questions:—'*If a son shall ask
bread of any of you that is a father, will he give him a
stone? or if he ask a fish, will he for a fish give him a
serpent? Or if he shall ask an egg, will he offer him a
scorpion? If ye then, being evil, know how to give good gifts
unto your children; how much more shall your heavenly
Father give the Holy Spirit to them that ask him?*' As if
He had said, 'What, then, will you merely repeat the
'prayer that God's name be hallowed? Are you not in
'earnest that it should be hallowed—that all the false,
'detestable names which have been substituted for the
'true name of a Father, or become mingled with it, should

' be separated from it ? Are you not really desirous that
' His kingdom should overthrow all the tyrannies and
' oppressions of the earth—that His perfectly good Will
' should triumph over your will and all other wills that are
' striving against it ? ' If you are, will you not go on asking
your Father for these blessings, in the assurance that it is
His purpose, because He is your Father, to bestow them,
in the assurance that He is educating you to desire, what
He desires, to work with Him for the overthrow of that
which He hates ? Will He not give you that without
which you cannot hallow His Name, seek His Kingdom,
do His Will—without which bread is nothing, forgiveness
a mere name, temptation irresistible—without which evil
must reign for ever ? Will He not give you His own Holy
Spirit ? Is it not this which such a Father would count
the good thing for His children ? Can you dream of anything better ? And surely the more you receive it, the
more you will ask for it ; the more you find it, the more
you will seek for it. This importunity, then, is not the
Baal importunity. It is that which we demand in different
spheres of labour, from every scientific man, from every
artist, from every sincere student in every profession. We
say to all, ' Be not slothful, be not discouraged by a
' thousand obstacles, by a thousand defeats. Onward, still
' onward. The truth is there. It will reward your diligence in
' wrestling for it when it seems most to deny itself to you ; in
' pursuing it, though the roads are most rugged.' ' *Seek, and
you shall find ; knock, and it shall be opened.*' I say these
exhortations are sound and wholesome, because God is a God
of Truth, and because He is our Father, and because He
has promised His Spirit of Truth to those who know that
without it they shall sink ever deeper into falsehood.

N

(3) There can be no better introduction than this prayer, and the comment upon it, to the next passage of the chapter—that in which Christ answers those who said, '*He casteth out devils through Beelzebub, the chief of the devils.*' 'Shall not your Father,' said Christ, 'give His *Holy* Spirit to them that ask Him?' 'By an *unholy* Spirit,' said the Pharisees, 'He casteth out these unclean and unholy spirits that have got the dominion over you.' Here is the point of that memorable answer of Christ :—'*Every kingdom divided against itself, is brought to desolation; and a house divided against a house falleth.*' Is it so, indeed?—is there a battle going on between the powers of evil? An ominous strife it is for them! They do not understand one another, then; they must destroy each other! '*But if I with the finger of God cast out devils, no doubt the kingdom of God is come upon you.*' 'If these works are not the tricks of some 'mighty power of evil, but the works of the Holy God—the 'God of Righteousness and Truth—do not doubt that you 'are standing before that God, that He is calling you to 'account.' Thus He explains all His exercises of power; to this test He brings them. Do they manifest the good Spirit in conflict with the evil spirit? Do they testify that the good must overcome the evil? He intimates that by this test the acts of *all* men must be tried. There were men of repute among the Jews who tried to cure diseases —perhaps who practised exorcism. Were *they* working, as He was said to be, in the service of an evil spirit? Was such a spirit enduing *them* with the powers which they claimed?

He does not conceal it. He had not come to make the world quiet. He had come to disturb a strong man who was keeping his palace, and whose goods were in peace.

He had come to bind that strong man, and to take from him all the armour wherein he trusted, and to spoil his goods He invited all to work with Him in that conflict. Not to engage with Him in it was to take part with the false spirit; not to join Him in gathering was to join with the spirit who was seeking to divide and scatter. The Lord told His disciples that those who were not against Him were with Him. If they cared for the name of the true God, though they might not assume His name, they were on His side. Now He says, that those who were not with Him in asserting the difference between the true God and all false gods—the uniting Spirit and the dividing spirit —were against Him. And then He goes on to describe, in awful language, the state of a nation, or an age, or a man, which has rid itself of one unclean spirit—the spirit, as most have said, and I doubt not truly, of idolatry; the spirit that tempts us to seek God in visible forms, but which has not sought any nobler, purer, diviner Spirit to replace what it has parted with; which therefore feels denuded of all the pictures and decorations that had filled its chambers of imagery; which goes wearily, restlessly about, seeking for something to people the vacant niches; to adorn the house that is empty, swept, and garnished. And then, in its dreariness and loneliness, the age or the nation or the individual soul invites spirits far more evil than the one of which it has been dispossessed. *'And they came in and dwelt there, and the last state of that man is worse than the first.'*

(4) *'And it came to pass, as he spake these things, a certain woman of the company lifted up her voice, and said unto him, Blessed is the womb that bare thee, and the paps which thou hast sucked. But he said, Yea, rather, blessed are they*

N 2

that hear the word of God, and keep it.' Could this poor woman understand the parable by which so many wise men have been puzzled? If she did understand it, must it not have had a sound of terror for her rather than of blessing? She may, or may not have comprehended the words. The face of the Speaker, the witness which it bore of gentleness and of power, was more to her than any language. It might be the most soothing or the most tremendous ever spoken; she had a certainty about the heart from which it issued that no explanations could have given or have taken away. Her words were the utterance of a simple nature. It was a woman's thought about the woman's blessedness in having such a Son. He turned her to the blessedness of a diviner parentage, of that higher life which comes from the Divine Word, when it has mastered and governed the heart within.

(5) But the heart of the age was not governed by that Word, rather was struggling with it. *'And when the people were gathered thick together, he began to say, This is an evil generation: they seek a sign; and there shall no sign be given it, but the sign of Jonas the prophet. For as Jonas was a sign unto the Ninevites, so shall also the Son of man be to this generation. The queen of the south shall rise up in the judgment with the men of this generation, and condemn them: for she came from the utmost parts of the earth to hear the wisdom of Solomon; and, behold, a greater than Solomon is here. The men of Nineve shall rise up in the judgment with this generation, and shall condemn it: for they repented at the preaching of Jonas; and, behold, a greater than Jonas is here.'* Everything here points to the condition of a land which had heard all Divine calls, which was hearing the divinest of these calls then, and was shutting itself up in

its pride and self-righteousness. All is pointing to the Divine purpose and power which had been manifested in past time, which would be manifested more wonderfully out of stones to raise up children to Abraham. Did God care only for the Jews? Did not their earliest prophet testify that He cared for the Ninevites? Did not the Ninevites hear when the prophet's own heart was hardened? Did God bestow wisdom on Solomon only for the sake of Solomon's countrymen? Did not the Queen of Sheba come to hear it? Had the Ninevites, had the Queen of Sheba the same blessing as the men of that generation? No! a greater than Jonas, a greater than Solomon was among them. Yet they did not repent. The highest wisdom seemed to them folly.

(6) '*No man, when he hath lighted a candle, putteth it in a secret place, neither under a bushel, but on a candle-stick, that they which come in may see the light. The light of the body is the eye: therefore when thine eye is single, thy whole body also is full of light; but when thine eye is evil, thy body also is full of darkness. Take heed therefore that the light which is in thee be not darkness. If thy whole body therefore be full of light, having no part dark, the whole shall be full of light, as when the bright shining of a candle doth give thee light.*' Words like these we have heard before, evidently with a somewhat different application. Here they belong, it would seem, strictly to the Jewish people. A light had been kindled on the earth; it was intended to shine forth on the world, not to be hid under a bushel. All were to come in and see the light; but alas! they had fancied that the light was in themselves. They had boasted of having what others wanted. Oh, what fear there was that the light so shut up, never rekindled from its source, would become the most absolute darkness.

But if any of you will come to the light, and let it stream
into you, your whole bodies shall be full of it. There shall
be no place dark.

(7) This sentence is the proper introduction to the discourse from which I have taken my text.

*'And as he spake, a certain Pharisee besought him to dine
with him: and he went in, and sat down to meat. And
when the Pharisee saw it, he marvelled that he had not first
washed before dinner. And the Lord said unto him, Now
do ye Pharisees make clean the outside of the cup and the
platter; but your inward part is full of ravening and wickedness. Ye fools, did not he that made that which is without
make that which is within also? But rather give alms of
such things as ye have; and, behold, all things are clean unto
you. But woe unto you, Pharisees! for ye tithe mint and
rue and all manner of herbs, and pass over judgment and the
love of God: these ought ye to have done, and not to leave the
other undone. Woe unto you, Pharisees! for ye love the
uppermost seats in the synagogues, and greetings in the
markets. Woe unto you, scribes and Pharisees, hypocrites!
for ye are as graves which appear not, and the men that walk
over them are not aware of them.'*

'What tremendous withering words!' exclaims the
modern critic. 'Can they have been really spoken at
'the house of one who asked Jesus to dine with him?
'How His temper must have been changed! What irri-
'tation must have been awakened in Him by the hostility
'which He encountered!' I admit at once that, if the
Pharisee were not abusing a trust which had been committed to him for the good of the nation, and if it was not
the King of the nation—his King—who was calling him
to answer for his trust, this language is wholly strange—

I can make no defence of it. If that were so, then I say the more Jesus cared for the poorest, the most suffering, the most sinful of the land—the more He had stooped to them—the more might we expect Him to speak in thunders to the consciences of those who were lifting up themselves, of those who were making themselves gods and hiding from the people the living and true God. If it were the great disease of the Pharisee, that he made all clean without and left all foul within, was our Lord merciful or unmerciful for telling him to his face that it was so? Was it merciful or unmerciful to remind him that the unseen God, the God of his fathers, demanded truth in the inward parts, and was willing to give what He demanded? Was it better for him to know, or not to know, that his money was not his to buy God's favour with, but his to be used as the almoner of God's bounty to His creatures? Was it well that he should wake up to discover in some dying hour, or when the land was perishing, that he had substituted mint, anise, and cummin for judgment and the love of God, or that the disguise should be torn from his eyes whilst he was yet full of ease and satisfaction? Was it good that he should go on receiving the greetings in the markets, and thinking himself the best of men, or that he should for a moment be discovered to himself in his rags and corruption? Was it well that more men should drop into the hollow graves which looked so fair without, or that the owners of the graves should be admonished to purify them from the bones and pollutions within?

(9) Did these words merely strike at the evils of a single school or sect? Were they not meant to reach all the

teachers of Israel—all who were busy with commenting
on the laws and letters of the Holy Book ?

‘ *Then answered one of the lawyers, and said unto him,*
Master, thus saying thou reproachest us also. And he said,
Woe unto you also, ye lawyers! for ye lade men with burdens
grievous to be borne, and ye yourselves touch not the burdens
with one of your fingers. Woe unto you! for ye build the
sepulchres of the prophets, and your fathers killed them.
Truly ye bear witness that ye allow the deeds of your fathers :
for they indeed killed them, and ye build their sepulchres.
Therefore also said the wisdom of God, I will send them
prophets and apostles, and some of them they shall slay and
persecute : that the blood of all the prophets, which was shed
from the foundation of the world, may be required of this
generation ; from the blood of Abel unto the blood of Zacha-
rias, which perished between the altar and the temple : verily
I say unto you, It shall be required of this generation. Woe
unto you, lawyers! for ye have taken away the key of know-
ledge : ye entered not in yourselves, and them that were enter-
ing in ye hindered.’

No sentence here is wasted. Each is aimed at some
special tendency of the time. Each is more intense than
the one that went before it. First, the infliction of hard
rules and practices, burdensome to the conscience of the
victim, not causing the least trouble to the imposer. Then
the complacent admiration for holy men who are safe out
of reach, who can no more utter the reproofs which en-
raged their contemporaries and brought death upon themselves. ‘ You joyfully build their sepulchres ; what would
you do if they stood up and confronted you !’ Then
the fearful assurance that the age, instead of being free
from the guilt of previous ages, as it fancied, was gather-

ing the guilt of them into itself, was cultivating all the murderous tempers and habits which had been their curse, was sowing wind to reap a whirlwind, such as they had not reaped. And this because the teachers of the divine law had that great master sin,—the sin of priests and possessors of knowledge in all times. They think that knowledge is given for their own use. They think the people are to be kept away from it, and fed on mere husks. So the key which might unlock divine treasures becomes rusty in their hands, and cannot move the lock. They cannot find their own way into the kingdom of God, and those that are longing for it they keep out.

Woes indeed these were—woes *for* the most grievous of all sins, but woes contained *in* the sins themselves. These religious teachers were their own tormentors, as well as the tormentors of the land. And this was their sorest misery. They longed to silence the voice which told them of their misery. They did not know that, in ridding themselves of the Judge, they would be ridding themselves of the Saviour. They did not know that He could take from them their pride, their hypocrisy, their hatred of Him and of His Father. Therefore, '*And as he said these things unto them, the scribes and the Pharisees began to urge him vehemently, and to provoke him to speak of many things : laying wait for him, and seeking to catch something out of his mouth, that they might accuse him.*'

Oh, my friends, may we take warning by that example ! If we believe that He who sat in the Pharisee's house was indeed the Eternal Son of God, may we open our ear to hear what He is now saying to the Churches ! In the cottage, where sisters are working and learning, may they know Him as the Inspirer of their work, as the Giver of their knowledge! May He teach us to pray, that we may pray aright! May He conquer the spirit which is dividing us by His uniting Spirit ! May that Spirit come and dwell with us, that the evil spirit of pride and malice may not enter into us and possess us ! May He enable us to listen to all the warnings which heathens who have repented at His call and profited by His Word send to us ! And if our religion ever becomes one of show and not of substance, of self-exaltation and not of humility, of death and not of life, may the words that have been fulfilled to other countries and ages ring in our ears and make us tremble, that we may turn with all our hearts to Him who can renew us by His grace, who can cause the light which He has kindled in us to shine forth on the world !

LECTURE XVI.

THE FIRE WHICH IS TO BAPTIZE THE NATION AND THE KING.

ST. LUKE XII. 49, 50.

I am come to send fire on the earth; and what will I, if it be already kindled ?   But I have a baptism to be baptized with ; and how am I straitened till it be accomplished !

THE words which were spoken in the house of the Pharisee were an open declaration of war.   It had begun before. John the Baptist had denounced both the sects as generations of vipers.   Jesus had provoked the wrath of this sect by His acts on the Sabbath day.   The suggestion, 'He casteth out demons by Beelzebub, the Prince of the demons,' proceeded most probably from them.   But He had not till now spoken to them directly of their habits of mind as those which were bringing down curses upon the nation, and which would destroy it.   He had not before showed men who assumed to be *the* worshippers of God—the teachers of the people how they should worship Him,—that they were essentially godless ; that they were undermining all godliness in the land.   Henceforth there can be no doubt of His meaning.   If the Gospel of His kingdom is true, their scheme of divinity and their code of ethics are false.   The establishment of one must be the ruin of the other.

I. If we construe the words at the opening of the twelfth chapter strictly, we must suppose that whilst he was talking

in the Pharisee's house, a great concourse of people had assembled, waiting to hear Him.   Before He speaks to them,
He must pour out the thoughts of which His heart is full
to His disciples.   '*He began to say to them, first of all,
Beware ye of the leaven of the Pharisees, which is hypocrisy.*'
He does not speak now as He had spoken when He was
face to face with the Pharisees and lawyers.   Then He had
laid open their special evils—those which arose out of their
belief in their superiority to the rest of their countrymen.
He speaks of a leaven which was affecting the whole land,
of which His own little flock were in as much danger as
any others.   That which was the disease of the Pharisee
was the disease of the time.   He calls that disease *hypocrisy.*
We have a reasonable horror of the name.   We consider
that it is applicable only to the worst men in the worst
times.   There is good excuse for that opinion ; yet it may
rob us of the force of our Lord's warning—we may put it at
a dangerous distance from ourselves.   The hypocrite is the
man who acts a part ; there is no more evil signification in
the word than that.   And oh ! how easy it is to be a hypocrite, if that is his characteristic ; how difficult it is not to
be one !   Do you not know with what terrible quickness
a child becomes an actor or actress ?   Do you not know
what we do to cultivate the acting talent, the acting habit in
them ?   Do you not know what a number of social influences
and contrivances are at work to convince men and women
that it is their business to be masquers, that their skill is to
be shown in the devising of masks ?

   To strike at the root of this hypocrisy, to point out the
remedy, this is the work which we ask from The King of
men, from Him who knows what is in man.   Jesus struck
at the root of all social hypocrisy, of all personal hypocrisy,

in Palestine, when He traced it to the religion which prevailed there. Then He pointed out the remedy in this sentence of everlasting might : '*For there is nothing covered that shall not be revealed, neither hid that shall not be known.*' The religion of the Pharisees consisted in a series of attempts to please, flatter, and bribe the Ruler of the earth. If He could be persuaded not to look too curiously into the acts of His servants, not to probe the secrets of their hearts ; if He could be induced to accept a compensation for this evil, on certain conditions to tolerate that ; if His commandments could be shown to bear different constructions for different persons ; if cases might be imagined to which they did not apply, or applied with various qualifications and mitigations ; if the creature could succeed in keeping the Creator at a distance from him, so that his secrets should not be brought to the light; their religion had realized its highest objects. Such a religion was leavening the chosen people, as it was under other aspects, with the most dissimilar professions under heathen forms of worship, leavening the old Roman Empire. The priests and lawyers in Jerusalem, the Pontifex and the Augur in Rome were alike acting a part. They rehearsed their parts in private ; they performed them in public. The Pharisees were at once the consummate practisers of the art, and the most systematic instructors in it.

But what if the Ruler of the earth could not be flattered or bribed ? What if *everything* that is covered *must* be revealed, if *everything* that is hidden *must* be known ? What if the very act of the Creator is to reveal, if He is bringing all things to light, if He hates darkness ? There is the whole question. Is it a God of light you serve, or a God of darkness ? Acting hypocrisy is an impossible kind of

service with the first, the only suitable one with the
second.

The apostles of Christ would have need hereafter to remember this distinction, when the thought would be presented to them, as it had been to all teachers in the former
days, that there was a certain lore which was meant for
them, the initiated few, and quite another lore for the vulgar
many. That poisonous doctrine, in which all imposture
lurks, is scattered to the winds for all who believe the words,
' *Whatsoever ye have spoken in the darkness shall be heard in
the light ; and that which ye have spoken in the ear in closets
shall be proclaimed upon the housetops.*' That is the maxim for
the ministers of a gospel. If they think the good news is
for themselves, and their little circle, it ceases to be good
news for themselves and that little circle ; if the world is
cheated of it they will find that it changes its character,
and takes the form of a curse to those for whose special
comfort it is reserved.

A new topic appears to be introduced in the next verse.
It is one, I think, which comes most naturally out of the
preceding one. Those who convey a message to mankind will
not have the ease and security of those who confine their
lessons to the select band. The whole body of religious
masquers will be in arms against those who proclaim God's
revelation of Himself, God's discovery of the thoughts and
intents of the heart, as the highest of all blessings to His
creatures. The battle will be deadly. ' *And I say unto
you my friends, Be not afraid of them that kill the body,
and after that have no more that they can do. But I will
forewarn you whom ye shall fear : Fear him, which after he
hath killed hath power to cast into hell ; yea, I say unto you,
Fear him.*' ' You will have all the power of those who have

' been denounced by me arrayed against you, all the power
' of those who are pursuing objects like theirs in every part
' of the world. But what is that power? What can it effect?
' At the utmost it can kill your bodies. If that is all, you
need not fear it. But that spirit of hypocrisy of which I
' am bidding you beware can do far more. Yield to that
' spirit, and it will destroy heart and soul as well as body;
' he prompts the murderers of the body, and after he has
' killed he has power to cast into hell. That, that is the
' dreadful enemy; you cannot regard that with too much
' dread and horror. Where is the protection from him?
" *Are not five sparrows sold for two farthings, and not one of*
' *them is forgotten before God? But even the very hairs of*
' *your head are all numbered. Fear not, therefore : ye are of*
' *more value than many sparrows.*" Utter absolute trust in
' God, that is the refuge from the evil and destroying spirit.
' Have you not a ground and warrant for such trust? You
' feel your own insignificance; you can put forth no claim
' of merit. But you are not more insignificant than the
' birds, are you? God cares for them. Whatever is their
' worth in the market, they do not fall to the ground without
' Him.' There is nothing in the argument to make the disciples think highly of themselves, nothing to exalt them
above other men. There is everything to remind them of
the prayer they have been taught to pray; there is everything to assure them that their Father in Heaven will give
them day by day what they need, and that His spirit is
stronger than the hypocritical and destroying spirit.

You must not confound the words which follow with
some words of similar sound, of which I spoke to you a
few Sundays ago. He said then, '*Whosoever shall be ashamed*
of me and of my words, of him shall the Son of man be

ashamed.' Here we read, *' Also* (or *but*) *I say unto you, Whosoever shall confess me* (rather confess *in* me) *before men, the Son of man will also confess him* (or *in* him) *before the angels of God : But he that denieth me before men shall be denied before the angels of God.'* If the last clause stood alone, we might treat the 'ashamed' and the 'denial' as equivalent expressions. But the previous clause, which has nothing that answers to it in the other passage, is the most prominent one here, and is that which unites this sentence to the rest of our Lord's discourse. That kind of trust in God's continual care and love for them would indeed raise them above the fear of their enemies. But how can a poor man, in the very moment when he is most crushed by those enemies, when the accusing spirit is tempting him and mocking him, entertain it? That spirit whispers to him continually that God has deserted him, that he has forfeited all right to depend on Him by his transgressions or his faithlessness. 'Confess in me,' says Christ. 'Assert 'your union with me as the Son of man. Forget your own 'nothingness in the recollection that you belong to the race 'of which I am the Head. And then the Son of man will 'confess in you before the angels of God. He will show 'you that you are one with His family in heaven and earth. 'It will be the denial of your fellowship with them, your 'attempt to establish some ground of worth or security for 'yourselves apart from Him, apart from your kind, which 'will separate you from the invisible world as well as the 'visible, from angels as well as men.' The courage to speak their gospel to men,—the courage which would raise them above the fear of men, would thus depend upon the degree in which they identified themselves with man in their common Lord and Saviour.

But the disciples of Christ might have turned these words to a wrong sense; they have been turned to such a sense in later days and generations. They might have said, 'See what worth He gives to the confession of Him. ' Those who assert the truth of His mission, those who call ' themselves by His Name, He will own hereafter. Those ' who refuse Him He will cast out of His Father's presence.' This was exactly the thought in another form which was working in the minds of the Pharisees. They hoped that God would reward them for accepting in great strictness a religion which had His sanction ; that He would condemn other people for not accepting that religion. The disciples of Jesus might suppose that He had come to introduce a religion under more terrible sanctions ; men would be rewarded for accepting it, punished for not accepting it. He adds immediately to the previous sentence respecting the confession and denial of Him one which, at first, appears to clash with it. '*And whosoever shall speak a word against the Son of man, it shall be forgiven him ; but unto him that blasphemeth against the Holy Ghost it shall not be forgiven.*' All interpreters have felt that this language must have some close relation to the words (with which it is directly connected by St. Mark), 'He casteth out devils by Beelzebub, the Prince of the Devils.' In another Gospel it is said that there shall be no forgiveness of this blasphemy, '*neither in this world, neither in the world to come.*' Taking this sentence with the rest of the passage, I cannot doubt that it tells us what the sin of the Pharisees and of the nation was ; why they were cast out of their stewardship in that age ; why the sentence upon them remains still. We say, 'They rejected Jesus ; they would not ' believe all the evidence which He brought from pro-

o

' phecies and miracles to attest His divine mission.' He
says, ' All words spoken against the Son of Man will be
forgiven ; ' but there is a blasphemy against the Spirit
of God—there is a confusion of good with evil, of light
with darkness—which goes down far deeper than this.
When a nation has lost the faculty of distinguishing hatred
from love, the spirit of hypocrisy and falsehood from the
spirit of truth, God from the devil, then its doom is pro-
nounced—then the decree must go forth against it.   I
believe that is the natural sense of these awful words here
and elsewhere ; if we give them that sense we are delivered
from imaginations which have darkened the Gospel to a
number of souls, and the warning to ourselves becomes
much more tremendous.

Fear and hypocrisy have always worked together.   The
dread of men's faces has been one great motive to hypocrisy ; the desire of their applause has been another.
The baptism with the Spirit of truth is the deliverance
from the spirit of hypocrisy.   That same Spirit is the deliverer from the spirit of fear.   ' *And when they bring you
unto the synagogues, and unto magistrates and powers, take
ye not thought* (be *not* anxious or troubled) *how or what
things ye shall answer, or what ye shall say.   For the Holy
Ghost shall teach you in the same hour what ye ought to say.*'
The meaning and worth of that promise were to be ascertained by later experience : only that experience could
enable the disciples to follow the windings of this discourse,
and to see how each part of it was adapted to some great
danger or necessity of theirs.   One thing St. Luke knew,
and has helped us to know.   This assurance of the Spirit's
presence did not cause those who depended on it most to
speak flighty words in the synagogues or before magistrates ;

rudely to defy them : to seize occasions of preaching to them.
Nothing can be more simple, business-like, respectful,
than the apologies of St. Paul. Must it not have been
so? Are not our apologies liable to be quibbling, rhetorical, passionate, just because we do *not* believe that a Spirit
of love and power, and a sound Mind, is with us to guide the
thoughts of our hearts, to teach us what is manly and
healthy, what is the product of our own fancy and vanity?

II. One principal poison which was working in the
veins of the Jewish commonwealth, and was hastening
its death, has been detected. Another was brought to
light by a question which appeared to interrupt the conversation.

'*And one of the company said unto him, Master, speak to
my brother, that he divide the inheritance with me. And he
said unto him, Man, who made me a judge or divider over
you? And he said unto them, Take heed, and beware of
covetousness : for a man's life consisteth not in the abundance
of the things which he possesseth.*'

Hobbes has dwelt upon these words as a confession
by our Lord that He was merely a religious teacher, and
that He aspired to no control over ordinary human affairs.
Undoubtedly He declined to interfere in the case in which
He was asked to interfere. He would not determine how
much of the inheritance belonged to the complainant, how
much to his brother. But His discourse on covetousness,
it seems to me, is the discourse of One who is laying the
axe to the root of a polity—of one who is come to establish a kingdom. How much it differs from the language
of one who is laying down a religious or ethical code of
precepts, I think you will perceive, if you examine it
carefully.

(1) The primary maxim of it you have heard. A man's
LIFE consisteth not in the abundance of his *possessions*.
The contrast between life and possession goes through the
whole of it.

A story illustrates this contrast.

'*And he spake a parable unto them, saying, The ground of
a certain rich man brought forth plentifully. And he thought
within himself, saying, What shall I do, because I have no
room where to bestow my fruits ?　And he said, This will I
do : I will pull down my barns, and build greater ; and
there will I bestow all my fruits and my goods. And
I will say to my soul, Soul, thou hast much goods laid up
for many years ; take thine ease, eat, drink, and be merry.
But God said unto him, Thou fool, this night thy soul shall
be required of thee : then whose shall those things be, which
thou hast provided ? So is he that layeth up treasure for
himself, and is not rich toward God.*'

This story may be called a parable, merely because a
single instance is taken to   hibit a general experience.
But I think you will find as we proceed that there is
another justification of the word. There is a spiritual
covetousness as well as a material covetousness. Both
were characteristic of the Jewish people. The man who
has goods laid up for many years may be an example of
one habit as much as of the other. But the point to which
I would especially call your attention is this. Moral and
religious teachers say much of the transitoriness of *life*.
Our Lord speaks of the transitoriness of the things which a
man has. '*Then whose shall those things be which thou hast
provided ?*' God is holding intercourse with the man himself. 'What art *thou ?* Do these things make thee better ?
Will they go along with thee ?'

(2) See how this remark bears upon the inference which our Lord draws from the story.

'*And he said unto his disciples, Therefore I say unto you, Take no thought for your life, what ye shall eat ; neither for the body, what ye shall put on. The life is more than meat, and the body is more than raiment. Consider the ravens: for they neither sow nor reap ; which neither have storehouse nor barn ; and God feedeth them : how much more are ye better than the fowls ? And which of you with taking thought can add to his stature one cubit ? If ye then be not able to do that thing which is least, why take ye thought for the rest ? Consider the lilies how they grow : they toil not, they spin not ; and yet I say unto you, that Solomon in all his glory was not arrayed like one of these. If then God so clothe the grass, which is to-day in the field, and to-morrow is cast into the oven ; how much more will he clothe you, O ye of little faith ? And seek not ye what ye shall eat, or what ye shall drink, neither be ye of doubtful mind. For all these things do the nations of the world seek after : and your Father knoweth that ye have need of these things. But rather seek ye the kingdom of God ; and all these things shall be added unto you.'*

'How contemptible a thing is the body ! How poor a 'thing is life ! And then think how God, by His infinite 'power, can crush both in a moment.' Such have been the arguments by which preachers in all ages have tried to withdraw their hearers to religious reflections. Our Lord takes the opposite course. 'How glorious is life ; how 'much grander than the mere meat which sustains it ! 'How grand is the body ; how much nobler than the 'raiment with which you clothe it ! And do you think 'God is indifferent either to the food or the raiment of His

' creatures ? Does He not feed the ravens ? Does He not
' clothe the lilies ? Are you afraid that He should ever grudge
' you what you want ? ' Here is the ground of His denunciation of the habits which He found prevailing among
the chosen people. They were heathenish habits. They
sprang out of distrust. The maxim of Solon, ' The Divinity
is an envious nature,' was at the root of them. The restless, feverish pursuit of things to eat and drink, the doubtful, miserable mind which accompanied that pursuit, would
cease if they once believed in the Lord God of their
fathers. Quiet, patient toil would then take the place of
craving for possession in the rich, of despair in the poor.
And here is His own Gospel. You have a Father. I
come to you, poor men, from Him. It is His pleasure to
give you a kingdom. You can claim your places as His
sons and daughters. You can know His righteousness and
His love, and be partakers of it, and show it forth. Assert
those rights. Seek to be subjects of His kingdom. The
outward things which you need will come to you as you
need them. They will be added to you.

(3) The foundation of the Kingdom is laid, then, in the
Nature of God, in His will to bestow the freest and
largest of His gifts on His creatures. Those who claim
their privileges as His adopted children may share this
nature. His Spirit will work in them to distribute rather
than to accumulate the things which they hold for a time,
and to seek their treasure in the unchangeable things which
are in Him. So read the verses which follow :

' *Sell that ye have, and give alms ; provide yourselves bags*
which wax not old, a treasure in the heavens that faileth not,
where no thief approacheth, neither moth corrupteth. For
where your treasure is, there will your heart be also. Let

your loins be girded about, and your lights burning ; and ye yourselves like unto men that wait for their lord, when he will return from the wedding ; that when he cometh and knocketh, they may open unto him immediately. Blessed are those servants, whom the lord when he cometh shall find watching : verily I say unto you, that he shall gird himself, and make them to sit down to meat, and will come forth and serve them. And if he shall come in the second watch, or come in the third watch, and find them so, blessed are those servants. And this know, that if the goodman of the house had known what hour the thief would come, he would have watched, and not have suffered his house to be broken through. Be ye therefore ready also : for the Son of man cometh at an hour when ye think not.'

How the precept, 'Sell that ye have, and give alms,' was acted upon by the disciples after the day of Pentecost, we know from St. Luke's other treatise. I pointed out to you, when I was speaking of the beginnings of the Church in Jerusalem, how entirely spontaneous the acts of selling and distributing were which the historian records ; how careful the Apostles were to tell their little flock, that the things which they had 'were in their own power,' and might be kept or parted with as they chose ; how dangerous the practice became when, as in the case of Ananias, it was thought to carry some merit with it, or be demanded by public opinion. Then it gave birth to the subtlest hypocrisy. A divine principle was exhibited in a particular and transitory form at that time—a principle which can never perish, and which must always find some form to express itself in, so long as the Church lasts. The principle is, that God is the ungrudging bestower of blessings, and that men are His stewards to distribute these blessings. So far as they enter into His mind, the delight will be in spreading abroad, not in accumulating. Their reward will be a continually growing knowledge of His character and purposes. Their treasure will be in whatever things are good, pure, true; their heart will be occupied with these. Here is warrant and encouragement for the servants. The King, the Bridegroom of your race, has set you your tasks. You are to watch over those to whom He has united Himself. You are to make them partakers of His gifts earthly and heavenly; those which are needed for their bodies, those which are needed for their spirits. And you are to remember that He Himself is at hand. These to whom you are ministering are not yours but His. He is Himself their chief minister. He has been so; He will be so. He will minister to you if you minister to Him. The sense of the nearness of the Son of man, of this great Bridegroom, is what must keep you watchful and earnest in your vocation. Lose that; think He is not near you, that He may not at any moment make you know how near He is; forget that He is the Son of man; and your house will be broken through. The spirit of covetousness will enter in and pillage it of all that is best and most precious within it.

(4) Peter knew, by this time, that he was to be the minister in a kingdom, however imperfectly he might understand the nature of that ministry or of that kingdom. He saw that these exhortations must apply to him and his brother Apostles. He wished to know whether they had any further application. He said, ‘ *Lord, speakest thou this parable unto us, or even to all ? And the Lord said, Who then is that faithful and wise steward, whom his lord shall make ruler over his household, to give them their portion of*

meat, in due season? Blessed is that servant, whom his lord when he cometh shall find so doing. Of a truth I say unto you, that he will make him ruler over all that he hath. But and if that servant say in his heart, My lord delayeth his coming, and shall begin to beat the menservants and maidens, and to eat and drink, and to be drunken, the lord of that servant will come in a day when he looketh not for him, and at an hour when he is not aware, and will cut him in sunder, and will appoint him his portion with the unbelievers. And that servant, which knew his lord's will, and prepared not himself, neither did according to his will, shall be beaten with many stripes. But he that knew not, and did commit things worthy of stripes, shall be beaten with few stripes. For unto whomsoever much is given, of him shall be much required: and to whom men have committed much, of him they will ask the more.'

The answer is very distinct. ' Wherever in any age or in
' any country men shall profess to belong to my kingdom,
' or shall call themselves my ministers, there may be that
' faithful stewardship of which I have spoken, there will be
' also the blessings of it. And in every such age and such
' country there will be the temptation to say, " *My Lord*
' *delayeth his coming.*" There will be the temptation in
' the ministers to act independently of their Master; to
' suppose that He has left them to do their own pleasure,
' to proclaim their own decrees, to tyrannise over those
' whom He came to deliver from tyranny. In every age
' and country those who call themselves His ministers, and
' claim to be entrusted with His treasures, will be the
' worst and cruellest oppressors of all, if they banish the
' Spirit of the Son of Man, and allow the spirit of covetous-
' ness to enter into them and possess them. But *He* will

'show that He is King of kings and Lord of lords. He will
'come to those ministers who have so exalted themselves,
'so sold themselves to His enemy, in an hour when they
'look not for Him. He will treat them as what they are—
'unbelievers. He will visit them with stripes which those
'who have had less committed to them can never suffer, of
'which they cannot even dream.' The language is terrible.
No words of ours can heighten or strengthen it. To us it
is spoken, and to all who bear our responsibilities. May
we meditate upon it in silence. And then the words which
come next will not be only fearful. There will be a promise at the root of them.

III. '*I am come to send fire on the earth, and what will
I, if it be already kindled ?*' I said in speaking of the
announcement of Christ by His forerunner that none
could answer to that name who did not baptize with fire.
We have seen a little of the need of this fire. The
vices of hypocrisy and covetousness had penetrated into
the very heart of the nation. No outward discipline could
suffice for the removal of them. The Spirit of the Son of
man must contend with these evil spirits. The battle
would be, as the prophet had said, with burning and
fuel of fire. That fire was already kindled which was
never to be quenched on the earth, which would encounter
the same foes in each new period—which would find
them most fierce and rampant in communities bound
together in the most holy names, professing the greatest
devotion. The nation was in the beginning of that fiery
struggle where it was to perish. But before its agony and
death were accomplished, there must be another agony,
another death. '*I have a baptism to be baptized with, and
how am I straitened till it be accomplished !*' 'I shall send

no fire on earth which I do not myself pass through.' The people cannot suffer apart from the King. Whatever pains He inflicts are pains to Himself. This is indeed the deepest of all mysteries. But it is the Christian mystery —the mystery of the divine charity. Take it away, and the Gospel ceases to be a Gospel. Men cannot enter into the Kingdom of Heaven; there is no Kingdom of Heaven for them to enter.

LECTURE XVII.

THE CITY OF THE GREAT KING.

St. Luke XIII. 34, 35.

O Jerusalem, Jerusalem, which killest the prophets, and stonest them that are sent unto thee; how often would I have gathered thy children together, as a hen doth gather her brood under her wings, and ye would not! Behold, your house is left unto you desolate: and verily I say unto you, Ye shall not see me, until the time come when ye shall say, Blessed is he that cometh in the name of the Lord.

I. I SPOKE last week of the fire which Christ came to kindle on the earth, and of the baptism with which He was Himself to be baptized. Words which He spoke at the same time, but which I reserved for this morning, tell us something of the nature of that fire and of that Baptism.

" *Suppose ye that I am come to give peace on earth? I tell you, Nay; but rather division: For from henceforth there shall be fire in one house divided, three against two, and two against three. The father shall be divided against the son, and the son against the father; the mother against the daughter, and the daughter against the mother; the mother-in-law against her daughter-in-law, and the daughter-in-law against her mother-in-law.*"

We try to soften this terrible prophecy by our comments. As if we could explain away facts which are notorious to every reader of history, to even one who has any experience of what is passing in his own time! As if we could convince any reasonable persons that there have not been, that there are not, these strifes in families; that the

Gospel of Christ has not provoked them, and does not provoke them still! Or as if our Lord, supposing He is the Prince of Peace, as we say He is, wanted our help to vindicate Him from the charge of being the Author of war! Surely we may trust Him with His own character. All that is required of us is, that we should let His words come to us in the fulness of their power and their condemnation. Goodness and gentleness do stir up what is opposed to them in us; we know that they do. Our sectarian animosities are kindled by the message of God's goodwill to men; we know that they are. Can we not understand then, how, coming among a set of hostile factions, which abhorred one another, but observed a conventional decency in their strife, Christ stirred up their rage to its very depths? Cannot we understand how the fury of both burned for awhile against Him—a hollow truce being established between them by the presence of a common enemy? Did it not revenge itself for that restraint afterwards? Did not every hearth and household become a battle-field in that war? This was the state of Jerusalem, as its own historian describes it in the latter days. He can give us the narrative calmly, Jew though he was. When Jesus looked forward to it, He was straitened with agony. He felt in every fibre of His own being what was coming upon His land. There may have been moments when the evil spirit thrust the thought full upon Him: 'Would it not be better to shrink from Thy task? If this 'is the effect of the Peace which Thou proclaimest, why not 'let them welter on without any announcement of God's 'kingdom?' Such suggestions have been continually made to His followers, when they have spoken of peace, and when those to whom they have spoken have made them ready for the battle. If He was tempted in all points like them, He cannot have been free from this kind of anguish. Nor will He have overcome the tempter with any other weapons than those with which He has furnished them. He must have said, for Himself and for them, 'My work 'is with the Lord, and my judgments with my God. In His 'own time my Father will accomplish His purpose. The 'hollow alliances of sects will end in more fierce and 'frantic war. But through that war will come, the discovery 'of the peace which passeth understanding, the peace 'which lasts in the midst of the world's tribulations; that 'peace will be established through the whole creation.'

II. Truly it did not require a prophet's eye to discern what was passing among the chosen people at that time.

'*And he said also to the people, When ye see a cloud rise out of the west, straightway ye say, There cometh a shower; and so it is. And when ye see the south wind blow, ye say, There will be heat; and it cometh to pass. Ye hypocrites, ye can discern the face of the sky and of the earth; but how is it that ye do not discern this time? Yea, and why even of yourselves judge ye not what is right?*' 'What, are the 'prognostics of the weather indeed so credible and trust-'worthy? Have you faculties for discovering these, and can 'you make nothing of the signs which shew whither this 'age is tending—whither the country, of which you are 'citizens, is tending? Cannot you even discern the facts 'which are going on within yourselves? Oh, believe it, the 'clouds do not portend rain, or the south wind heat, half so 'certainly as the accusing spirit who speaks in your con-'science warns you of storms which are approaching you.' Of this adversary, this accuser within, He speaks awfully in the next verse. '*When thou goest with thine adversary*

*to the magistrate, as thou art in the way, give diligence that
thou mayest be delivered from him; lest he hale thee to the
judge, and the judge deliver thee to the officer, and the officer
cast thee into prison.'* When you hear a voice within you
warning you of evils done by you, of evils that are coming
upon you, oh, let him not speak again, once, twice, thrice!
Agree with him quickly, whilst thou art in the way with
him. Confess the wrong. Ask to be set right. Tell God
of thy terrors. Ask Him to take them from thee. Else thy
spirit will become more rivetted in that evil, more and
more possessed by that terror. The Judge will deliver thee
to the officer, the officer will cast thee into prison. And
oh, that prison! the prison of the spirit, the spirit of the
man himself! My friends, if we know anything of what
that is, we shall enter into the force of the last words; we
shall confess their intense truth: *"I tell thee, thou shalt not
depart thence, till thou hast paid the very last mite.'* Yes,
the very last mite; till thou hast wholly, utterly given up
thyself. There is no redemption but in that.

III. Whilst He was speaking of these signs, which foretold
the downfall of the Jewish commonwealth—of those signs
which each member of that commonwealth might discover
in his own heart—*' there were present some who told Him of
the Galileans whose blood Pilate had mingled with their
sacrifices.'* It was an event, no doubt, which had occurred
recently; the minds of the people must have been full of
it. There could be no more ghastly exhibition of a Roman's
contempt for the rites which were most sacred in their
eyes; contempt mingled, as it generally is, with cruelty.
It was of a piece with much of Pilate's administration; he
had already done acts which shewed that, in his scorn of
the Jewish worship, he could forget the prudence of a

ruler, and transgress the maxims of toleration which the
Cæsars ordinarily recognised. Here, then, was a sign of
the times. Here was a warning of the desolation which
was coming upon city and Temple. But those who could
read the signs in the heavens so skilfully, could not discover the meaning of this sign. They supposed that the
Galilæans who had suffered these things were sinners above
all the Galilæans. God had given them over to the malice
of the Governor for some special enormities of which they
had been guilty. '*I tell you nay*,' said our Lord; '*but
except ye repent, ye shall all likewise perish.*' Understand,
from this event, the kind of punishment which is threatening you all. Understand, that unless you turn to Him
who has called you to know Him, and to be the witnesses of
Him to the world—unless you confess your abuse of that
calling—the sacrifices will be taken from you, and in the
most tremendous sense your blood will be mingled with
them. He went on to speak of another sign which had
been similarly explained. The tower of Siloam had fallen.
It had crushed eighteen men. Those eighteen had been
suspected of having drawn the sentence upon them because
they were sinners above all the inhabitants of Jerusalem.
Rather let all the inhabitants of Jerusalem see in that fall
a message from God, telling them that the towers of their
city would fall, that the whole nation would be crushed, if
it did not fly from its Mammon and Moloch worship to the
God of Abraham.

I do not in the least undervalue the lesson which is
commonly deduced from this passage against rash conclusions respecting those who are the subjects of any unusual
calamity. The lesson is there; it ought to be enforced;
but I believe it will be much more strongly and usefully

enforced, if we do not overlook the more prominent lesson which connects these words with all that went before, and with all that follow them.   For St. Luke says, ' *He spake also this parable;*' evidently meaning us to understand it as bearing upon the topic of which He had just been speaking. ' *A certain man had a fig-tree planted in his vineyard; and he came and sought fruit thereon, and found none.   Then said he unto the dresser of his vineyard, Behold, these three years I come seeking fruit on this fig-tree, and find none: cut it down ; why cumbereth it the ground ?   And he answering said unto him, Lord, let it alone this year also, till I shall dig about it, and dung it: And if it bear fruit, well : and if not, then after that thou shalt cut it down.*'   No reader of the Old Testament could misunderstand the general scope of this parable.   The nation's life had been associated again and again by the Psalmists and Prophets with the life of trees, of the fig-tree and the vine especially. The nation was asked why it did not bring forth such fruits as bore witness of a divine root, as answered to a divine tillage; why it brought forth wild fruits such as grew out of an evil—selfish root, or such as had received no benefit from tillage.   Our Lord adopts the old language. He explains the divine discipline upon human wills, upon the springs and sources of human action, by the discipline which is bestowed upon natural things.   He teaches that we are to refer the preservation of societies and the renovation of societies to a divine process, as we are to see in the degeneracy of societies and their dissolution the resistance to that process.   The Jewish nation was becoming sapless ; there was corruption at the core of it.   Still it was very dear to Him, who had watched over it in all generations, who had come to look after it now.   It was dear to Him,

P

for He had the mind of the great Husbandman, the Father from whom He had been sent. He must make new experiments upon it. He must see whether it would still reject all His appeals to it. Such language may clash with our theories of Omnipotence ; but it is the language of the Bible throughout. The whole of it is false, if it is false that God shows His might, not in crushing wills but in educating them ; that His punishments are themselves the expressions of His tenderness for the works of His own hand, of His determination not to cast aside the clay till He has shaped it into some vessel for His use. That *this* vessel, this chosen race, would be cast aside, is becoming all too evident. St. Luke could bear to recite the parable which pointed to that catastrophe, for he had entered into the language of his friend, the Hebrew of the Hebrews who had wished himself accursed for Christ for the sake of his kinsmen after the flesh. '*I say then, Have they stumbled that they should fall ? God forbid : but rather through their fall salvation is come unto the Gentiles, for to provoke them to jealousy. Now if the fall of them be the riches of the world and the diminishing of them the riches of the Gentiles ; how much more their fulness ?*'

But what were the proofs that the fig-tree had become sapless, that there was decay at its root? Here is one proof :—'*And he was teaching in one of the synagogues on the sabbath. And, behold, there was a woman which had a spirit of infirmity eighteen years, and was bowed together, and could in no wise lift up herself. And when Jesus saw her, he called her to him, and said unto her, Woman, thou art loosed from thine infirmity. And he laid his hands on her : and immediately she was made straight, and glorified God. And the ruler of the synagogue answered with indignation, because that Jesus had healed on the sabbath day, and said unto the people, There are six days in which men ought to work: in them therefore come and be healed, and not on the sabbath day. The Lord then answered him, and said, Thou hypocrite, doth not each one of you on the sabbath loose his ox or his ass from the stall, and lead him away to watering? And ought not this woman, being a daughter of Abraham, whom Satan hath bound, lo, these eighteen years, be loosed from this bond on the sabbath day? And when he had said these things, all his adversaries were ashamed: and all the people rejoiced for all the glorious things that were done by him.'*

In that act of Jesus came forth the tenderness and love which had cared for the man-servant and the maid-servant, which had ordained that man should rest because God rested, that man should work because God worked. In that speech of the Ruler of the Synagogue came forth that denial of a God of goodness and loving-kindness, that worship of a God who grudges blessings to His creatures, who insists upon one day for Himself and leaves His creatures to enjoy six days without Him—which had been accumulating in the nation for many ages, and was now reaching its climax. And Christ's awful exposure of the man who had no scruple about saving his property on the Sabbath Day, but had the greatest scruple about benefiting a fellow creature, showed to what god this ruler of the Synagogue had transferred his allegiance, what god was becoming the object of his countrymen's service. There was still a protest in the heart of the people against that service, a recognition of the invincible logic which confounded the ruler. *'The people rejoiced for the glorious things that were done by Him.'* The fig-tree was not yet dead. The

Dresser of the vineyard was still digging about it and dunging it.

And there was a profounder consolation, an infinite joy, in remembering that the divine seed was working, and that if that tree was dying, another tree which would spread its branches far more widely was springing up.

'*Then said he, Unto what is the kingdom of God like? and whereunto shall I resemble it? It is like a grain of mustard seed, which a man took, and cast into his garden; and it grew, and waxed a great tree; and the fowls of the air lodged in the branches of it.*'

Out of the perishing nation would arise the Universal Church; it would rise at the message of the Kingdom of Heaven delivered by fishermen; that would be the tiny seed from which it would grow. Even an humbler comparison (none could be too humble) might attest the mysterious working of the divine Word in the hearts of men. '*And again he said, Whereunto shall I liken the kingdom of God? It is like leaven, which a woman took and hid in three measures of meal, till the whole was leavened.*'

He goes onwards, still moving towards Jerusalem. At each step of the journey there has been an announcement of some great woe impending over the land—impending over those priests and rulers who might seem safe, whatever befel the rest of their countrymen. '*Then said one unto him, Lord, are there few that be saved?*' The question was a very natural one. It must have often been in their hearts, if it had not risen to their lips. What exactly it meant we cannot know, for probably he who asked it did not know. He had a vague terror of *some* great danger which might overtake him and all that were dear to him. It might be a danger to the body, it might be a danger to the spirit.

The scene of it might be in this world or in some other
world to which men would go after death. It might be temporary. It might be endless. It might come from the Son
of Man. He might be the Saviour out of it. All possibilities
were there; Christ's words had awakened the conscience to
activity; it gave its own force and sense to those words. Our
Lord's answer enabled the inquirer to know his own meaning as he did not know it before. And He said unto them:—

*'Strive to enter in at the strait gate: for many, I say unto
you, will seek to enter in, and shall not be able. When once
the master of the house is risen up, and hath shut to the door,
and ye begin to stand without, and to knock at the door, saying, Lord, Lord, open unto us; and he shall answer and say
unto you, I know you not whence ye are: Then shall ye begin
to say, We have eaten and drunk in thy presence, and thou
hast taught in our streets. But he shall say, I tell you, I
know you not whence ye are; depart from me, all ye workers
of iniquity. There shall be weeping and gnashing of teeth,
when ye shall see Abraham, and Isaac, and Jacob, and all
the prophets, in the kingdom of God, and you yourselves thrust
out. And they shall come from the east, and from the west,
and from the north, and from the south, and shall sit down
in the kingdom of God. And, behold, there are last which
shall be first, and there are first which shall be last.'*

If we took the last words of this passage first, we should
say at once, 'There is a direct answer to the demand, Are
'there *few* that be saved? Does He not say, They shall
'come from the east and the west, and from the north and
'the south, and shall sit down in the Kingdom of God?'
But this language would not have explained itself to the
mind or conscience of those who heard it, or of us who read
it, if it had stood alone.

He had warned them of active moral corruptions which were destroying the land and infecting the hearts of all its members. He had told them that against these he was waging war. Salvation from these was what they wanted. Let them remember what he had said of the leaven of hypocrisy, of that covetousness which was taking so many forms, putting on such religious disguises. Let them strive then to enter in at the strait gate—the gate of sincerity and trust which was so hard to find, which so many were missing. Let them understand that the Master of the house, the Lord of their hearts and spirits, was speaking to them there—was calling them to confess His government, to abandon the service of other lords for His. There might come a day when that voice would be heard no more—when the door through which He was calling them to enter would be shut. There would be then a confession in many hearts. 'He *was* our true Lord. These cheats and self-deceptions to which we have given up 'our souls are dying out; there is no help in them. ' These possessions, where are they going? are our rever- ' sions worth anything? Lord, Lord, let us have Thee ' now, since these have failed.' But He from within, that secret Lord of the heart and reins, shall answer, ' I know you not whence you are. You have never ' desired righteousness; you have never hungered and ' thirsted after truth. What have I in common with ' you?' And then comes the effort to gather comfort from the thought of all the religious duties they have performed —of all the privileges which they possessed and others were without: 'Can it be that Thou who didst preach to ' publicans and sinners hast no word for us who did so · many things to make ourselves acceptable to our Maker?'

But it avails not. The Voice sounds clear in the conscience : ' You have been workers of iniquity. These acts and ser- ' vices have not made you truer or better men. I tell ' you I know you not whence you are.'

Fearful words, surely; as fearful as ever were spoken, because they go to the very root of things—because they repeat a colloquy of the spirit in man with its Ruler, when all the disguises by which it has hidden itself from Him have been swept away. Therefore have they sounded in ever deepening tones through the ages; therefore must every one of us say, ' I am meant to heed them.'

But they did refer to that age, as the next verse proves. They pointed to the wailing and gnashing of teeth with which the exclusive, self-satisfied child of Abraham would regard the entrance of outcasts and idolaters into that Kingdom of God from which he was shut out. He might have still the external law, the Scriptures, whatever he had exulted in, as the proof of his distinction from the rest of mankind. He might have outward treasures, which would make him envied—and tormented. But the king- dom of the Living God, the eternal kingdom, under the shadow of which, in the hope of which, Abraham and Isaac and Jacob had dwelt, which they were sure would reveal itself more and more fully to the world—which they would rejoice in, after they had left the world—where was that? Gentiles would give thanks that the Lord was King, be the earth ever so unruly ; that He sat upon the water-floods, let the people be never so unquiet. Gentiles would expect a manifestation of His brightness and glory to the whole universe. And the brethren of the Psalmists and Prophets, the rightful inheritors of all their grand possessions and expectations, must be left to the anguish

of feeling themselves under capricious, tyrannical, human
rulers—of dreading, instead of longing, that God should
appear and that all things should be made subject to
Him.

To the Kingdom of God, then, we are brought back.
Shall only a few see that? Very many; more than you
dream of; men of every nation, and kindred, and tongue.
'*But there are last which shall be first, and first which shall
be last.*' How does that sentence strike at the judgments
of Jew and of Gentile; of the chosen nation and of the
Catholic Church! How does it encourage us to believe
that those whom we have supposed to be out of the pale
of salvation may be claimed as His by the Son of man
How does it force each of us to say, 'Mighty Lord! Master
' of the house! wilt Thou not save me from the pride
' and the scorn which have divided me from Thy brethren
' and from Thee!'

Jesus spoke of the Kingdom of Heaven. There were
rulers in Galilee who knew that their kingdom was not a
Kingdom of Heaven at all, and who did not like to hear
of one. '*The same day there came certain of the Pharisee
saying unto him, Get thee out, and depart hence: for Herod
will kill thee.*' These Pharisees were, doubtless, not sorry
to show the disciples of Jesus that there were kings who
exercised a power before which *their* King must bow. He
neither bowed before it, nor resisted it, nor fled from it.
'*And he said unto them, Go ye, and tell that fox, Behold, I
cast out devils, and I do cures to-day and to-morrow, and the
third day I shall be perfected. Nevertheless I must walk
to-day, and to-morrow, and the day following: for it cannot be that a prophet perish out of Jerusalem.*' Cunning
was the weapon of the Tetrarch; it was not His. He

had a work to do; He should do it openly. He must heal sicknesses; He must cast out devils. In a day or two His task in that region would be accomplished. Forward He must go. Herod would do Him no harm. He was indeed to die; but not by that hand, in that place. A prophet could not perish except in Jerusalem. Thither His thoughts, as well as His steps, were tending; the city of David, the city of murderers, was dear to Him above all others—had been dear to Him long before He came to it in that lowly guise with that troop of fishermen.

'*O, Jerusalem, Jerusalem, which killest the prophets, and stonest them that are sent unto thee; how often would I have gathered thy children together, as a hen doth gather her brood under her wings, and ye would not! Behold, your house is left unto you desolate: and verily I say unto you, Ye shall not see me, until the time come when ye shall say, Blessed is he that cometh in the name of the Lord.*'

There you see the King. Yes, do not fear to say it—the patriot King. He loves the world; He has come to gather in the nations. But *that* city had been chosen as the witness to all nations. Over that He had watched. Its kings had been raised up to show forth the righteous King of kings. Its prophets had been sent to declare that He reigns, let those who reign under Him be ever so unrighteous. They had been stoned and killed for that testimony. And still HE had sought to gather together that broken, divided people. '*But ye would not.*' You have refused the Reconciler; you have preferred strife and hatred to Him. And therefore the desolation must come. The Holy city, the Temple which is the sign of its holiness and unity, must be deserted of the divine Presence.

What! for ever? He points us to a time when this

fallen people should say, 'Blessed is He that cometh in the name of the Lord;' when the King and Deliverer should indeed be revealed to them. Is there anything hopeless in the counsels of the everlasting King? Are His purposes of grace and love finally defeated by the self-will of the creature? Let us trust that they will not be defeated. Else what is in reserve for you and me; for those who have resisted greater manifestations of divine Love, a larger and grander history of divine Patience than any which Jerusalem knew in its earlier days, or in that day?

LECTURE XVIII.

THE FEAST OF THE KINGDOM OF HEAVEN.

St. Luke XIV. 34, 35.

*Salt is good ; but if the salt have lost its savour, wherewith shall it be
seasoned ? It is neither fit for the land, nor yet for the dunghill ; but men
cast it out. He that hath ears to hear, let him hear.*

THIS 14th chapter opens with another act of healing on
the Sabbath Day. When I was preaching on the sixth
chapter, I considered these acts generally. I inquired why
they assume such prominence in the Gospels, why our
Lord attached such solemn importance to them, why they
awakened such bitter hostility against Him. There is a
difference, I think, between His treatment of those earlier
indications of the Pharisaic temper, and of those which
are presented to us in the chapter I considered last Sunday,
and in this. No doubt the principle which is enunciated
in the sixth chapter governs these cases as well as the
previous cases. '*The sabbath was made for man, not man
for the sabbath : Therefore the Son of man is Lord also of
the sabbath*'—that was the grand assertion of the true
humanity of the fourth commandment, that was the divine
exposure of all attempts to make the Godhead inhuman.
But in both these recent disputes with the Pharisees, the
argument takes this form : '*Which of you who shall have an
ass or an ox fallen into a pit, will not straightway pull him out*

on the sabbath day?' The repetition of this appeal, which
the Pharisees could not answer, shows, it seems to me,
what temper of mind our Lord was especially designing to
lay bare at this time. A self-seeking religion was undermining the nation. The habit of measuring acts by their
profit and loss, was the characteristic habit of the Pharisee.
Jesus detects it in this instance; He shows how little
what they held to be the law of God interfered with any
question of property; how stern it became when only the
health or life of a fellow-creature was at stake. If we
follow the windings of this chapter, I believe we shall find
that He is setting forth different illustrations of the self-
seeking spirit, and of the contrast between it and the mind
of the gracious God.

I. Jesus is at a feast. He sees the guests choosing out
the chief rooms. He puts forth, the Evangelist says, a
parable to them. We do not, at first, perceive why His
discourse should have that name. It reads like a simple
admonition applicable to those who frequented that feast
or any feast. *'When thou art bidden of any man to a
wedding, sit not down in the highest room; lest a more
honourable man than thou be bidden of him.'* And when
we go on to the next passage, we might easily say, ' Here
' is a sanction for calculations of worldly prudence. The
' conduct prohibited is treated as inconsistent with this.'
*' Lest he that bade thee and him come and say to thee, Give
this man place; and thou begin with shame to take the
lowest room. But when thou art bidden, go and sit down in
the lowest room; that when he that bade thee cometh, he may
say unto thee, Friend, go up higher: then shalt thou have worship in the presence of them that sit at meat with thee.'* My
friends, I do not in the least wish you to forget that our

Lord does announce this as the probable result of these two courses. I believe experience may have led many to the same conclusion, may perhaps have led some to aim at the humility which He enjoins. If it be so, must not these sagacious foreseeing men have gained a glimpse of some law which proves the eager longing for promotion— the natural desire for overtopping others—to be a mistake? What is that law? Our Lord proclaims it in the fullest, most distinct words: ' *Whosoever exalteth himself shall be abased, and he that humbleth himself shall be exalted.*' This is God's law, the law of God's kingdom. And therefore it discovers itself in all cases, in the least as well as the greatest. The commonest human feast is an illustration of it. The principle must reach that, or it is not a principle. It must be meant to govern a man's acts in all his relations, in all his circumstances. Some may recognize it in the higher regions of spiritual life and forget it in the lower; then they will always be in danger of losing it where they do confess its application. Some may learn the truth of the maxim in ordinary affairs, and then may trace it to its divine Source. They will be most likely to do so when they have obeyed the law instinctively; having always felt that they were deserving of the lower rather than of a high place. Those who have speculated on the advantage of seeming to be humble, may possibly get a reward from their hosts at earthly feasts; He who reads the heart will not say to such, ' *Friends, come up higher,*' at His feast. You will see, then, that our Lord did, on this occasion, speak a parable in the truest sense of the word. We might even learn from this instance what a parable is, how wide its range is. Our Lord would open our eyes to read in all the processes of nature with which we are most familiar, in all the earthly things with which we have most to do, in all our intercourse with our fellows, indications and expositions of the eternal Government. When the poet said that the law which guides the planets in their course is that very law which moulds a tear and bids it trickle from its source, we may be startled with the violence of the contrast. But he uttered an unquestionable truth, and one which has more practical force when it is referred to the mysteries of the spiritual world than to those of the physical.

II. Here, then, was one hint of the way in which the self-seeking, self-exalting spirit might work in little acts as in great ; how it had to be encountered in the little that it might not usurp dominion over the greatest. And He whose teachings were a continuous methodical education, who passed by insensible steps from one topic to another, always speaking to that which He knew was in His hearers —forcing nothing upon them—went on from this discourse concerning the choice of the chief room at feasts to speak of the highest hospitality, of that which is most in harmony with the spirit of the universal Benefactor. ' *Then said he also to him that bade him, When thou makest a dinner or a supper, call not thy friends, nor thy brethren, neither thy kinsmen, nor thy rich neighbours ; lest they also bid thee again, and a recompence be made thee. But when thou makest a feast, call the poor, the maimed, the lame, the blind : and thou shalt be blessed ; for they cannot recompense thee : for thou shalt be recompensed at the resurrection of the just.*' The privilege of doing good, of conferring blessings without the hope of a return, this He set before them, this He sets before us, as the grand privilege of all. We avail ourselves of it very seldom. The notion of giving in the expectation of receiving as much again, though a very sordid one, is apt to displace even in those who not only affect generosity but *are* generous the one which surely commends itself to our consciences and reason as the nobler. And there is a darker and sadder contradiction mixed with this. Our Lord's promise of a recompence at the resurrection of the just has been translated into the dialect of the money-market. He has been supposed to say, ' Make the sacrifice of giving feasts to the poor, and halt, ' and blind here, and God will pay you for it hereafter.' And so that hope of waking up after God's likeness and being satisfied with it, which has cheered and sustained all those who have really worked under the inspiration of God's Spirit for their fellow men, is quite set aside. The resurrection of the just is not the rising out of our-selves into fellowship with the divine Love; it is the prolongation and ratification of the great curse which has divided us from each other and made the earth miserable. Oh my friends! there is no language so pure and divine that men have not power to transmute it and wrench it into a justification of the sins which it denounces. If the Word of God were confined by the letters of Scripture, there would be no witness against our perversion of those letters. If God did not really baptize men with His Spirit and fire, but only gave us a holy book, the holy book would not only miss its interpretation; it would be made into an apology for the most unholy deeds. But in every generation the truth of the book has been confirmed by the divine power which has appeared to deliver the Church from those who have patronized it, worshipped it, trampled upon it.

III. *'And when one of them that sat at meat with him*

heard these things, he said unto him, Blessed is he that shall eat bread in the kingdom of God.' The thought of an age, of a state of society, in which men should really call the poor, the halt, the blind to their feasts, struck on this man's heart, and called forth in it wonder and hope. 'Yes ! 'that will be indeed a heavenly kingdom. One would like 'to be a citizen of that.' The rejoinder comes in a parable with which we are all familiar. 'You think it would be a 'great privilege to eat bread in the Kingdom of God. 'Listen then to a story.'

'*Then said he unto him, A certain man made a great supper, and bade many: and sent his servant at supper time to say to them that were bidden, Come; for all things are now ready.'*

In St. Matthew's Gospel the feast is one at a wedding. I believe the context of his narrative obliges us to think of this characteristic. It is the central point of the story; the accompanying particulars cannot be understood without it. St. Luke, by omitting it, shows me that he is directing our minds to another aspect of the subject. The nature of the feast is less in question than the freeness of the invitations to it and the temper in which those invitations are received. We must always remember, however, that it *is* a feast. Those who are called, are called to receive a blessing, to enter into an enjoyment. '*And they all with one consent began to make excuse.'* They do not excuse themselves from toil. They have no dislike to that. Toil is itself their excuse. '*The first said unto him, I have bought a piece of ground, and I must needs go and see it: I pray thee have me excused. And another said, I have bought five yoke of oxen, and I go to prove them: I pray thee have me excused.'* These are all honourable and useful occupations. And the third, who says, '*I have married a wife, and therefore I cannot come,*' evidently does not plead pleasure as his reason. Marriage he regards as part of the business and routine of existence, which gives him no leisure to take part in what might be a fit entertainment for a man with fewer cares.

Preachers who have partly perceived that *this* parable was not aimed at the dislike of work and preference for delight, by which some, especially in youth, are characterized, have evaded its force by describing the occupations which our Lord speaks of as belonging to the present world. ' He invites them to engage in religious duties— ' duties having reference to a future world.' I cannot see this distinction in the story. The man might be devoting himself to his piece of land or his oxen, on a calculation of what would be best for him in the time to come. He might be restraining himself from present gratifications for distant objects. The man who had married a wife might have a becoming sense of the obligation in both of them to frequent the synagogue. The worldliness I admit, but not a worldliness which was the least incompatible with a very punctual pursuit of what are called religious duties. Men who were busy with those duties, who carefully enjoined them on others, whose piece of ground or oxen or marriage would not have hindered them from making long prayers or going daily to the Temple, were especially the persons to whom this invitation was addressed, and 'who would not come.' Their religious duties were one of the strongest reasons which they alleged for their absence. And why? The call was to rejoice in a God who cared for His creatures, who had entered into fellowship with them, who would have them enter into fellowship with

Q

Him, who would have them share His blessedness—the
blessedness of distributing liberally, the blessedness of
raising those that were fallen. This was the feast of the
Kingdom of Heaven which the teachers and examples of
religion to the nation scornfully refused.

' So that servant came, and shewed his lord these things.
Then the master of the house being angry said to his servant,
Go out quickly into the streets and lanes of the city, and
bring in hither the poor, and the maimed, and the halt, and
the blind.'

Our Lord had urged rich men to call such as these to
their feasts. He now says that they were called and
would be called. He had blessed the poor. He had
Himself preached the Kingdom of Heaven to the outcasts
of the land. For this He had been described as evil,
a friend of publicans and sinners. Only men who had
nothing to boast of, who were needing a shepherd, who
did not count it a misery to them that others should be
blessed with them, heard His voice. They were willing
to be receivers, to take a gift from the Highest of all
not to insist that they had earned it.

' And the servant said, Lord, it is done as thou hast
commanded, and yet there is room. And the Lord said
unto the servant, Go out into the highways and hedges,
and compel them to come in, that my house may be filled.'
All interpreters have been inclined to treat this passage
as an announcement of the Gospel to the Gentile world—
the Gospel that since the Son of God had been born of a
woman, men of all kindreds and tribes might receive the
adoption of sons; that God sealed them by baptism with His
own name ; that He fed them with the flesh which was given
for the life of the world. That this sense must be in

the words, the fearful sentence which follows is proof sufficient : '*For I say unto you, That none of those men which were bidden shall taste of my supper.*' Here is that rejection of a self-seeking, exclusive nation—which would not receive benefits freely from God's hands, which would not be His instruments in imparting them—whereof our Lord has been speaking ever since He set His face to go to Jerusalem. Surely we lose nothing of the power and terror of the words for ourselves when we construe them in that literal and obvious way. Is not the Jewish habit of mind that to which every one of us is prone ? Does it not grow upon us, become deeper in us, through our familiarity with religious ordinances, through the repetition of the call to come and taste of God's feast ? Think of what it must have been to men who had believed God to be their enemy, to hear the news ; ' He invites you to His feast. He desires communion ' with you. He would have you read His mind to 'you in the food of every day.' What an Eucharistical song must have risen from all creation—from the world seen and unseen ! And we speak of the Eucharist as a religious duty which must be performed if we would escape perdition—not as the celebration of a wedding which the Son of God has made with our race ! Is not the temper which led the Jews to hate the feast, working in us Gentiles who seem to exult in it as our highest distinction ? Alas ! we do exult in it as our *distinction*—as the badge of our difference from other men, not as the witness of our union with all. Whilst it is so, can we really taste of the supper ?

And we can turn the words of the New Testament upside down, as the Jews turned the words of the Old

Testament upside down. What lessons have not Christians drawn, sometimes in theory, continually in practice, from the command, 'Compel them to come in?' 'Surely it must 'be good to make men Christians by force, if there is no 'other way.' Yes! if you *can*. Persecute them by all means, if persecution will make them partakers of the divine feast; if it is not shown by all evidence to be the best means of making them partakers of the feast of devils. '*They shall be willing in the day of my power;*' that was the faith in which Apostles preached. That was the compulsion which prevailed over the forces of the legions. Emperors, priests, mobs, have tried the other kind of compulsion: with what effect the records of God's judgments written in history have shown imperfectly, the judgment of the last day will declare completely.

IV. Jesus had preached of His kingdom to crowds, and had said that men of all kinds would be drawn into it. Now He seems to change His tone. '*And there went great multitudes with him: and he turned, and said unto them, If any man come to me, and hate not his father, and mother, and wife, and children, and brethren, and sisters, yea, and his own life also, he cannot be my disciple. And whosoever doth not bear his cross, and come after me, cannot be my disciple.*' How are we to explain such a passage as this? I believe it will explain itself better than we can explain it; if we want further help, we shall find it in the records of Christendom. There have been two facts which those records have brought prominently before us. In obedience, as they supposed, to this exhortation, men have abandoned human ties—father, mother, wife, children, brethren, and sisters—that they might do what? That they might save their own souls. In so doing, they have directly set at nought our Lord's command. I do not say they have exaggerated it. I say they have denied both the letter and spirit of it. That to which they have sacrificed all these human ties is precisely that which Christ commands them to sacrifice. They must hate all these, and *their own souls*. Our translators have taken here, as in another place, some pains to avoid the offence which would have been given by the use of the word ' soul.' They have changed it into ' life.' But when we are studying our Lord's meaning, we must adhere to His phraseology. It is clear, then, that monks and' nuns cannot be our guides in the interpretation of this passage. *They* have discovered no principle which reconciles it with Christ's stern condemnation of those who made a gift to the treasury and so excused themselves from obeying God's command to honour their father and mother.

But another fact has been also made evident by the experience of ages as well as of individuals. It has been found that, as men may relinquish the love of father and mother for the sake of themselves, so they may try to build the love of father and mother upon the ground of self. This love does not last. For love is the antagonist of selfishness. ' Therefore,' says Christ, ' If ' you would follow Me, abandon this experiment. Two ' powers are fighting for your allegiance—Self and the Son ' of man. Self, the enemy of all human affections, of all ' the bonds of human fellowship ; the Son of man, the ' Author and Sustainer of them all. Give up to Me, ' and for Me, all that has a selfish root. Plant your ' affections upon the divine root, so they will live and ' grow.' Such language may sound refined to divines who can indulge in all scholastical subtleties ; to devotees who think there is one law for them and another for mankind. It has not appeared strange or refined to humble men and women who have really taken up their cross and followed Christ in all lowly services—specially in services to the members of their own households. They have shown in their daily lives how, by giving up their souls to Him and not thinking of themselves, they were able to be true children and brothers and sisters and fathers and mothers. Their minds may have been exercised by this precept of their Lord, just as a student's mind is exercised by any problem in nature. But the exercise has been profitable in both cases. The reason and the will have been strengthened by the difficulty which they have had to master. In seeking they have acquired a power which they would not have had if the secret had been discovered to them without seeking. Our Lord gives two illustrations of His meaning.

'*For which of you, intending to build a tower, sitteth not down first, and counteth the cost, whether he have sufficient to finish it ? Lest haply, after he hath laid the foundation, and is not able to finish it, all that behold it begin to mock him, saying, This man began to build, and was not able to finish. Or what king, going to make war against another king, sitteth not down first, and consulteth whether he be able with ten thousand to meet him that cometh against him with twenty thousand ? Or else, while the other is yet a great way off, he sendeth an ambassage, and desireth conditions of peace. So likewise, whosoever he be of you that forsaketh not all that he hath, he cannot be my disciple.*'

This seems a hard test of discipleship, '*he must forsake all that he hath.*' May it not be just the blessing, if we knew it, which we are all craving for ? We have set about building many goodly towers, many gorgeous palaces. How they have all dissolved ! How our grand designs have mocked us ! Why ? Because there was always some selfish scheme beneath, which made the foundation weak, which showed itself in the feebleness and incoherency of the superstructure. There has been a mighty battle going on within us between two kings, the spirit and the flesh. The evil power has his twenty thousand. There appear but a poor ten thousand—troops ill-guided and disorderly—to oppose him. If we could give up ourselves, the Captain of the Host would descend to help us, the stars of heaven would fight against our foe. But we struggle to keep something of our own, something apart from Him. So the terrible twenty thousand win the day. Sealed as Christ's servants and soldiers, we are not His disciples, for we glorify self above Him who gave up Himself.

V. We have seen these various exemplifications of that self-seeking spirit which was destroying the chosen people. The moral is gathered up into the memorable sentence, ' *Salt is good : but if the salt have lost his savour, wherewith shall it be seasoned ? It is neither fit for the land, nor yet for the dunghill ; but men cast it out.*' The Lord of the earth had called out the seed of Abraham, to be the salt of His earth, to preserve it from decay and putrefaction. The salt was good ; it had the divine principle and power in it. But if this principle and power departed from it, if it acquired all the worst qualities of that which it was to purify, what could be done with it ? The land gained nothing from it ; the dunghill was not enriched by it. For the purpose which it was to serve, it had become useless.

Nay, was it not mischievous; was it not ministering to all the corruption which it was intended to counteract?

Therefore the house of Israel was cast out; it was treated as refuse, for it had become refuse. But the earth was not left without salt. A wider earth was brought into cultivation. The Catholic Church was the salt—so we have believed—which God appointed to purify that wider earth. Has this salt kept its savour? Is it doing its work? Has it not contracted the foulness of that which it was to regenerate? Has it not exhibited that foulness in its most concentrated form? Is the example of the past nothing to us? Are the words of Christ nothing? '*He that hath ears to hear let him hear.*'

LECTURE XIX.

THE JOY OF THE KINGDOM OF HEAVEN.

St. Luke XV. 31, 32.

And he said unto him, Son, thou art ever with me, and all that I have is thine. It was meet that we should make merry, and be glad: for this thy brother was dead, and is alive again; and was lost, and is found.

I should pay no homage to Passion Week if I chose another subject than that which comes before us this morning in the course of our readings in St. Luke. The Collect for the Sunday before Easter might have been formed upon the parable of the Prodigal Son; there is no sufficient commentary upon that parable but the Cross itself.

The words I have taken are addressed to the elder brother in the story. Who he was, what his dignity and his privileges were, how he cast them aside, we may learn from the last chapter. We must not forget what has gone before—what a contrast has been presented to us in all the discourses and acts of our Lord which the Evangelist has recorded.

Every step in the narrative has been a more full revelation to us of the mind of the nation which God had chosen as His witnesses to the families of the earth. Every step in the narrative has been a revelation of the mind of Him who chose them; of the principle and purpose of His government. The self-seeking spirit in its different aspects

was that which we considered last Sunday. A glimpse
was given us of the opposition between that spirit and
the spirit of Him who gave the feast to those who dwelt
in the streets and lanes of the city, in the highways and
hedges. But the difference was to be fully discovered
*when all the publicans and sinners drew near unto Christ
to hear Him.* They had not been attracted by any flatter-
ing promises. They had been told that unless they gave
up all that they had they could not be His disciples. But
there was a charm in those seemingly repulsive words.
Each of them carried a burden. That burden was himself. He was invited to cast it away ; to trust in another ;
to find the life which he had lost, in Him. There was that
in His look, His voice, His acts, His whole being, which
invited them to make this venture ; in very deed to trust
Him. '*And the Pharisees and scribes murmured, saying,
This man receiveth sinners, and eateth with them.*' There
was the offence. No objection could have been made
to mere teaching. The Scribes and Pharisees were themselves teachers of the people. There is no reason to suppose that they would have repulsed a tax-gatherer, even
an acknowledged evildoer, who came humbly and respect-
fully to learn what acts of penitence he might perform
for his previous misdoings, how he might hope to recover
God's favour, or some portion of it in the time to come.
But '*this man receiveth sinners, and eateth with them.*'
He puts Himself on their level. He identifies Himself
with them. He behaves to them not as His pupils, but as
His kinsmen. It was another mode of treatment altogether.
It must have arisen from another, nay, from a directly
opposite feeling and purpose. The difference He explained
by an instance.

I. ' *What man of you, having an hundred sheep, if he lose one of them, doth not leave the ninety and nine in the wilderness, and go after that which is lost, until he find it ? . . . And when he cometh home, he calleth together his friends and neighbours, saying unto them, Rejoice with me ; for I have found my sheep which was lost.*' We have heard how in his reasonings on the Sabbath day He contrasted the care which possessors felt for their property in the ox and the ass that had fallen into the pit, with their indignation at Him for helping a human sufferer.   There is in this parable, I conceive, a *hint* of the same kind.   ' What man of you would not take trouble to 'recover even a small loss?' But it is only a hint. The scribes read and studied the holy books.   The character and office of the shepherd appeared in every one of those books.   The great Lawgiver learnt his first lessons in the care of sheep ; the great King had the same training.   They were taught to feel for their flocks ; to feel for each silly member of the flocks.   So they came to apprehend a little of the feelings of the Lord of all to the nation of Israel, and to each individual of that nation ; so one was fitted to be His instrument in guiding them through the wilderness—the other in governing them when they were settled in the promised land.   The relation of the shepherd to his sheep was not that of one who was calculating their value.   They were dear to him ; his rod and his staff directed them ; he kept them together ; he knew each one ; he missed each straggler ; he would go any distance, into any dangers, in search of it.   The parable was, therefore, an old one.   But it could never become an obsolete one.   And now it came forth with a power which had never been in it before. ' You ask ' me why I eat and drink with publicans and sinners ? Are ' they not my sheep ?   Are not they all a portion of that

' flock which from generation to generation I have watched
' over ?   Can any of them be indifferent to me ? '

Evidently words of this kind suggested much more
than they expressed. 'Why, He is actually claiming to
' be that Shepherd of Israel whom the prophets spoke of !
' Does he really mean that ?   What is He making Him-
' self ? '   And presently His language becomes loftier still.
He tells us what the thoughts and feelings of the
heavenly Host are. ' *I say unto you, that likewise
joy shall be in heaven over one sinner that repenteth, more
than over ninety and nine just persons, which need no
repentance.*'   He speaks confidently, as one who knows.
And how entirely He reverses the conceptions of Heaven
which those whom He was addressing entertained !   The
highest joy they could think of was the joy of faring better
than others—of winning prizes which others failed to win.
The joy, He says, in heaven, is the joy of winning back
those who have wandered ; of recovering those who have
chosen the wrong way.   There is no joy, He intimates,
so heavenly, so much partaking of the divine Nature,
as this.

II. Once more the very lowest earthly symbol is used to
explain the highest rapture of blessed spirits. ' *Either
what woman having ten pieces of silver, if she lose one piece,
doth not light a candle, and sweep the house, and seek diligently till she find it ?   And when she hath found it, she
calleth her friends and her neighbours together, saying, Rejoice
with me ; for I have found the piece which I had lost.*'
Can it be ?   Can you imagine that the pleasure produced
by such a cause as this, awakened in the heart of a common
housewife, has anything in it that resembles the joy of
angels ?   Our Lord says so. ' *Likewise, I say unto you,*

there is joy in the presence of the angels of God over one sinner that repenteth.'   Their joy is like hers.   It is the joy of those who have sought after a treasure.   It is the joy of recovery.   It is the joy of those who cannot keep their happiness to themselves—who must call upon others to partake of it.   Is not *all* joy of this quality ?   Are not these its characteristics ?   Taken in the form which seems meanest, it must have this elevation.   Try to conceive the most selfish motive for it, still it only becomes joy by bursting the bonds of self.

Why is this so ?   Our Lord in effect answers, 'Because ' He who has given that woman her joy, who gives the angels ' their joy, finds His own in regaining hearts that have been ' lost, those that have counted Him their enemy; because He ' cannot joy alone ; He must call on all spirits to enter into ' His joy.'   It was a strange overthrow of the notions which the Pharisees had formed, which we form (oh ! how readily, how naturally), of an Omnipotent ruler, of a supremely happy Being.   But how it harmonises with all the previous revelations of His care for the stiffnecked and the rebellious ; with all the visions of prophets ; with all the human acts and feelings that had been recognised as most godlike !   How it bears witness of its worth to our consciences and hearts and reasons when it most shatters our vulgar— what we often regard as our sublime—conceptions of the majesty and the felicity of the divine nature !

It has been said, and I think most truly, that one of these parables fills up something that was wanting in the other.   There is more, doubtless, of tenderness and humanity in the yearning of a shepherd over his sheep than in the longing of a woman to find her piece of money.   But the sheep could bleat; it could signify where it was ; it might try to escape from its thicket, even find the track by which it had left the fold. So we might say that some movements on the part of men, some cries, or prayers, or sacrifices, disposed the mind of God to be merciful. The piece of money suggests no such thoughts. All in that story must depend on the zeal and patience of the seeker—upon her determination to remove the dust and rubbish, whatever was hiding the treasure from her. Nothing can urge her to her task but her own will. That is sufficient to make her spare no toil, however little the prize may seem to deserve it, or to requite it.

III. But both these parables are leading on to the third. It needs them to make its full sense intelligible, to prevent us from thinking, as we are very apt to think, more of the prodigal than of the father. Let us try to recall the different points in it, avoiding, as far as we can, any loose and vague sentimentalism, which is altogether unworthy of its simplicity and grandeur.

'A certain man had two sons: And the younger of them said to his father, Father, give me the portion of goods that falleth to me. And he divided unto them his living.' When these two sons are taken, as they generally are by interpreters, to signify the Jewish and Gentile divisions of mankind, there is a kind of revolt in the minds of earnest and affectionate readers of the Gospel. A scheme of the world's history seems a cold substitute for those family associations, those deep personal sorrows, which have linked themselves with this story in all periods. Such protests of the heart and conscience always deserve the most serious attention. If they cannot determine the sense of a passage, they may correct many of our imperfect judgments about it. The context of the Gospel seems to me altogether in favour of the opinion that the elder son *does* represent the Jewish people. And if so, nothing would seem more natural and reasonable than that he who asked for the portion of goods that fell to him should represent those who were not brought under the yoke of a covenant—who were allowed to seek after God, if haply they might find Him—to ask the heavens and the earth, and the sea, and the abyss below, whether He, or some form of Him, or some portion of His nature, was not in them. The Gospel to the outcasts of the Jewish race has already, in the parable I spoke of last Sunday, been hinted at as opening the way to a wider message still. The argument for mixing with publicans and sinners justified a message to the other sheep who were not of that fold. The appearance of this parable exclusively in the Gospel of St. Luke would be itself decisive evidence to me that the instinct of commentators on this point has not been a mistaken one.

But it will prove quite a mistaken one if the other instinct to which I have alluded does not work freely by the side of it. St. Paul's message to the idolatrous Athenians was, 'You see what your own poet has told 'you, that you are the offspring of God ; therefore you 'are not to conceive the Godhead in the likeness of art 'or man's device.' St. Paul told the Galatians that the Father had sent forth His only-begotten Son to emancipate and adopt them ; therefore they were not to be in slavery to the elements of the world. We may talk ever so learnedly about the calling of the Gentiles, but we destroy its force, we give another account of it than the Apostles give, unless we connect it with these passages. And if we do connect it with them, the parable may retain its beautiful domestic and human character—yes, and all its application

to individuals—whilst we treat it as unfolding the divine
method to the world. The Gentile races are sons who go
out of their father's house, each seeming to follow an independent course, each seeming to choose its own gods and
its own ways of drawing nigh to those gods. Still their
means of living, all their faculties, energies, impulses to
thought and to worship, are gifts from their Father. He
has bestowed these upon the younger son, however that
son may use them, as he has bestowed other gifts upon
the elder of which he must give account.

'*And not many days after the younger son gathered all
together, and took his journey into a far country, and there
wasted his substance with riotous living.*' These words
have had infinite applications; every one, perhaps, who
has heard them, has applied them in many different
ways. No one need contradict the other; those who
have learnt the meaning from their own experience
have understood it best. How the sense of an eternal
home, of a Father's house, is awake in childhood; how it
dies out as the youth begins to gather all together—to make
a world for himself; how he travels further and further
from the remembrance of home; how the divine treasures
of affection, hope, intellect, health, become dissipated;
how he loses himself in the intoxications of the senses:
here you have a story which is repeated again and again,
and always finds mournful facts in us and in our fellows
to illustrate and enforce it. And so the records of Gentile
mythology and Gentile history explain themselves to us.
We see what the cause of moral declension in the nations
of the old world was; how the feeling of the invisible
lost itself in visible worship; how the sense of unity broke
into a number of objects of terror or of beauty; how the

fear of a destroyer struggled with the hope of a deliverer; how the first overpowered the second; how the belief in justice contended with the dread of a Power which could overpower justice; how the lusts of the man darkened the images of the gods whom he adored; how he sought, by vile expedients, to avert the wrath before which he trembled; how superstitions grew to be more fearful; how moral corruptions always gained strength along with them; how protests against both mixed with an unbelief in those truths which the superstitions counterfeited, in the righteousness which the corruptions defied.

'*And when he had spent all, there arose a mighty famine in that land; and he began to be in want.*' The sense of a hunger, of an infinite want, oh my friends, in individuals and in nations, there are times when this becomes intolerable! Outward calamities may produce it; sometimes it comes only from discontent with the spiritual nourishment which is offered to the man or the people. So we may understand a little of those periods in the old world when men tried new religions, sought auguries about the future, tried to hold communications with the world which they could not see; all leading on to this mournful issue: '*And he went and joined himself to a citizen of that country; and he sent him into his fields to feed swine. And he would fain have filled his belly with the husks that the swine did eat: and no man gave unto him.*' The stye, the almost utter transformation of the man into the swine,— that would be the last scene of this sad eventful history if it were only a history of man's dealings. Thank God, it is not so. It is the history of a Father's dealings with a child whom He has created to desire other food than that of swine, whom He will not suffer to be filled with that

R

or with anything that man can give. Therefore, in the crisis of famine and of despair, begins that agony which our Lord describes as the process of the prodigal *coming to himself*. And with the arousing of self-consciousness,— with the terrible recollection, 'I exist,'—comes a sadder, deeper, more blessed recollection, '*How many hired servants of my father's have bread enough and to spare, and I perish with hunger!*' Yes! the dream of a father's house, of a home somewhere, is once again stirring in him. 'Those cattle on the hills, how peacefully they 'graze; these trees, how they put forth their leaves in 'spring; these streams, how they break their ice-chains " and flow freely as if they would flow for ever. Are not all 'these my father's? Does not he sustain their life? And ' I perish with hunger.' To hundreds of thousands of men and women in Christian Europe have these words revealed what was passing in them. Do they not tell what must have passed in the minds of the Samaritans, Ephesians, Thessalonians, of whom we read, when the good news, 'Children, you have a father,' burst upon them, and when any one of them formed that wonderful resolution, which has echoed through all ages, '*I will arise and go to my father, and will say unto him, Father, I am no more worthy to be called thy son: make me as one of thy hired servants?*'

Then follow the passages to which all else in the parable is subordinate. '*And he arose, and came to his father. But when he was yet a great way off, his father saw him, and had compassion, and ran, and fell on his neck, and kissed him. And the son said unto him, I have sinned against heaven, and in thy sight, and am no more worthy to be called thy son. But the father said unto his servants, Bring forth the best robe, and put it on him; and put a ring on his hand,*

and shoes on his feet: and bring hither the fatted calf, and kill it; and let us eat, and be merry: for this my son was dead, and is alive again; he was lost, and is found. And they began to be merry.

This infinite joy in the father's heart seems to us appalling when we read of it, and try to believe that it is an actual revelation of the Divine mind. It is high, we cannot attain to it; that is our natural language. And yet all Christendom is but an expression of this truth. What does the message of Christ's full and perfect sacrifice mean?—what do the Sacraments mean,—if it is not this? Are they not manifestations of One who of His tender love to mankind gave his only-begotten Son to take our nature upon Him, and to suffer death upon the cross. As I said at the beginning of my sermon, Passion Week is either a dream, or it is a translation into fact of this parable. It is a witness that the parable applies equally to both the sons of the father; to those who are near, and to those who are afar off.

IV. And so we come to the last part of it, which recalls the occasion that suggested it. The elder son is in the field. He hears music and dancing. He asks what it means. He is told that his brother is come, and that his father has killed for him the fatted calf. '*And he was angry, and would not go in; therefore came his father out, and entreated him. And he answering said to his father, Lo, these many years do I serve thee, neither transgressed I at any time thy commandment; and yet thou never gavest me a kid, that I might make merry with my friends: but as soon as this thy son was come, which hath devoured thy living with harlots, thou hast killed for him the fatted calf.'*

R 2

How plausible this reasoning sounds! How perfectly invincible it must have seemed to this dutiful son! And yet, if we examine it, what does it come to but this? ' I ' have been obedient, and I ought to be paid for my ' obedience. My brother has been disobedient. Why art ' thou glad that he has ceased to be disobedient? I see no ' cause for satisfaction in that. It causes me no delight.' Here is that flagrant opposition between the Divine purpose and the purpose of those who had been called to be the ministers of His will and purpose, which our Lord has been detecting in all His dealings with the scribes and Pharisees. ' The Father's joy is in the restoration of the ' lost. You have no such joy. You think the removal of ' their curse, of their sin, is an injury to you.'

But is this consistent with the words, ' *Son, thou art ever with me, and all that I have is thine ?* ' Thoroughly consistent. For what do those words signify but this : ' Son, ' I have called thee to know my goodness and loving-' kindness. I have called thee to be a dispenser of that ' knowledge to the children of men. I can give thee no ' greater treasure. I can make thee partaker of no higher ' bliss than my own. Thou wilt not have that ? Thou ' wishest for another kind of joy than mine ? Well, if ' thou choosest it thou must have it. Thou must try what ' that selfish joy is worth ; whether it satisfies thee better ' than the husks which the swine eat have satisfied thy ' brother. But before thou formest that terrible resolu-' tion I will come out and entreat thee. I will urge thee ' to partake of my festival. I will vindicate thy right ' to it. I will conjure thee to enter into thy Father's ' blessedness. Thou dost enter it when thou ownest the ' outcast for thy brother, when thou makest merry and art

' glad because he was dead and is alive again, he was lost
' and is found.'

So pleaded the Eternal Father by the mouth of Jesus
with His Jewish people. So pleads He with us in this
Passion Week. Do you want wages for your virtue, for
your faith, for your superiority to the•rest of mankind?
You must ask the devil for those wages ; for the service of
pride he will give you strictly and punctually the wages of
death. Do you desire the delight of the Father who so
loved the world as to give His only begotten Son for it ?
Do you want the delight of the Son who poured out His
blood for all men, who is the Saviour of all men? Do you
want the delight of the Spirit, who is seeking to bring all
to repentance and the knowledge of the truth? '*Son, thou
art ever with me, and all that I have is thine.*' Thou
mayest possess my own character. Thou mayest declare
my purpose to those who have lost themselves. Thou
mayest be my instrument in finding them. And if they
never hear thy feeble voice, thou needest not doubt that
they will hear the voice of the Son of Man; that by
hunger and misery He will remind them of their Father's
house ; that they will arise and go to Him ; that He will
meet them when they are a great way off; that He will
embrace them and bring them to His banquet ; that His
Spirit will enable them to feed on the perfect Sacrifice,
and to offer themselves acceptable sacrifices to Him.

LECTURE XX.

THE KING DISMISSING HIS STEWARD.

St. Luke XVI. 10, 11.

He that is faithful in that which is least, is faithful also in much ; and he that is unjust in the least is unjust also in much. If therefore ye have not been faithful in the unrighteous mammon, who will commit to your trust the true riches?

THERE are no parables which appear so unlike each other as those which we call the parables of the Prodigal Son and of the Unjust Steward. Yet the Evangelist who reports them to us, evidently discovered some close relation between them. One would gather from his narrative that they were spoken at the same time. If you remember how the first of these parables arose out of our Lord's discoveries of the moral diseases of the Jewish nation and its rulers, you will see more clearly how the story of the Steward and that of Dives and Lazarus carry on its lessons. I looked upon the parables in the last chapter as exhibiting, in the liveliest and fullest form, the contrast between the mind of the chosen people and of Him who had chosen them. He was a shepherd seeking after any one sheep which had wandered from His fold ; He was as earnest to reclaim a human heart, as a woman to find a piece of money which she had lost; finally, He was a Father looking upon the outcast who had wandered furthest from his home as a child, rejoicing to welcome him back. And the Jewish people, as represented by their scribes, their priests, their most religious men, held it a crime to receive sinners and eat with them. Their godliness consisted in avoiding those whom God was regarding with tender affection, whom He was making the mightiest sacrifice to deliver and to regenerate.

No explanation of the parable of the Prodigal was more consistent with this view of its object than that which has been ordinarily adopted. If the younger son who took his portion of goods with him into a far country reminded us of the world beyond the Jewish pale, the elder son who heard the music and dancing at his brother's return and refused to come in, showed exactly that temper of mind which our Lord had been detecting and exposing in the Jew himself. His privileges were not underrated. He had been admitted to know the will and purpose of God. All that his Father had was his. But if he believed his covenant, he believed that God's will was to bless all the families of the earth. That was the revelation of God which had been made to Abraham and his descendants. That was the call of Abraham and his descendants to work as God's ministers. They showed that they had no desire to see the families of the earth blessed. The blessing of others was an injury to them, a derogation from their rights. Their inheritance as the firstborn was put in peril.

I. What more natural than a transition from a story of this kind, to one which reminded the Jew that he was not a possessor of divine gifts at all, but merely a *steward* of them, that his honour as the elder brother was to assist in the distribution of his father's treasures, that if he looked upon his position in any other light, the position would be taken from him, the treasures would cease to be his?

Here we have what is at once the most obvious, and, I think also the deepest meaning of the parable of the Steward. Before we notice any particulars in it, let us fix our minds upon that name. For the Jew to believe that he was a steward—for us to believe that we are stewards—is the great necessity, the amazing difficulty. No other, we may depend upon it, is practically so serious, so profound, as that. Commentators have exercised their faculties laboriously upon one and another aspect of this story. They may have seen each others' mistakes ; one may have had a glimpse of our Lord's meaning which was hidden from another. But if they forgot the subject of the parable, or did not bring that home to their readers, their ingenuity in handling special points can have been of little avail.

On the other hand, if we take firm hold of the thought that we are studying the acts, punishments, resources of a steward, many perplexities of detail in the story disappear, and many opposing notions of it are harmonized. What goods, we ask, are these, which the steward was accused of wasting? Were they spiritual or material goods? Was it that knowledge of the Divine mind and purpose which had been imparted to the sons of Abraham ; was it the gold and silver which they might share in and traffic with like the other nations? The passage I took for my text gives the answer. The same law applies to both. '*He that is faithful in that which is least is faithful also in much : and he that is unjust in the least is unjust also in much.*' The second clause defines more clearly the doctrine of the first. '*If therefore ye have not been faithful in the unrighteous mammon, who will commit to your trust the true riches ?* ' The covetousness of the Pharisees extended from the lowest things to the highest; from the desire for present pelf to a calculation about the prizes after death which might be secured by a prudent investment of a certain amount of time and fortune here in religious duties and sacrifices. It could not be otherwise. The whole mind must be governed at last by the principle which has dominion over one part of it. This is what our Lord has affirmed so strongly elsewhere, and repeats in connexion with the words I have just read to you. *'No servant can serve two masters: for either he will hate the one, and love the other; or else he will hold to the one, and despise the other. Ye cannot serve God and mammon.'* Mammon must be the lord of both worlds, if he is the lord of either. If we admit him to make our earth for us, he will also make our heaven. The spirit of covetousness will be content with no half service, no divided allegiance. And in like manner our Lord teaches that the Spirit of love will be content with no half service, no divided allegiance. He asks for the little and the much; He asks to be owned as giving us our stewardship both in the unrighteous mammon and in the true riches, in all tangible as well as in all unseen treasures. Do not, then, let us try to separate in Christ's parables worlds which it is the very purpose of a parable to show us must be joined together. The outward and visible is always the sign of the inward and spiritual, whether grace or ungraciousness. The steward had wasted goods of both kinds; he had claimed them both as his own.

But the owner was not so far off as the steward supposed. He demanded an account of the goods. The steward knew that he was about to be dismissed. What was he to do? Could he become an independent man? Was he capable of standing on his own ground without any master? He knows that he was not. *He cannot dig.* Should he then tell his master that he had failed? Should he make a full confession? No! '*to beg he is ashamed.*' But there was another course open. Hitherto he had made no friends among his master's tenants. He had stood aloof from them; he had assumed the airs of one in his lord's confidence, having interests altogether apart from theirs. Now he felt the need of their help. When he had quarrelled with his employer, they might receive him into their houses. The method looks simple when it is once devised. He could earn their favour by reducing their debts. He could set them comparatively at ease. '*How much owest thou unto my lord? And he said, An hundred measures of oil. And he said unto him, Take thy bill, and sit down quickly, and write fifty. Then said he to another, And how much owest thou? And he said, An hundred measures of wheat. And he said unto him, Take thy bill, and write fourscore.*'

This was exactly what the Jewish nation did for the nations of the earth when it had lost its sense of a heavenly calling, when it ceased to feel itself a steward for mankind. Jews won themselves friends among heathen men who were weary of their own confusions, who were asking for some clearer light. But it was not by scattering the confusions, by pointing them to the light that lighteth every man. It was by lowering the standard which they had already; it was by substituting an easy atheism for a restless idolatry. For the hundred measures of oil they wrote fifty, for the hundred measures of wheat fourscore. It was the way to get friends; not an unsuccessful way, in that time or any other.

But this instinct of seeking friends our Lord says is a right instinct. He would cultivate it in His disciples. He would use the steward's example to show how the blessing is to be won. The steward had done wisely. Having given himself to mammon he had served mammon thoroughly. Having set before himself the object of winning men's favour, he had given himself up, soul and body, to that object. Could not they do the like? Might not they surrender themselves as heartily to the Spirit of love, as he had surrendered himself to the rival spirit? Could they not buy an everlasting home in men's hearts by showing them the truth, by delivering them from lies, as he had won a temporary home in their houses by disguising from them the truth, by encouraging them in lies? Might they not compel the god whom he worshipped, the unrighteous mammon, to be an instrument in their service?

There is, as I said in speaking of the Prodigal Son, a prevalent jealousy of all interpretations which give the parables a national sense, lest we should lose the personal sense which we are sure must be in them. I justified that feeling in the instance to which I referred then. I justify it in this instance. The same observation applies to both. This parable did not speak less livingly, less tremendously, to any individual Jew, because it described the condition of his people. Every individual Jew had a stewardship for which he must give an account. So neither does its fulfilment to them in the least weaken its force for us. Is the Church Catholic less a steward than the posterity of Abraham? Is the English nation less a steward than the Jewish nation? Is any of us in his vocation less a steward than any one of them? Are we less prone than they were to use our Master's goods as if they were our own? Are we less prone in our daily intercourse with each other, in our intercourse with the tribes of the earth, to lower the standard of justice, goodness, truth, which God has established in their consciences,—to put the fifty measures of oil, the fourscore of wheat, for the hundred? Might we not, if we would, be making friends of the other pattern, according to the opposite maxim, both among Christian men and among the men who have never heard of Christ or who disbelieve Him, by awakening them to nobler hopes, by setting before them a nobler life?

II. The sentences which connect this Parable of the Steward with the one of Dives and Lazarus are intelligible enough if they are viewed in this light, and are as much a comment upon one as an introduction to the other; otherwise they look like sentences thrown in by accident, not in the 'order' which St. Luke promised to observe. That we should be reminded just in this place of the covetousness of the Pharisees, and that that covetousness should be given as the reason for their deriding our Lord's words about the steward, is surely just what one might have expected, if the whole story turns upon a selfish attempt to appropriate blessings which were meant to be dispensed. That Christ should say to them, ' *Ye are they which justify yourselves before men : but God knoweth your hearts: for that which is highly esteemed among men is abomination in the sight of God,*' was consistent with the discovery He had just been making of a scheme of religion which was grounded upon self-seeking and ended in self-seeking, while the God whom the cultivators of that religion professed to worship was sending His own Son to seek after His creatures.

And the words which follow these, were not less directly addressed to *their* consciences and need not miss any of their force for ours. The Law and the Prophets had been sounding in the ears of the Jewish people; they boasted of the Law which their fathers transgressed; they gloried in the prophets whom their fathers killed. Then John came preaching, 'Repent, for the kingdom of heaven is at hand.' Since then there had been an eager crying for a kingdom of heaven. Numbers were pressing into it, dreaming that they should find in it some relaxation of the standard which Law and Prophets had set forth. But no! Heaven and earth would pass away before one tittle of the eternal law which bound heaven and earth together could fail. Jesus had come not to destroy the Law but to fulfil. For one example, which went very directly home to the Pharisee. He had come to make the bond which bound husband to wife more close and sacred. Those who worshipped the mere name of the Law, finding that it permitted—wisely permitted—letters of divorcement, were continually breaking loose from the obligations of wedlock, all the time pleading the authority of Moses, and fancying that they were obeying the Divine command. He who came to establish an inward righteousness which the Law could not establish, and so to fulfil the intent of the Law, could proclaim that there was a real moral adultery in such separations; that marriage was not dissolved except by a moral crime; that the man who sought the letter of divorce on any ground but that was making an adulteress of the woman whom he put away. This was an instance, a typical instance, of the way in which the Jewish rulers were using the Divine statutes to undermine the principle which they were created to enforce; an instance of the way in which they were using their knowledge of Scripture to weaken the conscience in their own people and in the people of other lands. Frequent as divorces were at this time in Rome, we have the testimony of the Jewish historian that they were at least as frequent in Jerusalem, and that the crime which our Lord said that they would foster did continually disturb the peace of families and the order of the State. It is our Lord who traces this result to the Pharisaical denial of any morality which was not legal and external, to that Pharisaical selfishness with which wedded love is incompatible.

III. All readers speak naturally of the 'parable' of Dives and Lazarus; all nevertheless seem inclined to regard it as an actual narrative of a rich and a poor man. We may now perhaps perceive why it is not safe to reject either of these convictions, why the parable must contain *more* than a mere story that it may vindicate its claim to be a story. In speaking to you on the Parable of the Sower, I maintained that it was an education—a divine education—for poor men or rich men if their minds were only awakened to the most obvious facts of nature. They knew the worth of that education when they began to connect nature with themselves, to regard the same Divine government as exercised in analogous methods over both. So here. I accept this story in its most literal sense as an example of facts which are occurring continually in this world, and as a revelation of what passes in the world after death. I cannot value it too highly in that character. But if it were only this, it would seem to me a loose fragment occurring in the midst of a continuous discourse. It would have no reference to the main subject of that discourse. I hold that it has a direct reference to that subject.

The more carefully we examine it in all its details, the more shall we find that it concerns the steward of whom we have just been hearing, the elder son of whom we heard last Sunday.

(1) '*There was a certain rich man, which was clothed in purple and fine linen, and fared sumptuously every day: and there was a certain beggar named Lazarus, which was laid at his gate, full of sores, and desiring to be fed with the crumbs which fell from the rich man's table: moreover the dogs came and licked his sores.*' Any rich man might certainly be clothed in purple and fine linen. But for the purposes of a parable, there would be a peculiar fitness in such vestures for a nation which is described in the Scriptures as one of kings and priests. The sumptuous fare may represent the luxury of any individual man. But these words occur in a song, which every Israelite knew by heart, which confessedly referred to the blessings of the race, which gave the form to the thoughts and language of a number of Psalms. '*He made him ride on the high places of the earth, that he might eat the increase of the fields; and he made him to suck honey out of the rock, and oil out of the flinty rock; butter of kine, and milk of sheep, with fat of lambs, and rams of the breed of Bashan, and goats, with the fat of kidneys of wheat: and thou didst drink the pure blood of the grape.*' Evidently whatever sense we give to the words of this song, the same we may reasonably give to the ' sumptuous fare ' of the parable, the only difference being that as our Lord spoke at a time when the nation had lost its civil freedom, the treasures which it possessed must be those which St. Paul enumerated when he said, '*Who are Israelites; to whom pertaineth the adoption, and the glory, and the covenants, and the giving of*

*the Law, and the service of God, and the promises ; whose are
the fathers, and of whom as concerning the flesh Christ came,
who is over all, God blessed for ever.*'

(2) And if the people who were chosen to know the one
God of all the families of the earth, the God who executeth
justice and righteousness on the earth, the God who is a
Creator and a Redeemer, are represented by the rich man—
the beggar at the gate must be the image of those tribes
that were bowing to gods who disliked some families of the
earth, to gods who were not just and righteous but spiteful
and malicious, to gods some of whom desired to enslave and
kill, some of whom were more gracious and merciful, but
were controlled by a power higher than all, which seemed
at times merely absorbed in its own happiness, at times
to be the envious beholder and the destined destroyer of
what men loved, of all their momentary gratifications, of
all their distant hopes. No mythology, no philosophy had
ever been able to cure these speculations, for they came
from sores in the conscience, from a sense of inward war,
from a prophecy that there must be a Righteous Being,
One who desired that men should be righteous,—if haply
they could feel after Him and find Him. But Lazarus had
never been so full of sores—at least the sores had never
been so obvious and so painful—as in that age of unbelief, of
moral corruption, of eager craving for signs and enchantments, of hopeless slavery, upon which the world, ruled by
the Cæsars, had now entered. There was, indeed, in that
time, a longing for any crumbs of consolation or infor-
mation which might be found anywhere. We have proofs
enough that the Roman masters, much as they may have
despised the Jews, did ask for those crumbs at their hands,
did try to understand their lore, did listen to the false

prophets who abused that lore and traded with the wisdom which it gave them. '*Moreover the dogs came and licked his sores.*' The animals and outward nature whispered to him the news which those who were trusted with it did not tell ' He who made these creatures and thee, does not forget ' them and will not forget thee.'

(3) '*And it came to pass, that the beggar died, and was carried by the angels into Abraham's bosom : the rich man also died, and was buried ; and in hell he lift up his eyes, being in torments, and seeth Abraham afar off, and Lazarus in his bosom.*' The beggar lies at the gate of the rich man no more. The blessing to Abraham becomes his blessing. He is carried into the very heart of that divine covenant which was given to one family for the sake of all the families of the earth. Is not this a faithful exhibition of the facts? Heathen nations have believed the God of Abraham to be their God; have confessed Jesus the seed of Abraham to be their Lord and King ; have said that He came to adopt them into His Father's family, to make them sons of God in Him. The language is at least consistent with the Gospel of the Kingdom of God, as the Apostles proclaimed it to the world.

(4) Does the account of the death and burial of the rich man answer less to the facts of history ? Does it answer less to the previous passages of St. Luke's narrative ? Is not that narrative (or rather the discourses which it records) declaring to us the symptoms of an expiring nation, the nature and source of the diseases which must at last extinguish it ? When the sentence went forth against it, what was it but putting into a grave that which had become putrid and was infecting the air?

(5) But life is not extinct when this burial has taken place.

S

There is a life in death. The torment which the beggar endured has become the rich man's. He has the frightful sores of conscience. He has the sense of being without God, of not knowing what His purposes are; whether He is not an enemy, whether He does not desire the misery of His creatures, whether Jehovah the Redeemer, or Mammon the Enslaver, is indeed the Lord of all. He has the feeling that a strange reverse has taken place in his condition; that he has fallen by some dire destiny; that others who were in an immeasurably lower state than his have ascended into a higher.

(6) Recollection of the past has not departed. At first it seems only to aggravate the misery of the loss.

'*And he cried and said, Father Abraham, have mercy on me, and send Lazarus, that he may dip the tip of his finger in water, and cool my tongue; for I am tormented in this flame. But Abraham said, Son, remember that thou in thy lifetime receivedst thy good things, and likewise Lazarus evil things: but now he is comforted, and thou art tormented. And beside all this, between us and you there is a great gulf fixed: so that they which would pass from hence to you cannot; neither can they pass to us, that would come from thence.*'

This craving for something to cool the tongue, if it were only a slight taste of outward civil rights, has characterised the Jewish race during ages of ignominy and cruel persecution at Christian hands. And all the while there has been a wish—I count it a noble wish—to receive the blessing from father Abraham—I mean to claim it as due to a people having a grand ancestry and glorious traditions, rather than to take it from the mercy of the Gentiles even if it must come through their hands. But *Abraham* can only answer by pointing to the advantages

which they had and which they have lost—can only speak
of the wide and impassable gulf which separates the
present from the past. Till they can look beyond their
ancestry to the Ancient of Days—till they can invoke not
Abraham, but the God of Abraham, that sad answer is the
only one which can reach them.

But there is another scene in the drama.

(7) ' *Then he said, I pray thee therefore, father, that thou
wouldest send him to my father's house : for I have five
brethren ; that he may testify unto them, lest they also come
into this place of torment.*'

I can find no key to the meaning of this sentence like
that which is supplied by some grand lessons which St.
Paul addresses to the Gentiles at Rome, in a passage from
which I have quoted on a former occasion.

'*Boast not against the branches.   But if thou boast, thou
bearest not the root, but the root thee.   Thou wilt say then,
The branches were broken off, that I might be graffed in.
Well ; because of unbelief they were broken off, and thou
standest by faith.   Be not high-minded, but fear : for if
God spared not the natural branches, take heed lest he also
spare not thee.   Behold therefore the goodness and severity of
God : on them which fell, severity ; but toward thee, goodness,
if thou continue in his goodness : otherwise thou also shalt be
cut off.   And they also, if they abide not still in unbelief, shall
be graffed in : for God is able to graff them in again.*'

The nations have been carried into Abraham's bosom.
They have become the fortunate brethren of the rich man ;
the successors to the stewardship which he has forfeited.
May not they fall from that honour as he has fallen ?
Will they not take warning from his fall ? Abraham
makes answer, '*They have Moses and the Prophets, let them*

hear them.' Moses and the Prophets will tell them what comes of exulting in great privileges; that men who had the revelation of the righteous God might turn to the vilest idols. Moses and the Prophets will tell them that they can only live by faith in God; that if they once begin to trust in themselves they must perish. He who had Moses and the Prophets, and did not hear them, replies, *' Nay, father Abraham : but if one went unto them from the dead, they will repent.'* The news of a Resurrection; the voice of one who had risen, that must prevail! Is there no conscience in us—in the beggars who have become princes— in the countries of idolators which now form a Christendom—that responds to the fearful sentence, *' If they hear not Moses and the prophets, neither will they be persuaded, though one rose from the dead ?'*

(8) I have endeavoured to follow our Lord's words step by step, and, instead of inventing a sense for them, to take that which is suggested by the context, that which associates them at once with the history of the time and with the Gospel of the Kingdom of Heaven. But, as I said before, no interpretation of this kind, however much justified by evidence internal and collateral, can warrant us in throwing aside the most palpable, most individual, meaning which has been ever found for the parable. If I thought I was weakening one application of it which has been made to any rich man clothed with purple and fine linen, to any beggar at his gate, I should distrust my apprehension of it altogether. But as I have shown in former cases, there can be no fear that a law which strikes at selfishness in spiritual treasures will not strike at selfishness in the case of material treasures. For men's unfaithfulness in little things corresponds to their unfaith-

fulness in great. And God's government is orderly and uniform. His dealings with nations must, as the Bible teaches us they do, proceed on the same principles and point to the same objects as His dealing with every human soul.

The relation between the past and future of the Jewish nation may be most fittingly set forth in the past and future of a man, by his condition here, and his condition after death. I assume that that is the *most* fit illustration of it, because it is our Lord's. And I assume that as He tells us of facts just as they are here, so He tells us of facts just as they are there. If He represents the selfish man as feeling the torment when he passes out of the world which was concealed from him in a great measure here, I take it for granted that it is even so. If He says that an utterly selfish man, who only cared for himself here, who at first only cares for the flames which are tormenting himself there, may be brought, through this discipline, to think of his brethren and care for them, I cannot reject the assurance of so mighty a moral change, merely because, without such an authority, I could not have conceived it. If I take our Lord Jesus Christ as my guide through mysteries which I cannot penetrate, if I suppose that He knows more than we know, I must conclude that a man who has been proof against all loving influences here, who had appeared to grow harder and more cruel under those very influences, may yet find the fatherly chastisement which will break his stubbornness and lead him to contrition. He who began to cry earnestly that those whom he had left behind him might not come into that place of torment, might have still a gulf separating him from Abraham. But that gulf must have been beginning to close up ; he was nearer in heart and mind to Abraham than he had ever been in the days when he was receiving his good things.

It is not, my friends, by quenching this hope for any individual man, or for any fallen nation, that we shall make ourselves purer, or shall deepen the awe of our minds. We may believe, we ought to believe, that punishment is inseparable from evil, that God will never withhold His punishments while evil lasts. Israel cannot be saved till it is saved from its distrust and hatred of God. When St. Paul says 'All Israel shall be saved,' he expresses his conviction that it will one day be brought to own that the perfect friend of man is the true image of God. The assurance that its disobedience will be at last overcome, cannot make it safe for the Christian Church to imitate the sin of Israel, and so to come into its torments. The trust that no sin, no selfishness, shall at last be found stronger than the divine love, cannot lead any man to cultivate that which is to be vanquished, or defy that which must prevail. Despair is the devil's instrument, not God's. He is the God of Hope.

LECTURE XXI.

HOW THE KINGDOM OF GOD COMES.

St. Luke XVII. 20, 21.

And when he was demanded of the Pharisees, when the kingdom of God should come, he answered them and said, The kingdom of God cometh not with observation: neither shall they say, Lo here! or, Lo there! for, behold, the kingdom of God is within you.

I. ANY one who reflects on the parables of the steward, and of the rich man, or on any of the facts of Jewish history which illustrate them, may exclaim in sadness and in bitterness, 'So then all things which seem blessings 'are really occasions of falling. Those who have most 'advantages of any kind are the greatest offenders. They 'stumble themselves—they cause others to stumble.'

He who knew what was in man—He who felt in Himself all the doubts and perplexities which could arise in any of us—anticipated these thoughts. His own spirit sounded the depth of them.

'*Then said he unto the disciples, It is impossible but that offences will come: but woe unto him, through whom they come! It were better for him that a millstone were hanged about his neck, and he cast into the sea, than that he should offend one of these little ones.*'

As if He had said, Yes! All these scandals which the children of Abraham are causing to each other and to the

heathen world are indeed very terrible.   How terrible they
are you cannot measure.   But you do yourselves no good
by complaining that you are exposed to them.   Prepare for
them as for enemies that must meet you, that you cannot
escape.   And then consider, ' The evil is not in receiving
' an offence, but in giving it.   The woe is to him through
' whom the offence cometh.   Think of that.'

II. My friends, here is indeed a maxim of the Kingdom
of Heaven.   There cannot be a simpler, there cannot be a
deeper or a more practical one.   Accept offences or scandals that meet you as inevitable.   Take care, each one of
you, that you are not the author of an offence or scandal.
Is it said then that you can have no control over those
which others cause, that you can do nothing to hinder
them ?   Hear what you may do if you observe the first rule.
' *Take heed to yourselves : If thy brother trespass against
thee, rebuke him ; and if he repent, forgive him.   And if he
trespass against thee seven times in a day, and seven times in
a day turn again to thee, saying, I repent ; thou shalt forgive
him.*'

Avoid giving offences, then you will forgive those who
offend you.   Forgiveness is your weapon against scandals.
Your temptation will always be to confound the evil which
is done with the injury which it inflicts upon you.   Separate
them by forgiving that injury ; so you lead the man to ask
how the evil whence the injury came may be taken away.
He rises from your forgiveness to the apprehension of a
forgiving God.   He perceives that there is one who desires
to send away sins.   It seems to me that our Lord struck
here at the very root of the Pharisaical doctrine—of that
doctrine which was always producing scandals, and could
do nothing to abate them.   Forgiveness in any real sense

of the word was not a part of their practice. It therefore
was not, and could not be, in any real sense, a part of
their creed. Forgiveness meant to them the indulging in
certain cases those who had offended. Up to a certain
point that might be a duty. It was a hard duty. After
a certain number of experiments they might assure themselves that God was satisfied. They had done all that
He required. Therefore forgiveness, when it was asked of
Him, meant the same kind of indulgence—a mere remission of punishment for injuries which He had incurred at
their hands. The dream of a God who delighted to forgive; who reclaimed by forgiving; who sent away not
punishment but sins; who made the hearts and consciences
of His subjects free from guilt; this did not enter into
their theology, as that which corresponded to it had no
place in their ethical code. But to reveal such a God
and His Kingdom was the work of Christ. His code of
morality is formed by His theology.

III. When the disciples heard the precept so new to their
ears, yet bearing such a witness of its truth to their consciences, that they should forgive their brother if he turned
to them seven times a day, and said, 'I repent,' they uttered
a very natural cry, 'Lord, increase our faith.' The words
expressed more than they knew of their own want. It
was exactly *faith* which they needed—faith in God's forgiveness; then forgiveness in its most inward sense, the
forgiveness from the heart, would be possible for them.
But there was a confusion in their minds which marred this
simple petition. They had thought of faith as a possession
or stock, which might be increased as a sum of money may
be increased by a present or a bequest. I judge that they
had this thought, partly from their language, partly because

we all of us have it ; still more from the answer which our Lord made them.

IV. '*And the Lord said, If ye had faith as a grain of mustard seed, ye might say unto this sycamine tree, Be thou plucked up by the root, and be thou planted in the sea ; and it should obey you. But which of you, having a servant plowing or feeding cattle, will say unto him by and by, when he is come from the field, Go and sit down to meat ? And will not rather say unto him, Make ready wherewith I may sup, and gird thyself, and serve me till I have eaten and drunken ; and afterward thou shalt eat and drink ? Doth he thank that servant because he did the things that were commanded him ? I trow not. So likewise ye, when ye shall have done all those things which are commanded you, say, We are unprofitable servants: we have done that which was our duty to do.*'

The grain of mustard seed, the tiniest of seeds, illustrates the nature of faith better than an accumulating heap. It is the greatest when it is least. The man feels that he has nothing, and can do nothing; therefore he relies on One who has all, and can enable to do what He wills him to do. Once let him think that he has any power of his own —*call* it faith, or what you please—the reliance vanishes ; the essence of faith is gone. While the man really depends on a strength which is not his own, he can bid sycamine-trees move into the sea ; mountains will be no hindrance to him.

Is that not a justification of all miracle workers ? What power have they ever pretended to which was so great as this ? To none which was half or a thousandth part so great. For they have pretended to exhibit their own great feats, their superiority to other men, the difference between them and their fellows. Therefore they have not been able to remove real hindrances, physical or moral, as those have done who have worked simply and obediently as the ministers of God's order. Such is our Lord's own correction of the tendencies which were sure to appear in His disciples, and to connect themselves with the efforts and the triumphs of faith. What was their faith given them for ? That they might indulge themselves with it ? That they might sit down to meat and enjoy themselves on the strength of it ? I trow not. They were simply labourers ploughing and feeding cattle for a master. Their faith was given them to serve Him with, that they might do His work. They would have what was wanted that they might do what was their duty to do; no more. In the performance of that duty difficulties that appeared quite insurmountable would disappear; nothing would be impossible to them. But if they began to be proud of themselves ; to think that they could do something more than was their duty ; that they might turn their faith into a luxury or an occasion of display : they would soon be reminded of their own insignificance ; they would be brought back to dependence and faith by severe lessons. The words, ' We are unprofitable servants ; we have done 'that which is our duty to do,' are often quoted by the champions of the Reformation against those who plead for works of supererogation. They have, no doubt, great point in this application ; but let us remember that the roots of that tenet of supererogation lie deep in all our natures, that they may send up shoots of various kinds. Those who speak of the efficacy of faith for justification may exhibit many of those shoots ; the Protestant soil is not less favourable to the growth of them than the Romish.

Those who glorify themselves on their faith come even more directly within the scope of our Lord's animadversion in this passage than those who glorify themselves on their works. And it is only by remembering that faith is the power by which God enables us to do what He wills us to do that we can escape either temptation.

V. I have inferred from the express words of St. Luke in the ninth chapter that all these discourses were delivered during our Lord's last journey to Jerusalem. You have seen how often our attention is called to the place whither His steps are directed ; how every woe, every expression of sorrow and anguish, every parable, has had some reference to it. We are reminded of it again in the eleventh verse. The incident which is recorded immediately after suggests another hint respecting the condition of the chosen people, another comparison between them and those whom they supposed to be enemies of God.

'And it came to pass, as he went to Jerusalem, that he passed through the midst of Samaria and Galilee. And as he entered into a certain village, there met him ten men that were lepers, which stood afar off: and they lifted up their voices, and said, Jesus, Master, have mercy on us. And when he saw them, he said unto them, Go shew yourselves unto the priests. And it came to pass, that, as they went, they were cleansed. And one of them, when he saw that he was healed, turned back, and with a loud voice glorified God, and fell down on his face at his feet, giving him thanks : and he was a Samaritan. And Jesus answering said, Were there not ten cleansed ? but where are the nine ? There are not found that returned to give glory to God save this stranger. And he said unto him, Arise, go thy way: thy faith hath made thee whole.'

The Jew dwelt much on the original crime of the ten tribes; on the mixture of Assyrian worship with the worship of Jehovah in those who had been settled in the land after the captivity of those tribes; on the opposition which they offered to the building of the temple at Jerusalem; on the carefulness of Ezra and Nehemiah to preserve the purity of blood in their race; on the schismatical temple at Gerizim. Not by arguments in confutation of this exclusiveness, but by living practical instances, is the way prepared for a message first to Samaritans, then to all who had no descent from the Patriarchs. How an habitual traditional faith may pass into a loss of all faith, how the formal acknowledgment of God may harden into Atheism; this was the fearful discovery which Christ was making to those who had inherited all blessings, who were exulting in their orthodoxy. How God may prepare 'strangers' to see Him in His acts, to confess Him, to give Him thanks for that which the others received as common things; this was the consolatory lesson which accompanied that melancholy one. The suddenness of their cure—what we call its miraculous character—had not the slightest effect in startling the nine Israelite lepers out of their moral torpor. They were glad to be freed from a plague, however the advantage might come. But there was no divine message to them in the deliverance. The hard trading temper of the rulers and the scribes had become theirs; they wanted certain things of the Most High; it might be freedom from punishment here or hereafter; it might be the acquisition of certain good things here or hereafter. They did not care to know Him. The Samaritan was overwhelmed by the blessing which was granted him; he had no right to it; what had he done to deserve it ? The gift must have come from the Source of health, and life, and gladness. It had come through a man who felt with him in his sorrow, who had healed him, it would seem, by some mighty power of sympathy. Surely this must be his ruler, the Lord of his spirit. And the God who spoke by this man could be no distant ruler in the clouds. Was it not He who taught Abraham to trust Him for himself and his seed after him ? The removal of the leprosy was to this man a revelation of God. His faith, the faith which was as a grain of mustard seed, did not glorify itself, but God who had saved him. He had been raised out of himself—he had become a new man.

VI. It is by no accident, I conceive, but in the most strict ' order,' that the words which we read next succeed to this story.

' And when he was demanded of the Pharisees, when the kingdom of God should come, he answered them and said, The kingdom of God cometh not with observation : neither shall they say, Lo here ! or, lo there ! for, behold, the kingdom of God is within you.'

The Pharisees had heard Him speak much of the King-dom of God as being at hand. They would like much to know when it was to appear. It seemed to be long in coming. The sneer was one in which they were sure to indulge ; it could not be without its effect on the disciples. We may hear and repeat the answer, not attaching much sense to it. The Samaritan leper had found the sense of it. The Kingdom of God had revealed itself to him. It had not come visibly, with observation. His spirit had bowed to it—had become its subject. And thou hard material Pharisee ! thou must learn what this Kingdom of God is as the Samaritan leper learned it, or thou wilt never perceive it at all, though it be about thee, though thou livest under the shadow of it, though thou art called as he is to enter into it, and be governed by it. If thou art looking for it in this place or that place, in the city or the desert, or the secret chamber, thou wilt not see it. Thou mayst calculate times and seasons accurately. Thou mayst guess from the sacred book what are the signs which shall herald the grand apparition. Thou mayst be picturing to thyself all the pomp and procession which shall welcome the Monarch, and the gifts and the punishments which He will dispense. But thou wilt know nothing of its nature till thou, like this stranger, this outcast, cryest for deliverance from a tyrant who is oppressing thee, and till thou thank God as thy Deliverer.

VII. Then He turned to the disciples, who needed counsel on this subject as much as the Pharisees. They had clung to Him; they had heard Him call Himself the Son of Man; they had entered in some slight degree into the force of that name; they had believed that the Kingdom of God would be His kingdom—would be a human kingdom—a kingdom for men. ' *But the days will come when ye shall desire to see one of the days of the Son of man, and ye shall not see it.*' That form which they had looked upon would be visible no more. Nay, it would seem to them as if they had lost Him —as if all signs of His presence were gone—as if the world were left—as if they were left—more desolate of Him than before. That would be a time of fearful temptation. They would hear voices saying to them, ' See here, or see there.' Impostures would beset them on all hands. They would be told, ' The Son of Man is ' revealing Himself to this seer, to this circle of initiated

' disciples.' Neither he nor they can teach you how to recognise your Lord. *'But go not after them, nor follow them.*
For as the lightning, that lighteneth out of the one part under
heaven, shineth unto the other part under heaven ; so shall the
Son of man be in his day.'

VIII. Hard it must have been for the disciples to understand that saying, even when they were preaching of the Son
of Man as the risen and ascended Lord of men and angels.
Hard it must have been to believe : ' Our words, the
' words which go forth from the mouths of fishermen
' and tentmakers, shall spread like the lightning from one
' part of the heaven to the other part of it; shall reach
' nations we never dreamed of; shall bring them to confess
' the Son of Man.' If they did grasp the conviction, it
could only have been through faith in the purpose of the
eternal God to establish the kingdom of His Son, for
neither then nor before will it have come with observation. They had to remember continually what He had
said when He was speaking of His triumph. *'But first*
must he suffer many things, and be rejected of this generation.'
A rejection not terminating with His death, only beginning
with it. The message of the Cross, the message of the
Resurrection, would be more scouted than He had been in
the days of His flesh. The rejection would come from the
same persons ; from the religious teachers and rulers of the
chosen nation first and chiefly ; then from the kings and
emperors of the world.

IX. *'And as it was in the days of Noe, so shall it be also in*
the days of the Son of man. They did eat, they drank, they
married wives, they were given in marriage, until the day
that Noe entered into the ark, and the flood came, and de-
stroyed them all. Likewise also as it was in the days of Lot ;

they did eat, they drank, they bought, they sold, they planted, they builded ; but the same day that Lot went out of Sodom it rained fire and brimstone from heaven, and destroyed them all. Even thus shall it be in the day when the Son of man is revealed. In that day, he which shall be upon the house-stop, and his stuff in the house, let him not come down to take it away : and he that is in the field, let him likewise not return back.'

That the words, ' days of the Son of Man,' point to some crisis which would affect the condition of mankind, no one who acknowledges the authority of the Speaker can doubt. Those who do not acknowledge His authority suppose that He expected such a crisis, or that His disciples expected it or believed that it had occurred, and therefore ascribed this language to Him. There is a perplexity in the minds of those who resort to the fraud or exaggerations of the Apostles or of the later Church for the explanation of these announcements. If what He said corresponds with some exactness to the events which happened when Jerusalem fell, they determine that it was a prophecy after the fact. But since they assume the prediction to be only satisfied by a destruction of the universe, they fall back upon the ignorance and simplicity of Him or His reporters, and suppose that their expressions prove them to have looked childishly forward to a catastrophe which never occurred, not to look back on one which did occur. We have a right, assuredly, to ask that they will determine which of these solutions they adopt, and will adhere to that ; not mix them loosely together, seeing that they are incompatible. But before we make that demand we must clear our own minds of a confusion which renders us often as irreverent to Christ, as inattentive to His express

T

language, as those who deem Him and the Evangelists to be impostors. Were the warnings derived from the state of men in Noah's age and in Lot's meant to warn the disciples of a calamity which was impending over them? Can you read any single sentence of the passage which I have read to you, or of the passage which follows it, and doubt that they were? Must not every one of those who listened to Him have supposed that they were? Leave for a moment the words respecting the past and consider these:—

X. '*In that day, he which shall be upon the housetop, and his stuff in the house, let him not come down to take it away: and he that is in the field, let him likewise not return back. Remember Lot's wife. Whosoever shall seek to save his life shall lose it; and whosoever shall lose his life shall preserve it. I tell you, in that night there shall be two men in one bed; the one shall be taken, and the other shall be left. Two women shall be grinding together; the one shall be taken, and the other left. Two men shall be in the field; the one shall be taken, and the other left.*'

Can any warnings be less vague, more distinct? They point to the field, the mill, the house, the house-stuff, the bed. Yet it is not the distinctness of one who had lived during a siege, and could relate some of the stirring and frightful incidents which had taken place in it; no *such* signs either of foresight or of deception are here. What we do observe, is a purpose to avoid the grand imagery of a falling universe, such as the analogies of the burning mountain might have supplied, and to fix the thoughts of the hearers upon minute and individual circumstances which might affect their own conduct.

But why then speak of Noah or of Lot? Ask Christ to tell you why He does not dwell as we might, if we

wanted to impress our hearers with a coming day of
judgment, upon the universality of the deluge, so far
as hills or valleys were concerned in it.   He speaks
of the condition of the people whom it overtook.   He
passes therefore naturally, and without an effort, to a
single city of the Plain, as if that contained precisely the
same lesson.   In each case there is a revelation of God's
purpose to put down evil and to vindicate right.   In each
case there is a stupor, indifference, hardness, lasting to the
very instant when the overthrow came.   Now, these characteristics of former crises or judgments were strictly
verified in the one which befell that age.   There was the
same incapacity of believing that the holy city could fall,
in its inhabitants, as there was that the city of the Plain
could fall, in *its* inhabitants.   The Lord of David, they said,
could not mean that David's conquest should be won by
sacrilegious Romans.   All our Lord's warnings have been
directed to remove this expectation from His disciples'
minds.   God would not prove Himself to be the Lord of the
city by such an interference.   He would Himself be its
Judge.   He would call His steward to give an account of
his stewardship.   He would manifest His Kingdom of
Heaven by putting down that kingdom on earth which
was most directly setting at nought all His purposes.
The downfall of the city, the casting out of the Jewish
nation, would be in the strictest sense a revelation of the
Son of Man.   It would fulfil the purpose of all previous
judgments.   It would declare God's eternal war with
unrighteousness in whomsoever unrighteousness might be
found.   It would declare His purpose to regenerate and
restore the human race, and to sweep away whatever
opposes its regeneration and restoration.   It would be like

all previous days of the Lord—a day of thick darkness, a day of glorious light coming forth from the darkness.

But can we afford, my friends, to rob ourselves of these divine predictions, that we may give all the terror of them to the Jews? We cannot, indeed! It is the very cheat, the very robbery which we *have* practised upon ourselves. The vague conception of some distant universal judgment, which we may describe in grand rhetorical phrases, has hidden from us those direct practical hints respecting a judgment, which might have helped the inhabitants of every city whereon any judgment has fallen, in Europe or in Asia, in the nineteenth century or in the first; which have actually verified themselves in every one. We have lost the special, the minute warnings which might have profited and consoled individuals so much, and shown them their position in the world's history. We have equally lost sight of the universal and the eternal. We have put the dream of a grand assize which merely appeals to the fancy, for the revelation of a Son of Man which speaks to every human conscience. We have forgotten that the trial day which the Jewish Nation passed through must come to the Universal Church. Does not this sentence apply to both?

'*And they answered and said unto him, Where, Lord? And he said unto them, Wheresoever the body is, thither will the eagles be gathered together.*'

LECTURE XXII.

WHO CAN ENTER THE KINGDOM OF HEAVEN.

St. Luke XVIII. 16.

*But Jesus called them unto him, and said, Suffer little children to come
unto me, and forbid them not: for of such is the kingdom of God.*

If the disciples had dreamed that the Kingdom of God
was to come with a pomp and glory which men would
observe, the last discourse of our Lord must have greatly
shaken that expectation. If they had supposed the day of
the Son of Man was to be one of mere brightness to them,
however dark it might be to those who were not disciples,
that comfort must have been overthrown. Calamities were
coming upon their country in that generation. They would
have their full share in these calamities. The danger could
not be escaped anywhere. Their nation was scattered abroad
in different parts of the world. It was perishing. Wherever
any part of the body was, there would the eagles be found
descending upon it. They might well faint at such tidings.

I. ' *He spake a parable to them to this end, that men ought
always to pray, and not to faint.*' The parable is of a widow
oppressed by a very powerful enemy. It is a case of the
weak against the strong. But the case is a very aggravated
one, for the law which should protect the weak against the
strong is in the worst possible hands. An unjust judge is

administering it. Nevertheless, the widow cries. There
is what should be a seat of justice in her city. She will
invoke it. The adversary goads her. She must appeal to
the tribunal, if it is ever so deaf. And the appeal is not
fruitless. The judge calculates that it is less troublesome
to do right than to be tormented with perpetual cries for
redress of wrong. The widow is avenged of her adversary
at last.

'*Hear*,' says our Lord, '*what the unjust judge saith. And
shall not God*,'—shall not He, who is all just—'*avenge his
own elect, which cry day and night unto him, though he bear
long with them?*' Cannot you trust Him to avenge you of
your adversary, who Himself has called you to seek Him,
who is Himself awakening the cry for help? '*I tell you
that He will avenge them speedily.*' Long as the time may
seem to the weary waiter, it will not really be long. He
will wonder afterwards how short the struggle was. '*Nevertheless, when the Son of Man cometh*,'—when there is that
revelation of which I have spoken, that discovery of the
true Friend of Man—'*shall he find faith on earth?*' Will
He be hailed in that character even by those whom He has
chosen to be His witnesses?

The history of Christendom has, I think, answered this
question. What does its existence mean, but this, that a
Son of Man has come, not merely by being born in a
manger, by dying on a cross, but in great power, by rising
from the dead, by ascending on high, by sending His
Spirit, by casting out the nation which had rejected Him
because He claimed to be the Head of all nations? But
where has been the faith that He has actually established
the Kingdom of Heaven on earth, that He has actually
avenged the widow who cried to Him of her adversary?

The Church has believed to a certain extent in Jesus as its own King.   Has it believed in Him as a Son of Man—as the King of Men?   And what kind of unity has it been able to maintain under Him as its own King, whilst it has lost sight of Him as the universal King?   Inevitably, it has set up a mortal king as a substitute for Him, or has been rent into a multitude of sects, with no real Head at all.   The Son of Man has come, and has not found faith on the earth.

II. The next parable helps us to understand why that faith has been so partial, and who have cherished it.

'*And he spake this parable unto certain which trusted in themselves that they were righteous, and despised others : Two men went up into the temple to pray; the one a Pharisee, and the other a publican.   The Pharisee stood and prayed thus with himself, God, I thank thee, that I am not as other men are, extortioners, unjust, adulterers, or even as this publican. I fast twice in the week, I give tithes of all that I possess. And the publican, standing afar off, would not lift up so much as his eyes unto heaven, but smote upon his breast, saying, God be merciful to me a sinner.   I tell you this man went down to his house justified rather than the other: for every one that exalteth himself shall be abased ; and he that humbleth himself shall be exalted.*'

No new sense can be found for this story or parable. The old sense is the true one.   The Pharisee is he who is satisfied with himself, who thinks himself above his fellows.   The publican is he who is dissatisfied with himself, who thinks himself below his fellows.   The Pharisee has no bonds from which he needs to be delivered; he thanks God for what he is.   The publican finds his sins a heavy burden; he cries for mercy to free him.   The one goes empty away. The one who wants mercy finds it. Nothing can be added to this common, generally admitted, interpretation. But we may gain much by connecting this parable with the passage which precedes it and that which follows it. The Pharisee cannot put faith in a Son of Man, for he wishes to be separated from men. He cannot see that the Son of Man is his avenger; of what adversary is he to be avenged? There is an Avenger for the publican, he sees that his own sin is his enemy. He goes down to his house justified, because he has had a glimpse of a Son of Man who is on his side, who is stronger than his enemy. When the Son of Man is manifested to the world, this conscious sinner can hail Him—can say, ' Here is the Lord I have waited for.' This parable shows at least one main part of the reason why the Son of Man has not found faith on earth, and sets before us one class of persons who have clung to Him in all periods.

III. But it has been found possible to change the publican into the Pharisee. Incredible as it seems, we may become proud of our consciousness that we are sinners. We may thank God that we are not as other men, who have not that consciousness. We may use it to destroy faith in the Son of Man. ' He has come to save *us* who feel our sin, ' who cry " Be merciful to us." *We* are in His kingdom ; ' over the rest He does not reign.' Of all kinds of exclusiveness and unbelief this has been, and is, the subtlest. It has assumed the most various shapes, adapting itself to the different modes of thought which have prevailed in Christendom ; nowhere has it been absent; it has been most rampant after strong awakenings of men to the sense of guilt, after fervent confessions of the need of One who can save to the uttermost. When that tide begins to ebb

the deposit is this pride of the publican, this self-satisfac-
tion in the discovery which was made to us, that we have
nothing of our own, that we can only exist by giving up
ourselves.

The next incident which is recorded was at the time,
and has been in all ages since, the most effectual protest
against this denial of Christ's dominion.

'*And they brought unto him also infants, that he would
touch them : but when his disciples saw it, they rebuked them.
But Jesus called them unto him, and said, Suffer little children to come unto me, and forbid them not ; for of such is the
kingdom of God.   Verily I say unto you, Whosoever shall
not receive the kingdom of God as a little child shall in no
wise enter therein.*'

The disciples might have a reasonable excuse· for re-
pulsing the mothers of these children.   They knew perhaps
that it was the habit of women in that land to bring infants
to an enchanter, that he might, by his word, or his touch,
work a charm on them, which would drive off some disease,
or secure them against disease.   Their Master was no such
enchanter ; let not these ignorant people fancy that He was.
So far well.   A desire to honour the truthfulness of Jesus
may have been mixed with their severity.   But there mixed
with it another element ; one of pride in themselves, not
of reverence to Him.   ' We are *men* ; we can understand His
' parables ; we can listen to His commands ; what can these
' infants do ? ' Here is that vanity of consciousness to which
I referred just now ; the secret thought—' He is our King
' because we are capable of choosing Him as our King. He
' has come to save us who are so good or so fortunate as to
' accept Him.' Bring out the thought clearly, and the
conscience of those who confess a Christ shrinks from

it ; but it is not brought out clearly ; it puts on cunning disguises.   The simple words, ' *Suffer little children to come unto me, and forbid them not, for of such is the kingdom of God*,' have done more to strip off the disguises than all arguments.   They have been owned as royal words. ' These ' children are Mine.   Whatever you may think of them, ' I claim them.   For your faith does not make Me your ' Lord.   You do not elect me to be a Sovereign.   If I am ' not King over children, I am not King over men.   If you ' do not receive Me as children, because you are weak, ' because you cannot depend on yourselves, your faith is a ' contradiction.   You do not mean what you say when you ' ask me to be merciful to you as sinners.   That prayer is ' a petition to be treated as children ; to be guided by the ' Divine Spirit because you cannot guide yourselves.'   It is on this ground, my friends, and not on any school reasonings, that the Church rests her Infant Baptism. Those who object to us for treating it as a charm should be listened to with all respect.   That is a great offence against Christ. But this Baptism has been a witness for the Son of Man and the universality of His kingdom, like no other. It has taught parents that to bring children into the world is not a horrible crime.   It has led them to see Christ and His redemption of humanity through all the mists of our teachings and our qualifications.   It has explained the nature of His Kingdom to the hearts of the poorest.   Christ has preached at the fonts, when we have been darkening counsel in pulpits.   On that subject the next story is a lucid commentary.

IV. ' *And a certain ruler asked him, saying, Good Master, what shall I do to inherit eternal life ?   And Jesus said unto him, Why callest thou me good ? none is good, save one, that is, God.   Thou knowest the commandments, Do not commit adultery, Do not kill, Do not steal, Do not bear false witness, Honour thy father and thy mother.   And he said, All these have I kept from my youth up.   Now when Jesus heard these things, he said unto him, Yet lackest thou one thing: sell all that thou hast, and distribute unto the poor, and thou shalt have treasure in heaven: and come, follow me. And when he heard this, he was very sorrowful: for he was very rich.'*

This young ruler has heard that Jesus is proclaiming eternal life to His disciples.   That is what he wants.   He could make great sacrifices to obtain that.   He is stopped at the threshold of his inquiry.   He has called Jesus 'Good Master.'   Mere ordinary words; a civil salutation. Is that word 'good' an ordinary word?   May it be used in a mere civil salutation?   *Good*—does not that describe God Himself.   Is there any one good but He?   A wonderful thought to be suggested to an ardent young man trained in Jewish lore, looking hither and thither for eternal life!   What! has not God spoken to your fathers? Is not He the Good?   Is there any life eternal but His life?

The lesson is pursued.   Has not this good God given you a law—that in which Psalmists and Prophets delighted to meditate?   Has not He told you not to commit adultery, not to kill, not to steal?   What humiliating doctrine!   Why, these commands the young man has kept from his youth up: these the most ordinary people might keep.   That obedience cannot purchase the transcendent blessing he is in search of.   Well! let him try *this* course then.   Let him sell all that he has, give to the poor and follow Christ.   Is he willing to do that?   Not quite.   Have the words, then, no effect?   Yes, a very great effect. He goes away sorrowful. What is so good for him or for any man as to be found out ; to be shown what his professions are worth ; to understand what he is clinging to and cannot part with. This young man may have been one of the disciples who did afterwards sell all that they had, and distribute to those who had need. But before he could do that he had to learn what treasure in heaven meant, and what keeping the commandments meant. That the one is not a selfish prize, but a common inheritance ; that dutiful, thankful obedience to a good God who watches over the life of His creatures, their marriage bonds, their property, is not an easy or ignominious service, but one involving the highest blessing—a participation in His Nature. Giving to the poor ! that would no doubt have been a great thing if he could have done it. But whilst he was exulting in the thought of his difference from the poor, whilst he was wishing to bargain for God's treasures—giving much, though not all, to secure them—what was his giving worth ? He was a rich man ; he had not yet discovered that to be a man was more than to be rich. Is not that the explanation of the next passage, which caused so much astonishment to the disciples, and has caused so much to all ages since ?

V. '*And when Jesus saw that he was very sorrowful, he said, How hardly shall they that have riches enter into the kingdom of God ! For it is easier for a camel to go through a needle's eye, than for a rich man to enter into the kingdom of God.*'

Our Lord does not say that it is hard for a rich man to be religious, or to pursue the rewards of a future state, though that construction has often been put upon the sentence. He says it is hard for him to enter into the

Kingdom of God; hard for him to take his station among other men; hard for him not to value himself on those things which lift him above his fellows; hard for him to become like the publican or the little child; hard for him to think not of what he has or may have, but of Him who is, and how he may know Him and be like Him. This is that passage of the camel through the eye of the needle, that entrance of the giant into the dwarf's cave, which is so difficult. And yet how can the Son of Man be acknowledged, how can the King of Men be seen in Him who humbled himself to the lowest estate, if the rich man does not feel himself on the level of the poorest, if his humanity is not that which is most precious to him?

VI. '*And they that heard it said, Who then can be saved?*' Surely a most natural question, full of profound interest and admitting but of one answer—that being, however, an all-sufficient answer. '*And he said, The things which are impossible with men are possible with God.*' To be saved from this self-exaltation, this inhumanity, is indeed impossible by any efforts of men, by any precepts of men, by any conventions of society. But God, who has appointed riches for men, who has intended that one man should have what another is without, who has organized Society on the law of mutual dependency and charity, does not leave rich men, any more than poor men, to be the victims of their circumstances. He awakens a hunger and thirst in them which nothing but His righteousness will appease. By a thousand methods of gracious discipline He makes them feel that the sorrows which cause the beggar's heart to ache are those which cause the rich man's heart to ache; that the sky and the air which they and the poorest share together are more than what they possess and the other wants; that the trees which their fathers planted were not planted for them; that the country which their fathers fought for and died for is worth more than any other inheritance they have bequeathed; that God is the peasant's God as well as theirs. So the camel is made to pass through the needle's eye; the rich man does enter into the Kingdom of God.

VII. The words, ' Who then can be saved?' indicated awe and humility on the part of the poor fishermen. But soon came the reaction of pride; *their* sense of being better than other men. ' *Then Peter said, Lo, we have left all and followed thee.*' We do not need the blunt question which is given by another Evangelist, ' *What shall we have, therefore,*' to perceive that the bargaining spirit of the ruler was working in the Apostle; that he thought the service of his Master was one which entitled him to large pay; that according to his notion of justice the amount of the reward should be proportioned to the amount of the sacrifice. This sense of justice, be it never so rude, never so mixed with the feelings of a hireling, never so inconsistent with the cry, ' Be merciful to me a sinner,' is not repulsed by Christ. Peter is not exaggerating the blessings to which he has been called, the blessings which are to compensate the loss of his nets and his trade; he is greatly underrating them.

' *And he said unto them, Verily I say unto you, There is no man that hath left house, or parents, or brethren, or wife, or children, for the kingdom of God's sake, who shall not receive manifold more in this present time, and in the world to come life everlasting.*'

To know what the Kingdom of God was, to be the herald of it to the world, was to learn the very meaning of kinsfolk and country, to have a glimpse of the glories of God's universe, to see the earth with clearer, brighter eyes. There was 'manifold more' in this present time. And that because above all, and beneath all, was the Eternal Life, the Life of Him who is, and was, and is to come—the Life which depended on no circumstances, which was affected by no changes, which would reveal itself fully in the world or age to come.

VIII. But then follows the correction of Peter's selfish calculations.

'*Then he took unto him the twelve, and said unto them, Behold, we go up to Jerusalem, and all things that are written by the prophets concerning the Son of man shall be accomplished. For he shall be delivered unto the Gentiles, and shall be mocked, and spitefully entreated, and spitted on : And they shall scourge him, and put him to death : and the third day he shall rise again.*'

We are going up to Jerusalem. Now, then, is the moment in which you think you may have the rewards of your service. Now you expect that the Son of David will take His crown and dispense His honours. Hear *what* that crown will be ; *what* honours are likely to await His ministers. All that you have read in the Prophets of the sufferings which they underwent in their day will be gathered up in the Son of Man whom they longed for. It is not only your countrymen who will heap scorn on their native ruler. They will call in the Gentiles to help them. He will be scourged. Yes! and He will die. There will be no heavenly powers to deliver Him. But He will rise out of death. It is the way to His Kingdom.

IX. Strange comfort this for men who had left all and

followed Christ, and were wondering how much better they should fare than the rich man for having done so! '*And they understood none of these things : and this saying was hid from them, neither knew they the things which were spoken. And it came to pass, that as he was come nigh unto Jericho, a certain blind man sat by the wayside begging : and hearing the multitude pass by, he asked what it meant. And they told him, that Jesus of Nazareth passeth by. And he cried, saying, Jesus, thou son of David, have mercy on me. And they which went before rebuked him, that he should hold his peace : but he cried so much the more, Thou son of David, have mercy on me. And Jesus stood, and commanded him to be brought unto him : and when he was come near, he asked him, saying, What wilt thou that I shall do unto thee ? And he said, Lord, that I may receive my sight. And Jesus said unto him, Receive thy sight : thy faith hath saved thee. And immediately he received his sight, and followed him, glorifying God : and all the people, when they saw it, gave praise unto God.*'

Here was a practical lesson. This blind beggar discovered what a Son of David, a true King of Men, must be ; one who can feel with His subjects, suffer with them, deliver them out of their plagues and torments. He had an adversary which hindered him from exercising the powers and privileges of a man. He had cried, and had found the avenger, the friend of His race—the one who could help the meanest member of it. Thus in that age, thus in every age, has the Son of Man been revealed to those whom He is not ashamed to call His brethren. Thus do publicans, children, beggars, find out His signs, and are led by Him to the Father from whom He has come, while the rich, who wish to buy the treasures of the

Kingdom of Heaven, go away sorrowful—whilst His disciples, looking for the pay of hirelings, understand nothing of His death or His resurrection. The rich ruler and the proud disciples, if they were brought to the level of the publican, the children, the beggar, might claim His Death and Resurrection with them—might enter into the same Eternal Life.

LECTURE XXIII.

St. Luke XIX. 41.

And when he was come near, he beheld the city, and wept over it.

I. How the Son of David was discovered by the blind
Bartimæus ; how He was invoked by that name to heal
a wayside beggar, we considered last week. As He enters
into Jericho, we hear of a rich man who bows before Him
as the poor man had bowed. But Zacchæus, though rich,
is a tax-gatherer. All the odium of his class belongs to
him. Probably he has deserved it. The complaint, '*He is
gone to be guest with a man that is a sinner*' taken in connexion with his own words, has struck most readers as
implying more than that Zacchæus had gained his wealth
in an unpopular occupation. But if it was so, there had
been awakened in him a craving for that which riches, well
or ill-gotten, could not buy ; yes, for a deliverance from
that which they had bought. The money-getter climbs
into a sycamore-tree, that he may get sight of one who, he
is told, is a Galilean Peasant. There is a witness in his
heart that this Peasant can do for him what no one
else can do. His King speaks to him in that Peasant.
'*Zacchæus, make haste and come down, for to-day I must
abide in thy house.*' He does not ask, as Bartimæus did,
that he may receive his sight ; but scales fall from his

inward eyes. The curse of riches and the use of riches, are revealed to him. He starts from a money-getter and a money-worshipper into a man. He does not repent of some vague general sin. He repents of that which has been besetting him. He casts that off in the strength of the friend whom he has found so near to him. '*Behold,*' he says, '*Lord, the half of my goods I give to the poor, and if I have taken anything from any man by false accusation, I restore him fourfold.*' Is he answered, ' Yes ; that resolution, ' if it is well kept, will procure the pardon of thy sins ; ' that surrender of thy goods may buy heaven for thee in ' spite of thy past wrong-doings ?' No ; but he hears words immeasurably more assuring and elevating than those. '*This day is salvation come to this house, forsomuch as he also is a son of Abraham.*' To be saved out of that money-worship which has degraded thee, enslaved thee, made thee incapable of entering into the glory of thy race, into thy citizenship as an Israelite, this is the highest gift which thy Prince can confer on thee. Now thou mayst walk the earth and look up to the heavens as a freeman. To give that freedom, I have come into the world. '*The Son of Man is come to seek and to save that which was lost.*'

II. They are approaching Jerusalem. There is a strange awe on the minds of the disciples. All these acts of royalty done on behalf of men who lie quite out of the path of ordinary teachers, whom the religious men of the land utterly scorn, increase their feeling that a revolution is at hand ; that the Kingdom of God is about to displace the kingdom of the Sanhedrim and the kingdom of the Romans. Therefore we are told, He added and spake a parable to them.

'*He said, A certain nobleman went into a far country to receive for himself a kingdom, and to return.*' The case might have occurred recently. It was one which they all knew had occurred, and was likely to occur. A member of the Herodian family, unable to maintain himself in the tetrarchy or kingdom which had been committed to him against his refractory subjects, travels to Rome that he may obtain a confirmation of it from the Cæsar, may strengthen and establish himself in it. He is a ruler, then, already. He leaves behind him a number of persons who acknowledge his authority, and wait for his return. To these he entrusts a certain treasure, bidding them make the most of it, and give him an account whenever he should call for it. The incidents which concern this kingdom cannot be detached from the parable ; they belong to the very essence of it. The disciples had thought that the Kingdom of God would immediately appear. Our Lord does not say now—He did not say before—It will *not* appear. He had said to the Pharisees, 'The kingdom of God cometh not *with observation.*' He illustrates those words to the disciples in reference to their own conduct. They would be shortly called to tell the House of Israel that the Son of David had come ; that God had established Him on His throne. But there would be no appearance of a throne. The King would seem to be away in a far country. His citizens would seem to have effectually banished Him. They who acknowledged His dominion would learn its reality by a deposit which He would entrust to them. It would not be a dead deposit, a treasure to be hoarded. It must be used ; it must be traded with. He would expect to find when He called for it, that they had laid it out to advantage. If it was kept hidden in a napkin ; He would know that they were not faithful to Him; that they did not really care for Him; that their loyalty was the loyalty of fear, not of trust.

You know that there are two different forms in which this parable is told in the Evangelists. In St. Matthew, various sums are given to the stewards. One has five talents, another two, another one. Here all have the same. I believe the observation of this diversity is very instructive and very helpful to the understanding of our Lord's purpose. When we read the Acts of the Apostles, we find the gift of the Spirit described as *the* great gift to the Church, *the* witness of the dominion of the Son of Man, *the* power by which His Apostles could show forth His Resurrection and His final triumph over His enemies. We also hear of *gifts* of the Spirit distributed variously to men according to the good pleasure of His will: the word of wisdom being entrusted to one, the word of knowledge to another, powers of healing to a third. The parable in St. Matthew, I apprehend, points to these last, and to the use which is made of them; the parable before us to the Divine Spirit itself, the endowment upon which all the others depended, which must be represented as one though its manifestations are manifold. When this Spirit came upon the Apostles, they spoke with undoubted confidence of a Divine kingdom. They knew that they were the subjects of one. They could call every man to confess himself a subject of the same. Every power and faculty within them was aroused, that they might fill their position. That which was torpid became active; that which had been bound with the ice of winter felt the breath and warmth of spring. Those who yielded to the stirrings of this life were raised out of themselves. It came forth in human sympathies. It drew their hearts to the Son of Man, from whom it was derived. To think of such a talent as intended to lie idle in a miser's chest was to deny its nature. It was made to grow, to become greater by exercise, to send its virtue abroad. The cultivation of it would be different. In one the pound would increase to ten pounds. There would be such an unfolding of spiritual energies, such a vigorous concentration and application of all the forces within, that every day would multiply them and the benefits accruing from them. In another, the results would be weaker; still there would be the expansion which betokens the presence of life. In each case, the reward would be proportionate to the power which had been acquired. For the reward is not repose, but fresh work, a larger sphere of usefulness and influence. The command over ten cities is given to the man whose pound had grown to ten pounds; the command of five cities to the man whose pound had grown to five pounds. The faculty of doing good, by an eternal law, is multiplied and magnified according to the use which is made of it. And then follows the deepest and most solemn moral of the story. Whenever this gift is not stirred up in the man, whenever it goes to waste, the cause is this. He suspects the Giver. He thinks of Him as '*a hard master, reaping where he has not sown, gathering where he has not strawed.*' The heathens called the Divine nature an envious nature. They supposed that the powers above grudged the prosperity of men below. This is a more subtle form of the same falsehood. The man who has been taught that God has bestowed His Spirit upon him dwells not on the grandeur of the trust, nor on the love of Him who has called him to be His fellow-worker, but on the peril of offending a Judge whom it is impossible to satisfy, who may crush him to atoms if he fails. All the time a voice, speaking to his conscience, is reminding him of his inconsistency. 'If thou hast such an inexorable 'Master, why dost thou not work more diligently to con-'tent Him?' He cannot; his limbs are palsied. Some power must move them, and the power is wanting, for trust is wanting, love is wanting.

The parable is two-edged. Those Jews who said, 'We will not have the Son of Man to reign over us,' were themselves exhibiting the temper which our Lord attributes to the man who hid his talent in a napkin. They would not use the mighty trust which God had committed to them for the good of the nations, because they thought of God as a hard Master. They first persuaded themselves that He frowned on the world, and only smiled on them. Then, by a just retribution, His smiles to them had the effect of terrible frowns. They felt that they ought to be doing something which they were not doing. They thought Him more hard and exacting to them than to the rest of the world, though that was doomed to perdition.

But this story was especially to remind the disciples that this temper would appear in *them*, the stewards of His more perfect covenant, of His highest treasure. The cause would be the same; the result would be the same. They would think of God as a hard Master first to mankind, then to themselves; consequently they would let the divine gift rust. They would suppose it a dead thing, to be returned to the owner, as if He had only endowed them with some words written in stones or in a book, not with a living Spirit capable of continually receiving fresh life, and of communicating it.

In both these applications the words which follow are very awful. '*For I say unto you, That unto every one which hath shall be given; and from him that hath not, even that he hath shall be taken away from him.*' They are translated for the Jewish people into these. '*But those mine enemies, which would not that I should reign over them, bring hither, and slay them before me.*' They were left to their enemies because they would not believe in a friend; they found the hardest of all masters because they would not serve the most gracious. It is added significantly, '*And when he had thus spoken, he went before, ascending up to Jerusalem.*' For now the time was approaching when there should be a formal declaration in that city. 'This is ' not the King we choose; we want one as nearly as possible ' the reverse of him.'

III. '*And it came to pass, when he was come nigh to Beth-phage and Bethany, at the mount called the mount of Olives, he sent two of his disciples, saying, Go ye into the village over against you; in the which at your entering ye shall find a colt tied whereon yet never man sat: loose him, and bring him hither. And if any man ask you, Why do ye loose him? thus shall ye say unto him, Because the Lord hath need of him. And they that were sent went their way, and found even as he had said unto them. And as they were loosing the colt, the owners thereof said unto them, Why loose ye the colt? And they said, The Lord hath need of him. And they brought him to Jesus: and they cast their garments upon the colt, and they sat Jesus thereon. And as he went, they spread their clothes in the way. And when he was come nigh, even now at the descent of the mount of Olives, the whole multitude of the disciples began to rejoice and praise God with a loud voice for all the mighty works that they had seen; saying, Blessed*

be the King that cometh in the name of the Lord : peace in
heaven, and glory in the highest.'

In every one of the Gospels the descent from the Mount
of Olives, and the entrance of Jesus into Jerusalem, is recorded as if it were a critical point in the narrative. Clearly
it could not be so if the object of the Evangelists had been
to present Him primarily as a Teacher or a Prophet. There
is nothing in the circumstances of that act which is characteristic of the Prophet ; you cannot conceive Elijah,
Isaiah, or Ezekiel taking that method of asserting his mission, if it had been ever so much denied. It recalls at once
the Judge or the Monarch. The command to fetch the
ass, *' The Lord hath need of him,'* has a special air of
authority and royalty. The people could not have raised
any cry but *' Blessed be the King that cometh in the*
name of the Lord,' or, *' Hosanna to the Son of David.'*
The garments spread in the way, however simple an
expression of reverence, could have but one signification.
If the shouts were from feeble voices, they were yet
felt by the Pharisees to be ominous of a new dynasty.
They said, *' Rebuke thy disciples.'* And His answer, *' I tell*
you that, if these should hold their peace, the stones would
immediately cry out,' was an emphatic declaration that when
there were none left to be witnesses of the real Head of
the city, the Corner-stone of the living temple, the material
stones would be found to have no cohesion ; they would
fall to pieces.

This thought was surely in His mind as He looked
down upon that dear and venerable city, and wept over it.
Preachers have chosen to paraphrase the words, and to
talk of the ' Redeemer's tears over lost souls.' When Jesus
speaks of the Son of man as coming to seek and save

that which was lost, I adhere to His language; I take it
to be the best.   When it is said, '*He beheld the city, and
wept over it,*' I understand that the City is meant, and not
something else.   If it seems to us an unworthy subject of
Christ's sorrow, that a divine polity which had lasted so
many generations—which God, and not man, had set up—
which had been the witness to the world that it is God, and
not man, who binds the societies of men into one, should
be about to pass away with its temple, its sacrifices,
all the outward signs of what it was within,—I think we
can have read sacred history to very little purpose.   See
whether every page of the Old Testament is not setting
forth to us the glory of national life.   See whether it was
not through their national life that patriarchs and prophets
were led to believe in Him who is, and was, and is to
come—who would be with the children as He had been
with the fathers—who would reveal Himself more to each
generation, till at last the earth should be filled with His
glory.   And now the Jew was deliberately casting aside
this marvellous education.   He was exalting a Mammon
God into the throne of Jehovah.   His religion was becoming another name for a selfish calculation of his individual interests.   Sects were rending the commonwealth
in pieces.   Do we want more than this to account for
Christ's tears, and for the words, '*If thou hadst known, even
thou, at least in this thy day, the things which belong unto
thy peace.*'   'Oh! that you would have owned Him, who
'would have healed your savage religious strifes, who would
'have bound you into one family, who would have shown
'you that the God of Abraham, and Isaac, and Jacob, is as
'truly your God as He was theirs.'   '*But now these things
are hid from thine eyes.*'   A thick impenetrable blindness is

coming upon you. You are cut off from the vision of the past. The brightness of the ages to come will be lost upon you. For when God's light is changed into darkness, when your desire is to conceal yourselves from Him, what else can look beautiful to you—what is there for you but ever-deepening gloom over heaven and over earth?

IV. *'For the days shall come upon thee, that thine enemies shall cast a trench about thee, and compass thee round, and keep thee in on every side, and shall lay thee even with the ground, and thy children within thee; and they shall not leave in thee one stone upon another; because thou knewest not the time of thy visitation.'*

Surely these are direct words; they cannot be reduced into figures. We cannot talk of casting a trench about 'lost souls,' or laying them even with the ground. The language belongs, if there is any truth in it, to a city and a temple. And therefore we read immediately after:

'And he went into the temple, and began to cast out them that sold therein, and them that bought; saying unto them, It is written, My house is the house of prayer: but ye have made it a den of thieves. And he taught daily in the temple. But the chief priests and the scribes, and the chief of the people sought to destroy him, and could not find what they might do: for all the people were very attentive to hear him.'

So Christ carried the war with Mammon into the very place where he was affronting the majesty of the Father. So He testified, that if Mammon was not cast out, God would depart from that place and leave it desolate.

The chief priests and the Pharisees felt that the battle was to be a deadly one. The Galilean was confronting them in their own capital. If He was the King He had found them out; He was calling them to answer for their government over the people. He might destroy them. First they would try if they could not destroy Him. The experiment must be made cautiously. ' *The people were very attentive to hear him.*' Their influence was trembling. There might be an insurrection. Who could say where it would end?

Oh, my friends! we cannot afford to divert this history from its direct purpose. Is not England a nation which Christ has cared for as much as He ever cared for Palestine? Is not London a city which He may weep over as much as He wept over Jerusalem? Have we known the things that belong to our peace? Have we asked Him to put down our factions, to give us His love for our hatred? Are there none that sell and buy in our temples? Must not *they* be purged?

LECTURE XXIV.

St. Luke XX. 1, 2.

And it came to pass, that on one of those days, as he taught the people in the temple, and preached the Gospel, the chief priests and the scribes came upon him with the elders, and spake unto him, saying, Tell us, by what authority doest thou these things? or who is he that gave thee this authority?

I. *'The people were very attentive to hear him.'* These were the last words which we heard in the 19th chapter. *'He was teaching the people in the temple, and preaching the gospel.'* These are the words which meet us when we open this chapter. The people are full of eagerness for a Kingdom of God. What it is they do not know. Something very different it must be from the kingdom of the priests; something very different from the kingdom of the Cæsars. Of such a kingdom Jesus, the Prophet of Galilee, is speaking in the very heart of the capital—in the temple itself. The news sounds like good news. Crowds listen to it.

There comes a grave procession of chief priests, and scribes, and elders. All the dignity of the Jewish religion and the Jewish nation is there; all that can awe the new Teacher. They have heard that He is talking of a kingdom; they have heard that He has assumed a right to purge the temple. They would like to know by what authority He did these things. Whence did he derive it? *'And he answered and said unto them, I will also ask you one thing;*

*and answer me ; The baptism of John, was it from heaven,
or of men ?'* John had come amongst them apparently
without any authority; he had wrought no miracle to
prove that he had a right to be heard. *Had* he a right to
be heard? He spoke of Repentance. He spoke of a
Kingdom of God. The people went out to him. Ought
they to have gone? Was his message an earthly or
heavenly one? *'And they reasoned with themselves, saying,
If we shall say, From heaven ; he will say, Why then believed
ye him not ? But and if we say, Of men ; all the people will
stone us : for they be persuaded that John was a prophet.'*
It was a calculation with them in all cases what answer
would be a safe one ; what the consequence would be of
saying 'Yes' or 'No.' On the whole, their reply came as
near the truth as a reply of theirs could come. The messenger might have been a heavenly one; they could not
positively say that he was not. Though he wanted the
proper signs of one, the people had an instinct that he
knew secrets which none but a divine teacher could know.
The true man, they thought, was sent by the true God.
The chief priests and scribes hated the people, and feared
what they hated. If the multitude grew violent, what
might it not do? They might be its first victims. It
was better to avow ignorance, though that was unpleasant
and might weaken their influence, than to incur this
peril. *'And Jesus said unto them, Neither tell I you by
what authority I do these things.'* You cannot find out
whence came the power of the man who called you to
repent. You cannot find out mine. My authority, like
John's, must prove itself. If it does not prove itself to
you, you will never know what it is.

II. And it did prove itself to them. *'Then began he to*

speak to the people this parable; A certain man planted a vineyard, and let it forth to husbandmen, and went into a far country for a long time.   And at the season he sent a servant to the husbandmen, that they should give him of the fruit of the vineyard : but the husbandmen beat him, and sent him away empty.   And again he sent another servant : and they beat him also, and entreated him shamefully, and sent him away empty.   And again he sent a third : and they wounded him also, and cast him out.   Then said the lord of the vineyard, What shall I do ?   I will send my beloved son : it may be they will reverence him when they see him.   But when the husbandmen saw him, they reasoned among themselves, saying, This is the heir : come, let us kill him, that the inheritance may be our's.   So they cast him out of the vineyard, and killed him.   What therefore shall the lord of the vineyard do unto them ?   He shall come and destroy these husbandmen, and shall give the vineyard to others.   And when they heard it, they said, God forbid.'   The parable took the old form.   To the readers of the divine book it recalled the song in Isaiah 'To my well-beloved, concerning his vineyard.' To those who dwelt among vineyards, and knew how vineyards were leased out, it was the liveliest instance of an actual trust which had been violated—of actual profits 'that were demanded, and refused.   It recalled the past history of the land, interpreting the messages of the prophets—the treatment of the prophets.   It brought distinctly before them their state of mind at that time.   They did hate Him who was speaking to them. Was it the same kind of hatred which their fathers had for the prophets ?   Was it not more intense ?   Why ?   A flash of light came into their consciences.   WAS it a Son of the great Husbandman who had been sent to them ?

Such flashes come and go. They provoke a momentary terror which soon passes into bitterer wrath. The cry, 'God forbid,' or 'Let it not be,' was the natural utterance of the terror. Oh, let us not be cast out of the vineyard! Let not our house be left desolate.

'*And he beheld them, and said, What is this then that is written, The stone which the builders rejected, the same is become the head of the corner? Whosoever shall fall upon that stone shall be broken; but on whomsoever it shall fall, it will grind him to powder. And the chief priests and the scribes the same hour sought to lay hands on him; and they feared the people: for they perceived that he had spoken this parable against them.*' Is it not the Heir you are rejecting? Have not your prophets spoken of a corner-stone of the nation, of one who alone could bind it together? Are you not trying to build up your nation without that corner-stone? Do you not think it will prove itself stronger than any one who dashes himself against it? Do you not think that if it falls upon your poor fabric the whole will be ground to powder? In those words we read the great Gospel to humanity; the announcement of the living Centre which was to unite all its arches, to knit its loose fragments into a whole. The chief priests and scribes read in it their sentence, which they must avert, if possible, by laying hands on the Reprover.

III. But there was a gospel also for *nations;* a gospel concerning the cause of national slavery; the true means of national emancipation. Thus was it preached:—

'*And they watched him, and sent forth spies, which should feign themselves just men, that they might take hold of his words, that so they might deliver him unto the power and authority of the governor. And they asked him, saying,*

*Master, we know that thou sayest and teachest rightly, neither
acceptest thou the person of any, but teachest the way of God
truly : Is it lawful for us to give tribute unto Cæsar, or no ?
But he perceived their craftiness, and said unto them, Why
tempt ye me ?   Shew me a penny.   Whose image and superscription hath it ?   They answered and said, Cæsar's.   And
he said unto them, Render therefore unto Cæsar the things
which be Cæsar's, and unto God the things which be God's.
And they could not take hold of his words before the people :
and they marvelled at his answer, and held their peace.'*

One can well understand the calculation which led to
this plot. ' He speaks of a Kingdom of God. The people
' suppose that He means freedom to the land ; freedom from
' Rome. Will He dare to avow that He does ? If not, His
' influence with the multitude is gone. Or else we have a
' direct charge to bring before Pilate.' The plot itself is well
laid. The messengers have a case of conscience. They do
not quite see their duty. Ought they to comply with the
demands of the tax-gatherer or to resist ? Of course He
will tell them frankly ; He is not afraid of any man. The
answer of our Lord is often represented as a kind of skilful
evasion. An evasion would have been fatal. The spies
were armed against that danger. *They* might evade. He
would, they were sure, make a direct answer. He met
them with defiance. He denounced them as hypocrites.
They had not come with a case of conscience. They knew
they had not. They had come to entrap Him.

But their question should be answered nevertheless. They
wished to know whether they were to pay tribute to the
emperor. What tribute did they pay ? Coins ? Let Him see
one of the coins. There is an image upon it. Whose image ?
The emperor's. There is a superscription upon it. Whose

x

superscription? The emperor's. Render to him by all
means that which is his. Your money is stamped by him.
Your dealings go on under his sanction. Do not withdraw
that from him. You cannot. He has proved his claim to
it. But render to God the things that are God's. Has
not He stamped His image anywhere? Is not His superscription to be discovered anywhere? Think where they
ought to be ; be sure that is His.

Here is the very principle of the Kingdom of Heaven ;
here is the proof that Christ did come to emancipate slaves
from the yoke of a tyrant, not to discourse about a religion.
The yoke of the Roman was upon the Jewish heart. That
was doing homage to the purple. That was coveting a king
just like the Cesars. And *therefore* they fancied that the
great bondage was the necessity of paying tribute. They
grudged their money. They yielded up themselves. While
this was so, there might be perpetual insurrections ; there
would be no freedom. They would be 'slaves by their
own compulsion.' They would lose the protection and
security of the Roman government ; they would bring
down its iron hand upon them. But they would not
recover their manhood ; they would not rise to be a nation.
The words have been heard through ages of Christian history. They have been perverted to various uses. They
have been turned into apologies for tyranny. They have
been turned into excuses for rebellion. The Cesar has
been taken disloyally and unpatriotically to represent a
native sovereign ruling according to law. God has been
blasphemously confounded with the ecclesiastical power—
often when it was most flagrantly violating justice, and
setting aside the maxims of Christ. But the grand truth
enunciated in the dialogue has asserted itself through all

these misrepresentations.   Tribute is not the cause of a nation's bondage, only the outward sign of it.   While it is debased, while it is confessing gold or outward power as its god, it cannot better itself by shaking off that badge of subjection ; it becomes worse, more anarchical, liable to fall under a grosser tyranny than that which it casts away. When the spirit is freed, when it bows to the God who sets free, the fetters fall from the hands.

IV. Both sects of the Jews were now to try whether they could not withdraw the people from the common enemy. The Sadducees might seem to have few resources for this purpose.   They obviously despised the multitude and its faith ; their lore was professedly for the refined.   But surely they were not wrong in thinking that they had arguments which would appeal very directly to the animal instincts of a crowd—to their broad notions of what was likely or unlikely.

' *Then came to him certain of the Sadducees, which deny that there is any resurrection; and they asked him, saying, Master, Moses wrote unto us, If any man's brother die, having a wife, and he die without children, that his brother should take his wife, and raise up seed unto his brother.   There were therefore seven brethren : and the first took a wife, and died without children.   And the second took her to wife, and he died childless.   And the third took her ; and in like manner the seven also : and they left no children, and died.   Last of all the woman died also.   Therefore in the resurrection whose wife of them is she ? for seven had her to wife.*'

So far as this argument was drawn from Jewish customs and the Mosaic law, it was very suitable for its immediate purpose.   The principle of it is the one which has affected, and does affect, the minds of all men, Jews, Heathens,

Christians, when they think of a life after death. 'Why 'should I not continue?' asks Butler. 'Are you not bound 'to show why the event you call death should break the 'thread of my individual existence?' 'Continue; how?' says the objector. 'Do you mean that all our relations, 'with the persons and things we see, are to continue? '*Whose wife then shall she be of the seven?*' that is the natural shape in which the doubt presents itself.

'*And Jesus answering said unto them, The children of this world marry, and are given in marriage: but they which shall be accounted worthy to obtain that world, and the resurrection from the dead, neither marry, nor are given in marriage: neither can they die any more: for they are equal unto the angels; and are the children of God, being the children of the resurrection.*'

When we first consider this reply, it has, I think, a mournful sound. We accept the inference which so many have drawn from it. We practically throw off Butler's doctrine of continuance. The future world is to be altogether unlike the present. All that has been most dear, most necessary, most human here, is to be wanting there. Then, as a maxim of practical conduct, are not those right who say, 'The more we can detach ourselves from the 'relations which are to terminate so soon the better. The 'hermit's life is the safe life.' Before we quite adopt that opinion, let us listen to our Lord's concluding words. '*Now that the dead are raised, even Moses shewed at the bush, when he calleth the Lord the God of Abraham, and the God of Isaac, and the God of Jacob. For he is not a God of the dead, but of the living: for all live unto him.*'

The God of Abraham, and Isaac, and Jacob! Was ever a greater honour put upon human relationships—upon this special relationship of father to son—than that? Was ever so distinct an assertion of the permanence of this relationship? We actually learn from it the very truth of immortality; we acquire from it the sense of our own continuance. The hermit cuts himself off from this evidence; his isolation from the present, his determination to be alone here, darkens his vision of the future. So we are brought to the secret of our Lord's words, to that which makes them a real confutation of the Sadducees' doubt, and of our doubt—a real message to the people, as well as to the earnest thinker. The Pharisee had the *dogma* of a Resurrection. Christ will not separate the Resurrection from God. The children of the Resurrection are the children of God. They live because He lives. Man continues because He continues. He has ordained the relations of men. Cannot they leave Him to take care of them—Him to maintain His own order? What have the accidents of those relationships here, what have the outward regulations concerning them, to do with their true nature as He sees it? Poor man! Do you fear that the wife or child that was bound to your heart here, will be torn from you there? That is a dream of death. That belongs to a death world. Is He not the living God? Is not the living God, the God of the living? Is He not the God of the fathers, and of the children?

'*Then certain of the scribes answering said, Master, thou hast well said.*' It might be merely the triumph of schoolmen feeling that their adversaries had been confuted by a few simple words—by the most familiar of all sentences. It might be the genuine witness of human hearts. 'Yes; 'that is, indeed, the Gospel of a Resurrection. We never 'believed it before, often as we have argued about it.'

Either feeling is compatible with the kind of awe expressed in the next verse. *'And after that they durst not ask him any question at all.'*

V. But He asked *them* a question ; the most searching that had perhaps ever been presented to them.

'And he said unto them, How say they that Christ is David's son? And David himself saith in the book of Psalms, The Lord said unto my Lord, Sit thou on my right hand, till I make thine enemies thy footstool. David therefore calleth him Lord, how is he then his son?'

If our Lord met doubts fairly and fully, even when they were raised by the most captious of His enemies—political doubts, such as that concerning the tribute, religious doubts, such as that concerning the resurrection—He also Himself provoked doubts. He led His disciples, and the scribes and the people, to compare passages in the Scripture which looked as if they were contradictory; to face the difficulties from which they would have been most inclined to shrink as perilous to the security of their faith. For faith in His teaching never means acquiescence. In the child it is not that, but trust from a sense of feebleness. In the man it scarcely begins till acquiescence and security end. Those who are comfortable and satisfied in themselves do not care to look beyond themselves.

No doubt is really so deep, so fundamental as this : 'How can David's son be David's Lord?' If the Jew had honestly grappled with it—if he had said, 'There must ' be a solution of it somewhere, or my Scriptures are false ; 'there must be a solution of it somewhere, or the testi- ' monies in my conscience are false ; since otherwise my ' Lord is not my brother'—if he had spoken thus with himself, he would have perceived that the puzzle was not a verbal one, and that no words could remove it. The Person in whom he discovered most of human sympathy, most of lowliness, would then have been recognised as having most Divine power—HE would have been the explanation of the riddle. But there was a reason why they could not accept this explanation. What was the reason ? Was it that they did not read their sacred books ? that they did not pore over the prophecies contained in them ? The scribes, who did this most, who were always reading the sacred books, always bringing forth interpretations of them, were those in whom this unbelief was the strongest, who revolted with the greatest horror from the notion that the Galilean peasant could be the Son of God. Is not the reason given here ?—' *Then in the audience of all the people he said unto his disciples, Beware of the scribes, which desire to walk in long robes, and love greetings in the markets, and the highest seats in the synagogues, and the chief rooms at feasts; which devour widows' houses, and for a shew make long prayers : the same shall receive greater damnation.*'

Those who loved to exalt themselves above other men could not confess Him as royal, as Divine, who stooped to be the servant of all. Those who devoured widows' houses could not accept a King who came to answer the cry of the widow and deliver her from the tormentors who assumed His authority. Those who craved to be seen of men could not abide the eye of the Judge who pierced through all veils into the secret heart. Therefore, upon that age of religious profession and self-glorification was coming greater damnation than had fallen upon all that had gone before it.

LECTURE XXV.

St. Luke XXI. 31.

*So likewise ye, when ye see these things come to pass, know ye that the
kingdom of God is nigh at hand.*

THE event which Whitsuntide commemorates has so many
aspects, that it is not wonderful if even an important
aspect should be overlooked. But it is strange that we
scarcely ever advert to the one which St. Peter puts most
prominently forward in his discourse on the day of Pentecost. An old prophet—the oldest, probably, of those whose
writings have come down to us—had spoken of an outpouring of the Spirit on all flesh, before a great and terrible
day of the Lord should come. St. Peter's mind is evidently
filled with the anticipation of such a day. The gift which
he and his brother-fishermen had received, the powers
which they were to exercise, had been expressly bestowed
to prepare them and their countrymen for such a day. Its
meaning and nature might still be obscure to them. The
Holy Spirit would gradually remove the obscurity. He
would show them what brightness and glory lay behind
the gloom which was thickening and which must at last
cover the land. If this be so, there can be scarcely a fitter
chapter for Whitsuntide than the one which comes next
under our notice. And Whitsuntide, in turn, will be the
best interpreter of it.

* Preached on Whitsunday.

There is much in it which recalls the latter part of the seventeenth chapter. Why should they have been separated? What need to repeat warnings that seem to have been given already?

I am very anxious that you should observe how much the coming of the Son of man, the downfall of the old polity, the discovery of the Kingdom of Heaven, is the subject of the whole Gospel, from the moment that the preacher in the wilderness spoke of an axe which was laid to the root of the trees, till Christ was lifted up. You perceive the order of the Gospels—of this Gospel especially—just in proportion as that fact becomes evident to you. But you will not forget that the former words were spoken as He went up to Jerusalem, because He was asked whether the Kingdom of God would immediately appear. They were suggested by an *approach* to the city. These are spoken while He is sitting by the Temple. You have heard that He began His work in Jerusalem by purging the Temple; that all His preaching has been in the Temple. The very first words in the chapter have reference to it:—

(1) '*And he looked up, and saw the rich men casting their gifts into the treasury. And he saw also a certain poor widow casting in thither two mites. And he said, Of a truth I say unto you, that this poor widow hath cast in more than they all : For all these have of their abundance cast in unto the offerings of God : but she of her penury hath cast in all the living that she had.*'

I do not doubt that the real charity of the widow was contrasted, as we have all supposed, with the ostentatious charity of those who gave alms to be seen of men. But I think her real reverence for the glory of the Temple, for the place in which God's presence dwelt, is also contrasted with the ostentatious care of the rich Jews to adorn the outside of the Temple with their goodly gifts. To these His attention is now drawn; these give the occasion to all the subsequent discourse. *'And as some spake of the temple, how it was adorned with goodly stones and gifts, he said, As for these things which ye behold, the days will come, in the which there shall not be left one stone upon another, that shall not be thrown down.'* The sentence had a very awful sound indeed. The eager question that follows shows how awful it seemed to the disciples. *'And they asked him, saying, Master, but when shall these things be? and what sign will there be when these things shall come to pass?'* Had not they heard this before? Was it new to them? They had been prepared for a great crisis, for a day of the Lord; but the destruction of the *Temple,* of the building which had borne witness for the God of Abraham, and Isaac, and Jacob, of the barrier, as it seemed, between idolatrous worship and the true worship, *that* was something altogether wonderful. Could the Kingdom of God be introduced by such a sign as that? Would it not be the sign that the Kingdom of God was utterly perishing from the earth?

(2) So assuredly it would be felt. And to this the warning in these verses refer. *And he said, Take heed that ye be not deceived: for many shall come in my name, saying, I am Christ; and the time draweth near: go ye not therefore after them. But when ye shall hear of wars and commotions, be not terrified: for these things must first come to pass; but the end is not by and by.'* When the city was threatened, there would be an expectation of some Deliverer, some Anointed One from heaven, to drive away the hosts of the

heathen. 'He surely *must* come to save the Temple. God
cannot let that perish.' The disciples would be open to
these deceptions as well as others. They expected the
revelation of a kingdom more than any. When they heard
of wars in Palestine, of commotions elsewhere, they could
not doubt that these were announcements of it. Their
Master might be descending Himself to deliver His Father's
House, and to make it the centre of the earth. He might be
sending some angelic messenger to do that work. Who could
say whether this or that man might not have the authority
which he boasted, which he probably believed, that He
had ? The words, ' *Go not after them nor follow them,*' which
had been spoken before, might well, therefore, be repeated.
The Christs who appeared because the Temple was falling
would be deceivers like the rest. It was not to be saved.
Till it fell, the end of the age had not come, however
many preparations there might be for it. To these preparations He directs their thoughts.

(3) ' *Then said he unto them, Nation shall rise against nation, and kingdom against kingdom : And great earthquakes
shall be in divers places, and famines, and pestilences ; and
fearful sights and great signs shall there be from heaven.*' The
time between the day on which our Lord spoke these words
beside the Temple, and that in which the Temple fell, has
been described by a dull Jewish historian and by the most
profound of Roman historians. If the former tells of the
bloody and fruitless encounters of his countrymen against
the forces of the empire, the other tells us of the convul-
sions in the empire itself, of the ruin which was threatening it from its own defenders, of the German race which
it could not subdue and which might at last subdue it.
Both alike testify of the physical calamities which make

a guilty and infidel, and therefore superstitious age, tremble more than any political trials; which *seem* to come more directly from the powers above. The warnings in this discourse point to much more general and grand events than those in the seventeenth chapter, which alluded to the stuff in the house, to the women grinding at the mill. By those who have the opportunity of comparing what Josephus and Tacitus have written with this passage in the Gospel, and who are eager to build some argument upon their likeness, surprising coincidences will be discovered. These will, of course, be turned the other way by writers who think that a Galilean peasant could have no rare gift of insight or foresight. They will see everywhere the fraud of disciples who change known facts into predictions. What I said before applies here. I can find no such coincidences between the events and the discourse as an inventor would have cared to introduce. No special incidents are thrust in which might make the imposture credible. But I do not expect this observation to have the least weight with those who deny that there is any supernatural order in the universe. They must endure improbabilities rather than accept what seems to them impossible as the solution of them. My appeal would be here, as before, to those who reverence the authority of Jesus, who believe Him to be indeed the King and Prophet of the universe. Do they want to strengthen their own faith in Him, by finding confirmations of it from Jewish or Gentile historians ? Surely that cannot be. Do they want then to make others believe in Him by referring to those historians ? But our way of appealing to them has the opposite effect. We suggest the notion that language which, read by itself, would sound broad and simple, has been the result of the deepest artifice.

How, then, may we use the Roman and Jewish historians ? Thoughtfully studied, they will show us what a crisis was betokened by the facts which they are making known to us ; how much more wonderful a one than we have ever fancied it to be ; how completely it was the shaking of an old order ; the announcement that some other must take its place. And if we say to ourselves, ' But how was it ' this, seeing that the Roman world did not pass away then ' —seeing that the Germans did not for many centuries ' trample it down ? ' the answer seems to me this. The convulsion was in the heart of the body politic. Its *belief* was shaken. The Temples which had expressed the relation between the visible and the invisible world, were tottering. This was the proof that a revolution had begun which all the subsequent ages would develope, which would not cease to work till the fabric of the polity, as well as of the worship, of the world was thrown down. Suppose, then, with these thoughts on our mind, we go back to this discourse about the Jewish Temple and its fall ; we may find in it not a superficial likeness between the records which we have been reading elsewhere, but the very key to those records, that which makes them coherent and intelligible. If the fall of the Jewish Temple was indeed the manifestation of the Son of Man, the unveiling of Him who was the Head of the nations, the living Bond between heaven and earth, we can understand why all lands should have participated in the shock of that time ; that the events of it, however disjointed they may have seemed to contemporaries, and may seem to us, were all conspiring to exhibit the *true* centre of the divine and human order ; that the departure of the *apparent* centre of that order was *the* sign in which the disciples were to recognise, and we are to recognise, the end of an age, the beginning of that for which it had been the preparation.

(4) '*But before all these, they shall lay their hands on you, and persecute you, delivering you up to the synagogues, and into prisons, being brought before kings and rulers for my name's sake. And it shall turn to you for a testimony.*'

The Apostles in after days must often have been puzzled to connect their words—words spoken in fear and trembling by such weak lips—with the doings of the great world, with the earthquakes, political or physical, of which they heard reports. Their enemies did not suffer them to forget the connexion. Was not the traitorous sect which preached salvation to the Gentiles when all Jewish patriots were praying God to destroy the Gentiles, the cause of the calamities that had overtaken the holy land? Were not the tribulations of the empire owing to those who turned away men from the service of the gods? These cries would reach the Cesars, and in spite of their tolerant maxims and their contempt, would induce them—that they might conciliate their Jewish or Gentile subjects—to interfere with the preachers of the Kingdom of Heaven. A time would come when it would openly confront the kingdom of the Cesar, and be recognised as its antagonist. But even in this generation the Apostles would be brought not only before synagogues, but before kings and rulers for His Name's sake. Their trials would '*turn to them for a testimony*' of the grandeur of the work in which they were engaged, of the strength in which they were to perform it.

(5) ' *Settle it therefore in your hearts, not to meditate before*

what ye shall answer : For I will give you a mouth and wisdom, which all your adversaries shall not be able to gainsay nor resist.' Here is the Pentecostal promise ; the assurance that the Spirit with whom their Master had been baptized should be with them ; the warning to trust in His calm wisdom, utterly to distrust the rash and vain suggestions of their own fancies ; to seek the true zeal which God inspires instead of that zeal which is often inspired by the devil. They would need this strength, for ' *Ye shall be betrayed both by parents, and brethren, and kinsfolks, and friends ; and some of you shall they cause to be put to death.'* To be put to death—that might be borne ; but to be betrayed by parents, and brethren, and kinsfolks, who could help them to bear that ? Only He who was shortly to say to His own dear circle, ' *One of you shall betray me.'*

(6) ' *And ye shall be hated of all men for my name's sake. But there shall not an hair of your head perish. In your patience possess ye your souls.'* Hated they would be by all kinds of men, by Gentiles as much as Jews ; hated by both for declaring that they were one in Christ ; hated, therefore, expressly for His name's sake. But how could it be that not a hair of their heads should perish if some of them were to be put to death ? That paradox could only be explained if their Master's words were fulfilled ; if He was given up to death ; if He rose from the dead because death could not hold Him. Supposing they had, indeed, a Prince of Life, One mightier than the grave and hell, they might trust their bodies as well as their spirits to Him. And so they might in patience possess their souls, waiting for their own redemption, waiting for the world's redemption.

(7) '*And when ye shall see Jerusalem compassed with armies, then know that the desolation thereof is nigh. Then let them which are in Judea flee to the mountains ; and let them which are in the midst of it depart out ; and let not them that are in the countries enter thereinto. For these be the days of vengeance, that all things which are written may be fulfilled. But woe unto them that are with child, and to them that give suck, in those days ! for there shall be great distress in the land, and wrath upon this people. And they shall fall by the edge of the sword, and shall be led away captive into all nations: and Jerusalem shall be trodden down of the Gentiles, until the times of the Gentiles be fulfilled.*" We have here only the more distinct announcement of that which has been told so often before ; that which it was so hard and so necessary for the disciples to understand and to believe. That Jerusalem should be trodden down of the Gentiles, could that be ? We read the words lightly ; we turn them merely into some commonplace lamentation over Jewish unbelief, some not more serious expression of thanksgiving for our blessings. But have we ever thought what it was that a heathen empire should tread down the city which had for generations declared that the God of Righteousness, the God of Salvation, is the Lord of the whole earth—that there is none other God but He—that men cannot make gods for themselves ? Was there nothing tremendous in that ? No shaking of heaven as well as earth ? And may there not be something more than we have dreamed of in the words, '*Until the times of the Gentiles be fulfilled ?*' If you ask me *what* is in it, I would reply, 'Let us meditate 'earnestly on what the Gentiles have gained by that 'overthrow of the Jewish Temple—what it signified to

'them and to mankind.' Then we may learn the import of these words, as no preacher or commentator could represent it to us. That you may pursue this meditation successfully, and under the highest guidance, study these words :—

(8) '*And there shall be signs in the sun, and in the moon, and in the stars; and upon the earth distress of nations, with perplexity; the sea and the waves roaring; men's hearts failing them for fear, and for looking after those things which are coming on the earth: for the powers of heaven shall be shaken. And then shall they see the Son of man coming in a cloud with power and great glory. And when these things begin to come to pass, then look up, and lift up your heads; for your redemption draweth nigh. And he spake to them a parable; Behold the fig-tree, and all the trees; when they now shoot forth, ye see and know of your own selves that summer is now nigh at hand. So likewise ye, when ye see these things come to pass, know ye that the kingdom of God is nigh at hand. Verily I say unto you, This generation shall not pass away, till all be fulfilled. Heaven and earth shall pass away: but my words shall not pass away.*' When you hear these words read to you on the Second Sunday in Advent, does not the thought sometimes strike you, 'Oh, no doubt that is to happen some day. We ' suppose the Son of man will come in a cloud with power ' and great glory. But the news is very vague—the coming ' is a long way off. Divines have not settled the when and ' the how. They are always disputing about some point ' connected with the Advent of Christ. Till they have ' arrived at some agreement among themselves, they can- ' not expect us to be much moved by the tidings, even ' though they are uttered by such lips,—though they are

Y

' accompanied by such solemn declarations that the words
' cannot pass away.'

My friends, these things are said, and will be said, till
we have courage to face the question, 'And did not the
' Son of man come as He says that He would in that
' generation ?' Were not the signs in the sun and moon,
the distress of the earth with perplexity, the failing of
men's hearts for fear, the vague looking into the future,
the wailings after Him,—was not the breaking up of
the Temple, with its goodly stones,—the witness that,
however hidden by clouds from mortal eyes, He was
there in power and great glory ? If so, the disciples had
a right to say, ' Our redemption is drawing nigh. This
' is the token that He, whose glory Isaiah saw in the
' Temple, who preached to us in the Temple, is Himself
' coming forth as the living human Temple of the Eternal
' God. As surely as the shooting forth of leaves in
' trees that had been dried and bare betoken the ap-
' proaching summer, so surely do these Churches of Jews
' and Gentiles, rising out of a dying age, and exhibiting
' all the energies and fruits of youth, testify that the
' Kingdom is establishing itself in our earth; that it will
' survive whatever perishes ; that of it there can be no
' end.' If so, Christ's words were fulfilled in that generation, as He said they would be. If so, they will not pass
away, though heaven and earth should pass away. If so,
we are living in the days of the Son of man, and every
crisis that has befallen Christendom has been an unveiling
of Him whom it had forgotten. If so, there may come a
day when the times of this Christendom shall be fulfilled,
when its temples and all the outward establishments which
have testified of the living God and the Son of man, and

have often been used to hide Him from the hearts of men, shall pass away with a great noise, that the Divine Temple may stand forth in its glory.

(9) My friends, Whitsuntide has been testifying to us from year to year of that Revelation of the Spirit of God— of that indwelling of the Spirit in human temples, which was to prepare the way for the fall of the Temple made with hands. It has been telling, year by year, of a Church composed of men of all kindreds and tongues which rose out of the Jewish nation at the voice of the Spirit. It has been telling us that we are members of this Church—that we are Temples of the living God. The disciples of the first age were in danger of forgetting that they had been brought unto this glorious state, that they had been made members of this Universal and Eternal Kingdom; that they were witnesses of it to mankind. Those who, we should have supposed, were continually reminded by persecution of their calling, had yet need to hear these words :—' *And take heed to yourselves, lest at any time your hearts be overcharged with surfeiting, and drunkenness, and cares of this life, and so that day come upon you unawares. For as a snare shall it come on all them that dwell on the face of the whole earth. Watch ye therefore, and pray always, that ye may be accounted worthy to escape all these things that shall come to pass, and to stand before the Son of man.*' Do we not need these warnings—we who live in a world not less luxurious than that of the early Cæsars, not less exposed to religious self-exaltation and religious strife than that of the Jews in the days when the Temple was falling? We have both perils to encounter at once. May the Spirit of God enable us to encounter them! May He make us worthy to stand before the Son of man!

LECTURE XXVI.

THE KING IN HIS AGONY.*

St. Luke XXII. 41, 42.

And he was withdrawn from them about a stone's cast, and kneeled down and prayed, saying, Father, if thou be willing, remove this cup from me: nevertheless not my will, but thine, be done.

THERE was a time when divines fancied that they could maintain the doctrine of the Trinity by quoting separate texts of Scripture in support of it. That Name, into which generations of men and women and children have been baptized—that Name which, if it means anything, must denote Him in whom we are living and moving and having our being,—was supposed to rest on some passages of the Holy Book, or rather upon our interpretation of those passages. Such a habit of mind favoured all irreverence and all unreality. God confounded it. The text on which controversialists relied most was found to be a spurious one. They fought for it as long as they could; at last they were compelled to abandon it.

The loss of such a feeble buttress has proved an inestimable blessing to us. We are suspecting—as yet it is only a suspicion—that awe and worship may have more to do with our faith than disputation. As we have been less able to follow the Fathers of the Church in punishing or denouncing those who dissent from our opinions, we have learnt a little more of what they meant when they spoke

* Preached on Trinity Sunday.

in their most rapturous devotions, on their dying beds or at the stake, of the Trinity as the infinite, all-embracing charity, to know which, to dwell on which, is the reward of the spirits in glory, the ground of all trust and hope for sinners upon earth.

'*Father, if it be possible, let this cup pass from me, yet not as I will, but as thou wilt.*' There is a revelation of the distinction of Persons, of the unity of substance in the Godhead, which we may dwell upon in silence. My fear is, that I should weaken the force and emphasis of this record by discoursing of it. I shall avoid that danger best if I use these words as a key to the events of the last Passover. I shall take the story exactly as it is set down by St. Luke. I should wish you hereafter to compare him with the other Evangelists, and not to evade any of the difficulties which the comparison will suggest. But you will make the comparison most fairly, if you have first pondered thoughtfully on one narrative : you will then look into points of detail seriously, but without exaggerating their importance. And you will find that the great principles which St. John unfolds in those discourses at the Last Supper which he alone reports, are the necessary interpretation of the acts that are recorded here.

I. The people still flocked to the Temple. Each morning Jesus came from the Mount of Olives and spoke of the Kingdom. Was He preparing them for the festival that celebrated the deliverance from Pharaoh ? Would that be the signal for His revolt ? The priests must have feared it. Vaguely, perhaps, the people may have hoped it. Would it be better to arrest Him before the day came ? Might not they increase the danger if they made the attempt openly before the multitude ?

II. '*Then entered Satan into Judas surnamed Iscariot, being of the number of the twelve.*' That is all we are told; it is all we need to be told. The tempter may have presented this thought to the man once and again: 'You 'could give up your Master; the priests would pay you 'well if you did.' He may have driven back the suggestion. It may have been enforced by many arguments: 'Is this Kingdom of God ever to come? Has Jesus the 'powers for which you have given Him credit? If He 'can save Himself He will. May not the priests know 'more about what is right than you ignorant peasants?' Whatever the voice of the evil spirit said, whatever answers were made to that voice, he prevailed. The man sacrificed himself. The dark power became his master. '*And he went his way, and communed with the chief priests and captains, how he might betray him unto them. And they were glad, and covenanted to give him money. And he promised, and sought opportunity to betray him unto them in the absence of the multitude.*' That was the great object. The priests lived in the dread of a people whom they did not love, as they lived in the dread of a God whom they did not love. It was soon to be proved that the multitude was far less dangerous than they had supposed. *That* enemy might be brought over to be their servant.

III. '*Then came the day of unleavened bread, when the passover must be killed.*' The disciples of Jesus must have anticipated that feast with a mixture of fear and hope. They could not doubt it would be a crisis in their lives. But what would come of it? Would they be established as the ministers of a great King? Would the King Himself, according to the strange prediction which they had heard, not understood, be given up to the Gentiles?

'*And he sent Peter and John, saying, Go and prepare us the passover, that we may eat. And they said unto him, Where wilt thou that we prepare? And he said unto them, Behold, when ye are entered into the city, there shall a man meet you, bearing a pitcher of water; follow him into the house where he entereth in. And ye shall say unto the goodman of the house, The Master saith unto thee, Where is the guestchamber, where I shall eat the passover with my disciples? And he shall shew you a large upper room furnished: there make ready. And they went, and found as he had said unto them: and they made ready the passover.*'

The command to prepare the feast is the command of a Master. But it is addressed to friends. It does not sound like a royal edict, or as if He meant to arouse the multitude. He is withdrawing from His preaching in the Temple into an inner circle. At the same time He is illustrating the spirit of the original commandment in Exodus. If the Passover was to be a national feast, it was also to be a family feast. Each household was to prepare the lamb and to eat of it together. The nation had lost its freedom: it had lost its unity. What was the source of its freedom, the centre of its unity, this little band was to learn and to proclaim. The proclamation, as we hold, has gone forth into all lands. An illustrious historian of our day, writing with no theological interest, only bearing witness to facts, bids us compare the great feast at the beginning of the French Revolution which was to inaugurate the new age of fraternity, with this festival in the upper chamber at Jerusalem. I know not a deeper or more pregnant suggestion. It seems to me worth whole volumes of Christian evidences. But if we use it rightly, we shall not turn it into an argument for the confutation of objectors. *We* are the infidels who need to be persuaded that the Elder Brother of the race has appeared, that He has established a real fraternity for men. *We* have lived as if He had offered His sacrifice that we might be less of a family, that we might be more of enemies, than Jews or heathens.

IV. '*And when the hour was come, he sat down, and the twelve apostles with him. And he said unto them, With desire I have desired to eat this passover with you before I suffer; for I say unto you, I will not any more eat thereof, until it be fulfilled in the kingdom of God. And he took the cup, and gave thanks, and said, Take this, and divide it among yourselves: for I say unto you, I will not drink of the fruit of the vine, until the kingdom of God shall come.*'

That intense longing to hold this feast with His disciples, shall we call it a mere human longing? Or shall we separate it, as some do, from the craving for fellowship which is experienced by every peasant, and which has been felt, certainly with not less strength, by those leaders and teachers who have seemed most to dwell apart? Shall we say that it is profane to associate the thoughts and conflicts of Christ with our thoughts and conflicts? We must adopt one of these alternatives, if we do not believe that the human is the perfect image of the Divine; that Jesus possessed the very mind of Him who had been in all ages seeking for communion with the sons of men, whose very nature excludes the notion of solitude; that He felt, in its depth and fulness, the need which human beings have of communion with each other. What was the Passover but the witness that the Highest of all had seen the affliction of His people, had heard their cry, and had come down to deliver them? What was it but the witness that He had established an intercourse with them from age to age? What was the Paschal sacrifice but the bond of this union between the redeemed nation and Him who had stooped to it—but its acceptance of Him as its King and Lord, instead of the Egyptian ruler? For Christ to desire that He might keep the feast of that union, of that dedication, once more with those whom He had chosen to be the witnesses of the Divine kingdom to His countrymen—was not this in the highest sense to do the will of the Eternal Father? Was it not to justify all ties by which the Most High had bound together His creatures—to give society its true consecration?

V. '*And he took bread, and gave thanks, and brake it, and gave unto them, saying, This is my body which is given for you: this do in remembrance of me. Likewise also the cup after supper, saying, This cup is the new testament in my blood, which is shed for you.*'

He desired to eat the Passover before He suffered, not because it was to be abolished, but because it was to be fulfilled in the Kingdom of God. The maxim of His early discourse has never been forgotten. No tittle of the law is to perish. No tittle of the family covenant is to perish. He has come, not to destroy, but to fulfil. Here is the point of the transition. The nation which He had redeemed out of the house of bondage is sinking into a worse bondage, must sink into death. But the symbols of the national redemption are translated into the symbols of human redemption. The purpose of the calling out of the family of Abraham will be manifested. All the families of the earth will be claimed as God's family.

And if the nation is to die, the King of it is to die. If the sacrifice that commemorated the conservation of the nation in its first-born is disappearing, it is only because *the* Sacrifice—the Sacrifice of *the* Firstborn—is about to be accomplished. If the body and blood of Jesus do unite God to man, Heaven to earth—if they have been presented by a Son to a Father—if the Spirit of the Son and Father teaches our spirits to remember that reconciliation and to partake of it, then indeed the unleavened bread and the Paschal wine have been fulfilled in the Kingdom of God—then the New Testament has taken the place of the Old—then the Lord's Supper has been a true message to men of all peoples and tongues. The disciples in the upper chamber could not tell what the words meant for themselves till they could say to Jews, Greeks, and Latins, ' They are for you.'

VI. Then comes the sudden cry : ' *But, behold, the hand of him that betrayeth me is with me on the table. And truly the Son of man goeth, as it was determined : but woe unto that man by whom he is betrayed !* ' ' Yes ! the traitor ' is amongst us, in the little flock itself. We have not left ' him in the crowd at the Temple ; he is here in the upper ' chamber. He has stretched his hand to receive the bread ' and the wine.' A witness, surely—*the* witness—that by no narrowing of circles, by no fencing of tables, can you exclude the most false disciple or apostle. Is there not more in these words ? Is not the deepest problem of the universe in them ? ' *The Son of man goeth, as was determined.*' Could you bear to think otherwise ? Was that which we believe to be the most blessed event in the world's history not intended, not appointed, by the Father of all ? Was He not the Author of the sacrifice ? Was

it not, in the highest sense, the fulfilment of His will?—
'But woe to that man by whom the Son of man is betrayed.'
Could you bear to think otherwise? Could you believe
that the man was merely the agent of the Divine purpose
—that his *sin* was not an act of his will? You must
maintain both these propositions, however hard you find
it to reconcile them. Perhaps, if we read these words
more strictly—perhaps, if we thoroughly believed in our
Lord's death and resurrection—we should see how the
gracious determinations of God are to prevail over the
stubborn resistance of the human will. I used to think
that Judas only was the betrayer, that he is the man of
whom it is said, ' He had better never have been born.'
The words now come to me in a more terrible, yet in
a more hopeful, sense. The covetous man, I think, dwells
in each one of us—is the enemy of the Son of man in
each man. Good were it for each one of us, good were
it for humanity, if that traitor had never been born. But
may he not die? May not God's purpose triumph? May
not the Son of man have all enemies at last put under
His feet?

VII. There was a moment in which this thought of the
traitor within seems to have seized strongly on the minds of
the disciples. *' And they began to inquire among themselves
which of them it was that should do this thing.'* Could any
one say, ' I may not be the betrayer?' Blessed, inspired
suspicion ! From what sins, what betrayal of Christ, might
we not each of us have been saved, if we had cherished it
instead of transferring our fears and our accusations to our
brethren ! Were the Apostles, then, much more humble, less
ambitious, than men of later generations? Hear :—

' And there was also a strife among them, which of them

332   LECTURE XXVI.

should be accounted the greatest.' What, there? at that
feast? Yes, my friends, and almost before their self-
questioning about the betrayal was over! That cannot
have been invented. No compiler of a legend could have
brought such contradictions together. And no reader of
his own heart can doubt that they exist there; that they
may appear in this rapid succession; that one will spring
up in revenge for the other, as a kind of compensation
for what seems an injury we have done to ourselves.
'Betrayers! how can that be? Has He not told us that
we are to have seats in His Kingdom?'

VIII. *'And he said unto them, The kings of the Gentiles
exercise lordship over them; and they that exercise authority
upon them are called benefactors. But ye shall not be so: but
he that is greatest among you, let him be as the younger; and
he that is chief, as he that doth serve. For whether is greater,
he that sitteth at meat, or he that serveth? is not he that sitteth
at meat? but I am among you as he that serveth. Ye are
they which have continued with me in my temptations. And
I appoint unto you a kingdom, as my Father hath appointed
unto me; that ye may eat and drink at my table in my
kingdom, and sit on thrones judging the twelve tribes of
Israel.'*

Did our Lord arrest the quarrel of His disciples about
precedence by telling them that they had been wrong in
considering Him a King; that He was not really a King;
that His Kingdom of Heaven was only a figurative one,
or only one to be enjoyed after death; that they must
dismiss the dream that they were officers of a kingdom,
for it would soon be scattered to the winds? No! in that
dreadful hour He did not unteach all His previous lessons.
He ratified them. He asserted that He had come to

establish a real Kingdom; that it was appointed for Him; that He appointed it for them; that they were to sit and judge in it; that the twelve tribes of Israel would be tried by them. What, then, did He correct in them? That which He had always been correcting in them—the vulgar notion, so natural to them and to us, that a kingdom is a society in which men are enjoying honours and high places, or contending for them. The Gentile monarchies, wherein those who exercised authority were called benefactors, were not the types of the Divine monarchy. There the Chief of all stooped to be the Servant of all. They had been called to share His temptations. He had passed through the great temptation of being asked to take the kingdoms of this world and the glory of them, instead of waiting for the Kingdom which His Father had appointed for Him. If they remembered Him, and resisted as He resisted, they would have power such as no rulers of men had ever exercised. They would do the work which the twelve tribes had been appointed to do. When the voice of the twelve tribes was silent, they would bear witness why the Kingdom had been taken from them, and how permanent and universal it was.

IX. Those who have been with Him in His temptations were now to be sorely tempted themselves. '*And the Lord said, Simon, Simon, behold, Satan hath desired to have you, that he may sift you as wheat: but I have prayed for thee, that thy faith fail not: and when thou art converted, strengthen thy brethren.*' It was an enemy that desired to sift the Apostle. It was Christ who was on the tempted man's side, asking that the temptation might be for his strength, not his ruin. Think of that lesson, my friends. Many dark passages in our lives would become clear if we read them by that light.

'*And he said unto him, Lord, I am ready to go with thee, both into prison, and to death. And he said, I tell thee, Peter, the cock shall not crow this day, before that thou shalt thrice deny that thou knowest me.*'

Peter had what a great man has called the 'fore-feeling of his capabilities.' He had that in him which could and would go to prison and death. He had also that in him which would make him a denier. The chaff must be separated from the wheat. The Holy Spirit, not the Evil Spirit, would conduct that sifting, burning process. The man must be made to know what he is in himself, what he is in union with the Son of man. So he would be able to strengthen his brethren.

X. I think the passage which follows would have been far more intelligible to us if it had been taken along with this. '*And he said unto them, When I sent you without purse, and scrip, and shoes, lacked ye any thing? And they said, Nothing. Then said he unto them, But now, he that hath a purse, let him take it, and likewise his scrip: and he that hath no sword, let him sell his garment, and buy one. For I say unto you, that this that is written must yet be accomplished in me, And he was reckoned among the transgressors: for the things concerning me have an end. And they said, Lord, behold, here are two swords. And he said unto them, It is enough.*'

The Apostles had been sent forth to preach the Kingdom of Heaven. They had the powers which could show what the Kingdom was. They had wanted nothing that was necessary for their work. Did they fancy they should have those powers or those supplies for their necessities now? Let them not dream of it. They would have no swords given them to overcome their enemies. Their Master Himself would be numbered with the transgressors. The end of all the plots of His enemies against Him, of all the purposes of His Father concerning Him, was approaching.

This language would find its interpretation before many hours were over. The disciples would know what the helplessness was which He told them of; how utterly changed their condition was since that day when they went forth in triumph as heralds of a kingdom, and found even the spirits subject to them. At present their minds are only fixed upon the words, 'He that hath no sword, let him sell his garment and buy one.' They fancied He must mean them to go forth on that Passover-night, when nothing could be bought, and procure swords. They produce two. Might not these be enough? He answers, probably with a sad smile, 'Enough.' As if He had said, 'My poor 'children! do you really suppose that I want you to do 'battle for me with those swords of yours? You will soon 'see what you have to encounter, and what you and your 'swords are good for.' Wonderful things have been said and sung about those two swords. They are, we are told, the civil and ecclesiastical powers. I suppose the authors of that interpretation wish us to understand how impotent both have proved themselves whenever they have attempted to establish the Kingdom of God and overthrow its enemies.

XI. Then follows the passage which I have regarded as the central one of this history.

'*And he came out, and went, as he was wont, to the Mount of Olives; and his disciples also followed him. And when he was at the place, he said unto them, Pray that ye enter*

not into temptation. And he was withdrawn from them
about a stone's cast, and kneeled down, and prayed, saying,
Father, if thou be willing, remove this cup from me: never-
theless not my will, but thine, be done. And there appeared
an angel unto him from heaven, strengthening him. And
being in an agony he prayed more earnestly: and his sweat
was as it were great drops of blood falling down to the
ground.'

The Passover-feast, which He had desired with so great
a desire, is over. He has had a few hours of fellowship
with the twelve. There has been darkness in that room,
the sense of betrayal, the prospect of desertion. Still, He
had broken the bread and given it to them. He had told
them of a Father. He is now but a stone's cast from them,
yet He feels alone. These disciples cannot watch with
Him. The priests hate Him; the people are losing trust
in Him. And is the Father there? Is He not left to Himself? 'Father, I cannot bear it! Let this cup pass from
me.' That is the hour of real, though unfelt victory.
'Nevertheless, not my will, but Thine be done.' The
agony is intense: the Angel from Heaven may soothe
the sufferer, but cannot save Him from the bloody sweat.
He arises, and bids the disciples pray that they may not
enter into temptation; as if He who was always tempted
then knew for the first time the whole meaning of temptation; as if He who was always praying then understood
the necessity, and yet almost the impossibility, of prayer.
My friends, have we not here what this day would teach
us? If we think of the Son without the Father, we leave
Him in His agony; if the Father is without the Son, what
is He but a phantom wrapped in His own greatness
standing aloof from all human sorrow? if there is no

Spirit uniting them, how was the Son sustained in His hour of darkness, how can we be sustained in ours?

XII. '*And while he yet spake, behold a multitude, and he that was called Judas, one of the twelve, went before them, and drew near unto Jesus to kiss him. But Jesus said unto him, Judas, betrayest thou the Son of Man with a kiss?*' It is still the same language. Jesus speaks of Judas not as betraying Him, the Master, the Friend, but '*the Son of Man.*' Judas was giving up *the* Man, the King of Men, the source of all that had been manly in himself. The kiss, the mockery of love, was the sign that he was cutting himself off from his kind, declaring war with it, retreating into his own outer darkness. '*When they which were about him saw what would follow, they said unto him, Lord, shall we smite with the sword?*' They did not wait for an answer. They took it for granted. '*And one of them smote a servant of the high priest, and cut off his right ear. And Jesus answered and said, Suffer ye thus far. And he touched his ear, and healed him.*' So ended the valour of the disciples—their grand attempt to defend Christ's person, and establish His Kingdom with a sword. It ended in the scorn of their enemies, in the rebuke of their Master, in their own shame. Is there no lesson for us there, my friends? May the like scorn and the like shame pursue every such experiment when it is made by us! The rebuke certainly will.

I am afraid, however, that the high priests and rulers have been on the whole more frequent models for the imitation of the Christian Church than the disciples. '*Then Jesus said unto the chief priests, and captains of the temple, and the elders, which were come to him, Be ye come out, as against a thief, with swords and staves? When I*'

Z

was daily with you in the temple, ye stretched forth no hands against me: but this is your hour, and the power of darkness. Then took they him, and led him, and brought him into the high priest's house. And Peter followed afar off.' Those to whom He spoke no doubt argued with themselves that one who disturbed the minds of the people respecting a divine kingdom was far worse than any thief. They believed that they were doing a high act of religion in silencing Him,—an act of religious prudence in assaulting Him at night, not amidst the crowd in the temple. And those who judged of right by success must have thought God was on their side. The thing they desired comes to pass. The dreaded teacher does nothing to save himself. His followers prove cowards. There is no resistance in the people. The worshippers of the god of darkness they who thought him the lord of all, had their way. It was their hour.

XIII. *'And when they had kindled a fire in the midst of the hall, and were set down together, Peter sat down among them. But a certain maid beheld him as he sat by the fire, and earnestly looked upon him, and said, This man was also with him. And he denied him, saying, Woman, I know him not. And after a little while another saw him, and said, Thou art also of them. And Peter said, Man, I am not. And about the space of one hour after, another confidently affirmed, saying, Of a truth this fellow also was with him: for he is a Galilean. And Peter said, Man, I know not what thou sayest. And immediately, while he yet spake, the cock crew. And the Lord turned, and looked upon Peter. And Peter remembered the word of the Lord, how he had said unto him, Before the cock crow, thou shalt deny me thrice. And Peter went out, and wept*

bitterly.' The story is told by every Evangelist. Not one
felt that he had a right to suppress it, or that he could
bring out the full Gospel of the Divine King without it.
I think Christendom has confirmed their conviction.
Whilst it has in terms confessed St. Peter to be the rock
on which the Church stands, it has felt the immense
worth of this testimony to the absolute feebleness of the
highest Apostle when he was not resting upon another
rock than himself. Who can tell the worth of it as an
education of St. Peter in his high calling to tell all men of
a rock on which they might build, and against which the
gates of hell shall not prevail? By this story, as by the
Virgin's song, the Church Catholic in all ages has been
warned of some of her own greatest temptations. She
has carried a practical warning against them in her very
heart. Protestants can do little service to their Romanist
brethren by denouncing any of their most confused convictions, by weakening their admiration of any person.
How much good might they do if they showed that they
only refused to acknowledge St. Peter as head of the
Church, lest they should set aside his confession and share
his denial, lest they should rend the Church in pieces
which he sought to unite in its true corner-stone!

The special point in St. Luke's narrative is the memorable passage in which the Lord is described as looking
upon Peter. I see no reason, from the description of the
place in which Peter was standing, why the actual eyes
of Him who was before the Sanhedrim may not have been
turned towards His disciple. Nevertheless, I cannot
doubt that he who, in any age, weeps bitterly over a
denial of Christ, does so because the eyes which are as
flaming fire, which read the thoughts and intents of the

heart, have been fixed upon him, and have brought him
to confession and repentance.

XIV. '*And the men that held Jesus mocked him, and
smote him.   And when they had blindfolded him, they struck
him on the face, and asked him, saying, Prophesy, who is it
that smote thee?   And many other things blasphemously
spake they against him.*'   When we read such words as
these in a country which has for centuries confessed Him
who was blindfolded as the King of kings, the King by
whom its kings reign, ought we not to ask ourselves
sometimes, 'What should we have done if we had been
' living at a time when all the rulers of the land, all the
' religious men of the land, counted Him an impostor
' and a blasphemer ?'   Oh, my friends, if that question
leads us to some startling thoughts about ourselves, to
some fears lest we might have been among the mockers,
then let this be the use to which we turn that apprehension.   Let us remember who said,—who will say,—
' Inasmuch as ye did it to the least of these my brethren,
' ye did it to me.'   Let us ask that we may be preserved
from the spirit of scorn and mockery towards any
human creature, lest we should find that we are not
essentially unlike the men who struck Him on the face,
and said, ' Prophesy, who is it that smote thee ?'

XV. Hitherto it has been night. The day has just dawned,
and this is the first spectacle which the light discloses to us.
'*And as soon as it was day, the elders of the people and the
chief priests, and the scribes, came together, and led him
into their council, saying, Art thou the Christ? tell us.
And he said unto them, If I tell you, ye will not believe :
and if I also ask you, ye will not answer me, nor let me go.
Hereafter shall the Son of Man sit on the right hand of the*

power of God.' The question is, Art thou the Christ? He
had forbidden His Apostles to say that He was the Christ.
He does not care to use that name before the Sanhedrim.
For would they understand it? Would they believe Him
if He told them what the Christ was—if He spoke of One
who baptized with the Spirit? Or if He asked them to
tell Him what they meant by the Christ, would that avail
anything? He falls back then upon the old name. He
affirms what He has been affirming by all His acts and
words, that there is a union between God and man. He
has been revealing God in the lowliness of the man. He
declares that the man shall sit on the right hand of God.
The Priests seize upon the sentence. It was not just what
they expected. They wished to convict Him of claiming
royal rights, as the Son of David; that charge they will
renew when they go into Pilate's judgment hall. Now,
they perceive the opening for a more dreadful charge, one
of which the Sanhedrim can take cognizance. *' Then said
they all, Art thou then the Son of God? And he said unto
them, Ye say that I am. And they said, What need we any
further witness? for we ourselves have heard of his own
mouth.'* He had not of His own accord taken that awful
dignity. As always, He disclaimed glory for Himself.
He emptied Himself of all titles ; when He spoke of His
Father it was that He might say He could do nothing
of Himself. But now that He is adjured to speak, and
that to speak is to die, He accepts before men that name
which had been proclaimed in His baptism. Henceforth
it becomes inseparably linked with the Passover night,
with the agony, with the Sacrifice. And that name, my
friends, will become dearer to us, the more we associate
it with the Divine agony ; the more we think of the

Son and the Father going together to the great Sacrifice;
the more we ask for the Spirit that we may offer ourselves
acceptable sacrifices.   So we shall be able to confess the
glory of the Eternal Trinity, and in the power of the
Divine Majesty to worship the Unity.

LECTURE XXVII.

THE KING ON THE CROSS.

St. Luke XXIII. 38.

And a superscription also was written over him in letters of Greek, and Latin, and Hebrew, THIS IS THE KING OF THE JEWS.

THAT the Gospel is the Gospel of a Kingdom we have been reminded at every turn of St. Luke's narrative. When we come to the history of the Crucifixion we may be tempted to forget that name; we may even shrink from it. Are we not to hear the cries of a Victim? Should not the Sacrifice be the prominent thought in our minds? Do we not, at least in the hour of darkness, lose sight of the King?

The Evangelist never does; he will not suffer us to do it. The superscription upon the Cross is for him the simplest expression of the truth which the Cross was proclaiming to the Jewish nation—to all nations, Greek and Latin as well as Hebrew. He reads in that superscription the meaning of previous history and of subsequent history. It does not distract his mind at all from the sufferings of Jesus; it explains His sufferings. It does not hide from him the nature or the worth of His Sacrifice. It shows how real the Sacrifice was, and how it was accomplished. If we observe the incidents recorded in this chapter as they arise, we shall see how they all tend to this point.

I. ' *And the whole multitude of them arose, and led him unto Pilate.*' The Sanhedrim would rather, no doubt, have enforced its own decree. Having declared Jesus guilty of blasphemy, they would have inflicted the punishment for blasphemy ; but either the Governor or the people might have interfered, and the Passover was not the time for incurring such a risk. It was far safer to quell their Jewish pride, and ask the Gentile to destroy their enemy as his own.

II. ' *And they began to accuse him, saying, We found this fellow perverting the nation, and forbidding to give tribute to Cesar, saying that he himself is Christ a King.*' This was to be the charge. Let us remember distinctly that Pilate could care for no other. They had the mortification of finding that he did not care for that. This sudden zeal for Cesar, this anxiety about his tribute, in men who were habitually impatient of the foreign yoke, always expecting some deliverer, must have struck a shrewd worldly man, used to different forms of hypocrisy, familiar now with the special forms of it which prevailed in Jerusalem, as very suspicious. His question, ' *Art thou the King of the Jews ?* ' was equally contemptuous to the accused and the accusers. ' Art thou the Person before whom the Ruler of the world ' is to tremble ?' What the answer implied, whether it was or was not, a denial of the imputation, was nothing to Pilate. The charge seemed to him ridiculous on the face of it. He dismissed it at once with the sentence, ' *I find no fault in this man.*' I am not afraid lest *he* should overthrow my authority or my master's. The priests felt the rebuke ; it irritated them ; besides, they had no time to lose.

III. ' *And they were the more fierce, saying, He stirreth up the people, teaching throughout all Jewry, beginning from*

Galilee to this place.'	Pilate knew what it was to struggle
with men full of religious fury.	He would avoid the battle
if possible.	He caught at the word 'Galilee.'	Perhaps he
might shift his task upon another.	'*And as soon as he
knew that he belonged unto Herod's jurisdiction, he sent him
to Herod, who himself also was at Jerusalem at that time.'*
The men were very unlike.	Pilate, merely indifferent—the
weary Roman unbeliever of the age of Tiberius.	Herod,
like the rest of his family, curious and speculative, with
an uneasy conscience and intellect, breaking through moral
laws—all the more eager to find out whether there was
any connexion between the visible and the invisible world,
what one or another man had to say about it.	The
prophet of Repentance he had listened to and silenced;
his successor, it was said, exhibited wonders, real or pre-
tended, which it would be worth while to witness.	'*And
when Herod saw Jesus, he was exceeding glad : for he was
desirous to see him of a long season, because he had heard
many things of him ; and he hoped to have seen some
miracle done by him.'*	It was mere disappointment.	'*Then
he questioned with him in many words ; but he answered him
nothing.'*

IV. '*And the chief priests and scribes stood and vehemently
accused him.'*	The nature of the accusation is not stated ;
it was obviously the same as that before Pilate, otherwise the mockery which followed would have had no
significance.	'*And Herod with his men of war set him at
nought, and mocked him, and arrayed him in a gorgeous
robe, and sent him again to Pilate.'*	The absurdity of His
kingly pretensions struck Herod as it had struck Pilate.	A
prophet or an enchanter would have been treated respect-
fully, perhaps half credited ; but who could dream of such

a person exalting Himself to a throne? If He or any of His followers had that madness, this, it seemed to Herod, was the best method of curing it. So far the two Judges were agreed, and their sympathy as to the right method of treating the case, as well as Pilate's courtesy in deferring to Herod's judgment, removed a long-standing grudge between them.

V. It must have been almost in despair that the priests came again before the Governor's judgment seat, and heard him announce the sentence, '*Ye have brought this man unto me, as one that perverteth the people: and behold, I, having examined him before you, have found no fault in this man touching those things whereof ye accuse him: No, nor yet Herod: for I sent you to him: and lo, nothing worthy of death is done unto him.*' In other words, He is evidently a fanatic, with no evil intention, capable of doing little harm. '*I will therefore chastise him, and release him.*' He believed, no doubt, that the people would be pleased, if the priests were offended. They would accept the release of a favourite teacher as a boon to them. If His teaching was seditious—if He did, as was said, forbid them to pay tribute—the indignity of the chastisement would check the mischief better than any more violent punishment. The Governor was seeking the alliance of those whom the priests feared against them. In that critical moment the thought seems to have been suggested to them—or perhaps they had already kept the proposition in reserve if it should be necessary—that they might win the favour of the multitude to their side.

VI. '*And they cried out all at once, saying, Away with this man, and release unto us Barabbas: (Who for a certain sedition made in the city, and for murder, was cast into*

prison).' A brigand, a leader of insurrection, taken with
arms in his hands, must surely be a greater witness for
the popular cause than One who had quietly yielded to
the officers that were sent to seize Him. If the Governor
could be forced by their voices to give him up in homage
to the feast, would not that be the greatest of all triumphs?
The priests had not been mistaken in their calculations.
The name of Barabbas once heard gave a direction to the
minds of the multitude, already more than half persuaded
that Jesus had not the power which they had ascribed
to Him. It was one of those impulses which so often
lead to the most sanguinary deeds.

VII. '*Pilate, therefore, willing to release Jesus, spake again
to them. But they cried, saying, Crucify him, crucify him.*'
The words are often taken to indicate a serious wish in
the people that Jesus should suffer the most cruel kind of
death. If we study the reports of the different Evangelists
I do not think that impression will remain on our minds.
'Give us the man we want; what becomes of the other we
'do not care. Treat Him as you like '—that was evidently
the sense of the popular cry. The cruelty was given to it
by the priestly instigators; in the rest it was a dull, blind
instinct, which wants some object to care for, and which,
if it lights upon a worthless one, will, through mere
indifference, suffer any other, even the most beautiful, to
perish. That is the history of the process by which men
inspired with religious hatred can turn a people into a
mob, and divert passions which might be generous into
the instruments of all fury and malice.

VIII. The sense of justice and law, which could never
wholly forsake a Roman, if he were individually ever so
worthless, was aroused in Pilate. It was mixed, no doubt,

with intense contempt both for the Jewish rabble and the Jewish priests. *'And he said unto them the third time, Why, what evil hath he done ? I have found no cause of death in him : I will therefore chastise him, and let him go.'* He was himself perplexed. Supposing Jesus had forbidden to give tribute to Cesar, the *people* would not be likely to demand His crucifixion for that offence ; if they were, they would not be asking for Barabbas. Was it impossible to make them consider for what crime they would inflict so tremendous a punishment ? No ! the time was passed for any such consideration. The priests had taught the people to shriek. Shrieks, they knew, would be the best arguments with a Governor whose justice was a tradition, not a principle, in whom it would always yield, at last, to fear or policy.

IX. *' And they were instant with loud voices, requiring that he might be crucified. And the voices of them and of the chief priests prevailed. And Pilate gave sentence that it should be as they required. And he released unto them him that for sedition and murder was cast into prison, whom they had desired ; but he delivered Jesus to their will.'* There are many passages introduced into the story of the arraignment before Pilate by the other Evangelists, especially by St. John, which throw a clear light upon the incidents that are recorded here. They all bear upon His claims to be a King. When He said, in answer to the question of Pilate, *'Art thou the King of the Jews ? ' ' My kingdom is not of this world ; if my kingdom were of this world, then would my servants fight,'*—it has been supposed that He disclaimed the title in any ordinary sense that could be given to it. I apprehend that He said precisely what He had been saying since He first went, in the power of the

Spirit, into Galilee. He had come to proclaim the Kingdom of God, not a Kingdom which stood by outward force,
not a tyranny civil or ecclesiastical; just the opposite of
that : a Kingdom which was to emancipate, not enslave ;
a Kingdom, therefore, before which the kingdoms of the
world, civil and ecclesiastical, would have to bow. For
it did assume to be, in the strictest sense, a Kingdom over
the world, a Kingdom over the bodies as well as the spirits
of men ; a Kingdom over every region in which the tyrants
were exercising dominion. Whether this pretension was
true or false was now to be tried. The priests demanded
the test, Pilate granted it, Jesus accepted it. When the
Jews chose Barabbas instead of Jesus, were they rejecting
their King ? Were they destroying themselves as a people
and becoming a gang of murderers by that act ?

X. '*And as they led him away, they laid hold upon one
Simon, a Cyrenian, coming out of the country, and on him
they laid the cross, that he might bear it after Jesus. And
there followed him a great company of people, and of women,
which also bewailed and lamented him. But Jesus, turning
unto them, said, Daughters of Jerusalem, weep not for me, but
weep for yourselves, and for your children. For, behold, the
days are coming, in the which they shall say, Blessed are the
barren, and the wombs that never bare, and the paps which
never gave suck. Then shall they begin to say to the mountains, Fall on us ; and to the hills, Cover us. For if they do
these things in a green tree, what shall be done in the dry ?*'

A mysterious worth has been perceived in the words
spoken *on* Calvary. Surely their depth and awfulness
cannot be measured. The words spoken *on the way* to
Calvary deserve equal reverence. But I do not think they
have received it. They associate our Lord's death with

the miseries that were coming on the land. They clearly represent His death as a prelude to the death of the nation. Christian teachers have shrunk from language which seems to lower and to narrow the signification of the event which they feel to be the grandest in the world's history, the one which most concerns all human beings. We may honour the sentiment; but if we have followed St. Luke carefully thus far, we cannot participate in it. In his story Jerusalem has never been separated from any of the Revelations of the Son of Man. The hour when Christ set His face to go to Jerusalem is the critical one in his narrative. We have heard from him how Christ declared that a prophet could not perish out of Jerusalem; how He wept over Jerusalem; how He entered Jerusalem as the heir of David's throne; how He spoke of the fall of Jerusalem as a day of destruction, and yet as a day of Redemption; to be awaited with trembling, as the darkest that had been known; to be hailed with hope and joy as the beginning of a new life to the world. Those who feel the discourse to the daughters of Jerusalem out of place amidst the records of the Passion, cannot look upon the Passion as the Evangelists look upon it; they must separate it from all the other steps in the manifestation of the true King.

That King bids the daughters of the land in which He has been revealing Himself not to weep for Him, but for the people who have cast Him off. He speaks of a judgment approaching them which shall make women regard the curse of being childless as a blessing, in which those who had counted God their champion and the foe of other men, should ask the hills to hide them from Him. He bids them understand that as yet there was sap in the

tree, there were some in the land who could weep for its
sins.   It would become utterly dry, all sorrow would be
staunched as well as joy; only the hatred which was
working His death would remain.   Oh, my friends, let
not that vision be exchanged in our minds for any vague
rhetoric such as preachers and writers concerning the
Crucifixion sometimes indulge in.   The actual women, the
actual Cross, the actual hills and mountains, these have a
power which belongs to no figures of speech.   What our Lord
said as He turned to the women was fulfilled in the holy
city, has been once and again fulfilled in cities that have
been accounted very holy in Christendom.   They are words
which cannot pass away.   May He who spoke them enable
us to think of them, and to ask ourselves what lessons we
are to draw from them.   If ever they should seem to be
coming near to our land, to our own very selves, may the
recollection of His Cross sustain us under the pressure
of them.

XI. ' *And there were also two others, malefactors, led with
him to be put to death.   And when they were come to the
place which is called Calvary, there they crucified him, and the
malefactors, one on the right hand, and the other on the left.
Then said Jesus, Father, forgive them ; for they know not
what they do.   And they parted his raiment, and cast lots.
And the people stood beholding.   And the rulers also with
them derided him, saying, He saved others : let him save himself, if he be Christ, the chosen of God.   And the soldiers also
mocked him, coming to him, and offering him vinegar, and
saying, If thou be the king of the Jews, save thyself.*'

It is not for us to speak of this record.   It must speak
to us.   It has spoken to all generations of men.   And
beneath the message which it has brought to each separate

human heart there has been this. Here is He who would not make Himself a King, or use His power as a King, to save Himself, because He *was* the King; because all who were mocking Him, soldiers and rulers, were His subjects ; because He cared for them and therefore gave up Himself; because He cared that the forgiveness for which He asked as a Son should be revealed and proclaimed to the universe. How little do we know yet of the force of that prayer, ' *Father, forgive !* ' But if we are Christians, we believe that it was uttered by Him whom the Father heareth always. We must believe that if any petition was ever asked according to the will of God, it was that petition, offered up when He was fulfilling that Will to the very utmost.

XII. ' *And a superscription also was written over him in letters of Greek, and Latin, and Hebrew, THIS IS THE KING OF THE JEWS.*' You will feel, I think, now, that I had some right to take this sentence as a central one; as one which explains the accusation and the condemnation of Christ, as one without which the history of the Passion would be imperfect and incoherent. It must seem a fiction —it can seem nothing else—to those who separate Jesus from the Christ. Instead of complaining of their denial, is it not better for us who say that He is the Christ to accept the testimony of the Roman Governor, and really to believe that the King whom the Jews rejected is the King of Hebrews, Greeks, and Latins ? Must not we repent of our desire to divide the crucified man from the Ruler of the world before we can hope to convince any others that they have erred by their imitation of us ?

XIII. There was one, at least, St. Luke tells us, who discovered the King upon the Cross. ' *And one of the malefactors which were hanged railed on him, saying, If thou be Christ, save thyself and us. But the other answering rebuked him, saying, Dost not thou fear God, seeing thou art in the same condemnation ? And we indeed justly ; for we receive the due reward of our deeds : but this man hath done nothing amiss. And he said unto Jesus, Lord, remember me when thou comest into thy kingdom. And Jesus said unto him, Verily I say unto thee, To-day shalt thou be with me in paradise.'* The evil-doer had been vanquished by many a lust, had been a miserable slave. Often he had heard a voice reproving him and recalling him. Whose voice was it ? Was there power in it ? Here he has learnt the secret. This is He from whom the voice came. This is the Deliverer, the Conqueror. He must reign. Would He refuse him, the outcast, as His subject ? *'Lord, re-member me when thou comest into thy kingdom.'* Come into it He would, some time or other. What says the answer ? That very day the robber should be with Him in Paradise. Where is that ? What is that ? How can the man in his agony debate such questions ? What need that he should ? What can it signify ? 'Thou shalt be *with me.* ' Dost thou want more—in anguish or in bliss, in darkness ' or in light—than to find that I am near thee, as I am ' near thee now ? '

XIV. In darkness it seemed, not in light. *'For it was about the sixth hour, and there was a darkness over all the earth until the ninth hour ; and the sun was darkened.'* You will read, in the margin of your Bible, 'land' instead of ' earth.' There can be no doubt, I conceive, that that was the meaning of the Evangelist. He had no dream of that universal darkness in which Gibbon supposes that Christians believe, and of which he says that some record

A A

must have been preserved, at least by so great an observer of natural phenomena as Pliny. We shall weaken, not strengthen, the narrative, if we attribute that force to it. If the darkness had been general, its significance would have been less. The local, direct impression of it would have been lost. And make the earth which it covered as large as you will, it must have been limited to that time. The darkness about the Cross over the region in which the crime was perpetrated has been felt throughout all ages, has been a witness to all. It has indicated that sympathy of Nature with man which we are, at times, compelled to recognise. It does not turn that sympathy into a mere startling phenomenon, which makes us forget the Light of the world in thinking of the natural sun.

XV. '*And the vail of the temple was rent in the midst. And when Jesus had cried with a loud voice, he said, Father, into thy hands I commend my spirit: and having said thus, he gave up the ghost.*' That the visible Temple would disappear, that its destruction would be the sign of the Son of Man's manifestation, this we have been led by former passages and by the whole context of the Gospel to believe. It was for later times to read the meaning of this sign. St. Luke merely announces it in the fewest possible words. And the words which follow he did not dare to weaken by any comments of his own. What that loud cry was of which he speaks we learn from the other Evangelists, not from him. But it is he who tells us what we especially long to know, that the voice, '*My God, my God, why hast thou forsaken me?*' ended in this: '*Father, into thy hands I commend my spirit.*' If we confess Him as the King of the Universe, how many spirits must He have commended to the Father with His Spirit? How many of those who have seemed to others and to themselves to be forsaken by the Father!

XVI. '*Now when the centurion saw what was done, he glorified God, saying, Certainly this was a righteous man. And all the people that came together to that sight, beholding the things which were done, smote their breasts, and returned. And all his acquaintance, and the women that followed him from Galilee, stood afar off, beholding these things.*' What a Roman soldier, what a few Galilean women said or thought of the deed and the sufferer, St. Luke tells us. He adds no comments. If we think of Christ as he did, we shall be content that our words, like his, should be few.

XVII. '*And, behold, there was a man named Joseph, a counsellor; and he was a good man, and a just: (The same had not consented to the counsel and deed of them;) he was of Arimathea, a city of the Jews: who also himself waited for the kingdom of God.*' Many legends have clustered round the name of Joseph of Arimathea; he is especially a British saint, associated with trees and flowers that grow on our soil. But which of these stories bring him as near to us as the account of what he was and what he sought for in the land of his fathers? The just man who groaned under the evil deeds which he saw sanctioned and done by those in high places, by rulers of the Sanhedrim, by chief priests of God's own appointment; the man who would not consent to a wicked deed because it was called religious and was done to preserve religion; the man who waited for the Kingdom of God, in which eternal goodness and justice should prevail;—this, my friends, is the true British saint, though he may have wrought no miracles in Glastonbury; in him we recognise a true human brother, because the

A A 2

Divine Spirit showed him what he needed, and what men in all times and in all countries most need. '*This man went unto Pilate, and begged the body of Jesus.*' That body must be a sacred body. If it was only the body of a righteous man, as the Roman centurion felt that He who had died on the Cross certainly was, it was sacred, worthy to be ' *wrapped in linen, and laid in a sepulchre that was hewn in stone, wherein never man before was laid.*' It must be that. Might it not be more than that? Might it not be the body of that King of the Jews of whom the superscription on the Cross bore witness? If He was that King, was the Kingdom of God, for which Joseph had waited, at an end? Had that death scattered the dream for ever? Joseph would wait still. Others would wait too. The Passover, which spoke of a Redemption, might even promise a Redemption of the body. The Sabbath, which spoke of man's rest and God's rest, might point to a rest such as there could not be in a tomb.

' *And that day was the preparation, and the sabbath drew on. And the women also, which came with him from Galilee, followed after, and beheld the sepulchre, and how his body was laid. And they returned, and prepared spices and ointments; and rested the sabbath day according to the commandment.*'

LECTURE XXVIII.

THE KING TRIUMPHANT.

St. Luke XXIV. 5.

And as they were afraid, and bowed down their faces to the earth, they said unto them, Why seek ye the living among the dead?

JOSEPH of Arimathea waited for the Kingdom of God. God, so he read, so he believed, is the Living God, the Author of life to all things, the Renewer of life day by day. God, so he read and believed, called out the seed of Abraham to be the witnesses of Him against all dead gods —all gods who cannot impart life, who can only be endued with the semblance of life by those who worship them. Yet Death *had* triumphed over the works of God's hands. Death had triumphed over all men whom God had made in His image. There had come into the world One who spoke of Life, Eternal Life; One who said that God had sent Him to bestow this Life on men. And now Death had laid hold of Him. In the darkest form it had come to Him. He had not driven it back. He had cried out in agony, '*My God, why hast thou forsaken me?*' He had been taken down from the Cross. There could be no doubt that His Spirit had gone. His body was laid in the tomb hewn out of the rock. The waiting, therefore, had, to all appearance, been in vain. There was a Kingdom of Death; that was universal. How could there be a Kingdom of God, in the sense in which prophets had spoken of it, in which Jesus had borne witness of it? The women who

had watched beside the Cross rested the Sabbath day
according to the commandment. Could it have been rest?
Yes, the unrest of vague expectation was over. The death
which they thought must be averted, in which they could
not believe, had actually come. There is a kind of rest in
that necessity. The Sabbath, dull and leaden as it may
have looked, at least said: 'The struggle is past. Nothing
that you can do will bring Him back.' If you say rest
without hope is impossible, that may be true also. I think
it is. The Sabbath spoke of God. While they kept the
commandment, there was a dim sense that He was still the
living God. If He was, there must be hope.

I. ' *Now upon the first day of the week, very early in the
morning, they came unto the sepulchre, bringing the spices
which they had prepared, and certain others with them. And
they found the stone rolled away from the sepulchre. And
they entered in, and found not the body of the Lord Jesus.
And it came to pass, as they were much perplexed thereabout,
behold, two men stood by them in shining garments: and as
they were afraid, and bowed down their faces to the earth,
they said unto them, Why seek ye the living among the dead?
He is not here, but is risen: remember how he spake unto
you when he was yet in Galilee, saying, The Son of man
must be delivered into the hands of sinful men, and be crucified, and the third day rise again.'*

If this were true, if it could be true, the message of a
Kingdom of God might not be a mere dream; the witness
which the Sabbath bore to a communion between man and
God, in rest and in work, might not have deceived them.
You think these poor women may not have known all the
reasons which have induced learned men to say that it
could not be true. Oh, my friends, does not every woman

and every man carry within a sense of the power of death which is stronger than all these arguments, which really gives them their weight? Death does not want philosophers to assist him in proving how invincible he is. He makes the peasant understand that well enough. And if either peasant or philosopher ever understands anything else —if either peasant or philosopher is led to protest, 'Death 'cannot be the Lord of this living universe—Death cannot 'be, and shall not be, my Lord,'—it must be, I suspect, because there are other voices besides his speaking to the heart of every man, which he must listen to, even when he is most inclined to turn away from them.

Did the voices come to these women only from those two persons in shining garments who were sitting in the tomb? If the Resurrection were a truth, it was no contradiction that such persons should speak to them, for then the visible and the invisible world cannot be hopelessly divided. But angel voices saying, 'He is risen,' could not of themselves break the strong spell of custom—could not of themselves answer the cry of the heart, 'It cannot be. 'The news is too good to be true. We dare not trust to it.' No! if this marvellous report of the women, told in such plain words as these, urging no probabilities in its favour, has defied the opposition of Jewish and of Gentile scorn— of all the power of Jewish and Gentile priests as well as rulers—if it has established itself in the heart and conscience of the most civilized countries of the world—if it has moulded their civilization, transfigured their art, changed the thought and tone of all books, won priests and rulers to lend their very questionable, often their very mischievous aid, in enforcing the belief which made its way in defiance of those to whose functions they have succeeded—if all this has come to pass, the echo of those angel voices which spoke to the women cannot be all that has been ringing through these ages. Other messengers, whose shining garments could not be seen, must have been holding converse with the hearts and consciences of the sons of earth. A man is sometimes heard crying in his despair, ' I am told that I must believe this news of a Resurrection; ' that men will punish me here, that God will punish me ' hereafter, if I do not. But I cannot. Milleniums of deaths, ' the sights of daily corpses, prevail against all your argu- ' ments, all your terrors.' There comes to that man a message : it may be brought by books or pictures, by sunset or sunrise, by the spring that maketh all things new ; it may be brought by the remembrance of mothers, by the pressure of hands that are cold, by the conviction that poverty and injustice cannot be for ever. But however it reaches him, this is the tenour of it : ' Brother man, He is ' risen. The God of Life does not force thee to think so by ' threats of destruction. He sends thee the good news that ' death and destruction have tried their power against the ' Son of Man, thy Lord, and that they have not prevailed, ' and shall not prevail.' Is not that an angel message, a still small voice, but bearing a witness of its origin which the storm and the earthquake do not bear ?

II. '*And they remembered his words, and returned from the sepulchre, and told all these things unto the eleven, and to all the rest. It was Mary Magdalene, and Joanna, and Mary the mother of James, and other women that were with them, which told these things unto the apostles. And their words seemed to them as idle tales, and they believed them not.*'

The disciples describe themselves as incredulous. Modern

critics say that men such as they were must have been
credulous. 'Would they not have had the superstitions of
'their country? Did they not belong to the most ignorant
'part of it? Did they not think that their Master was
'like no other man, and that all the laws of the universe
'would be cast aside in His favour?' Assuredly they had
all the superstitions of their country; an unspeakable
dread of death, a sense of the power of death and of
darkness would be the strongest of these superstitions.
A glimpse into the secrets of the unseen world, an apparition coming from it, this they were not unlikely to accept.
This they tell us they did accept as possible when they saw
their Master. They had no doubt believed that their Master
was different from other men. They had thought that He
had saved others, and would certainly save Himself. He
had not done it. There had been no exception in His
favour. Death had met Him as he meets other men, only
in a more ghastly form. What is more, these Galileans,
with their partial notions of Him, went forth, saying,
'This Resurrection is *not* an exception in His favour. His
'Resurrection is yours. He has overcome death and the
'grave for you, Jews and Greeks, barbarians and Scythians,
'bondsmen and freemen.' This was the Gospel which they
preached. With this they encountered the magicians,
enchanters, the death-worshippers of all kinds who were
spread through the Jewish and Gentile worlds. With this
they became instruments in establishing the society of
modern Europe. Must they not be honest when they tell
us that the words which were the warrants for such convictions, which led to such effects as these, seemed to
them at first as idle tales, that they believed them not?

III. How, then, was the incredulity overcome? St. Luke

tells us a simple story which explains the alteration, which I think, no arguments have ever explained :—

'*And, behold, two of them went that same day to a village called Emmaus, which was from Jerusalem about threescore furlongs. And they talked together of all these things which had happened. And it came to pass, that, while they communed together and reasoned, Jesus himself drew near, and went with them. But their eyes were holden that they should not know him. And he said unto them, What manner of communications are these that ye have one to another, as ye walk, and are sad ? And the one of them, whose name was Cleopas, answering said unto him, Art thou only a stranger in Jerusalem, and hast not known the things which are come to pass there in these days ? And he said unto them, What things ? And they said unto him, Concerning Jesus of Nazareth, which was a prophet mighty in deed and word before God and all the people : And how the chief priests and our rulers delivered him to be condemned to death, and have crucified him. But we trusted that it had been he which should have redeemed Israel : and beside all this, to day is the third day since these things were done. Yea, and certain women also of our company made us astonished, which were early at the sepulchre ; and when they found not his body, they came, saying, that they had also seen a vision of angels, which said that he was alive. And certain of them which were with us went to the sepulchre, and found it even so as the women had said : but him they saw not.*'

These two disciples had talked much with each other, had tried to put facts together, had considered what glimpses of hope the women's story afforded. No light had come to their minds. It was all sadness and perplexity. The Stranger who joins them seems chiefly anxious to draw out their thoughts, to let them express all which is troubling them. But when He has done that, He appears suddenly to assume the right of a reprover and a Judge.

' *O fools, and slow of heart to believe all that the prophets have spoken! Ought not Christ to have suffered these things, and to enter into his glory?* ' ' Did you think that He was to ' redeem Israel, and that He was not to struggle with the ' enemies who held Israel in slavery? Did you think He ' was to be a King, and that He was not to suffer with His ' subjects? Is not that the path which all the prophets ' and kings have travelled? Has not that been the way to ' their triumph? Did they not teach you that *the* King, ' *the* Prophet, was to do and suffer perfectly what they ' had done and suffered imperfectly?'

' *And beginning at Moses and all the prophets, he expounded unto them in all the scriptures the things concerning himself. And they drew nigh unto the village, whither they went: and he made as though he would have gone further. But they constrained him, saying, Abide with us: for it is toward evening, and the day is far spent. And he went in to tarry with them.*'

So the dead letters of Scripture which these disciples had mused on so often, which had been interpreted to them by so many scribes, started into life. What had been maxims, or dogmas, or allegories, became portions of a human and divine history. A Person was the centre of that history, One who as the Book said had been, and was, and would be. But where was He now? Could the Stranger tell them? To know that would be more than to trace Him through all the records of other days.

' *And it came to pass, as he sat at meat with them, he took*

*bread, and blessed it, and brake, and gave to them. And
their eyes were opened, and they knew him ; and he vanished
out of their sight. And they said one to another, Did not
our heart burn within us, while he talked with us by the way,
and while he opened to us the scriptures ? And they rose up
the same hour, and returned to Jerusalem, and found the
eleven gathered together, and them that were with them,
saying, The Lord is risen indeed, and hath appeared to Simon.
And they told what things were done in the way, and how he
was known of them in breaking of bread.'* Thus were these
disciples prepared to believe in a Resurrection. There was
a Christ. He ought to have suffered. That must be the
way to His Kingdom. And this Christ was with them.
They might know Him. He ate their bread. He blessed
it. Did He only while they saw Him? Did He not
bless their bread always? Did not their hearts burn while
He told them how He had been the same throughout all
ages ? He could be no apparition. They might go and
tell the disciples at Jerusalem that He was among them, a
living Person in a living body.

IV. The Apostles, too, were beginning to believe. But
the feeling or dream of an apparition which might just for a
moment have looked upon them out of a world of shadows
still haunted their minds, still quenched the acknowledgment of a substantial Presence.

*' And as they thus spake, Jesus himself stood in the midst
of them, and saith unto them, Peace be unto you. But they
were terrified and affrighted, and supposed that they had seen
a spirit. And he said unto them, Why are ye troubled ?
and why do thoughts arise in your hearts? Behold my hands
and my feet, that it is I myself: handle me, and see ; for a
spirit hath not flesh and bones, as ye see me have. And when*

*he had thus spoken, he showed them his hands and his feet.
And while they yet believed not for joy, and wondered, he said
unto them, Have ye here any meat ? And they gave him a
piece of a broiled fish, and of an honeycomb. And he took it,
and did eat before them.'*

'They supposed they had *seen* a spirit.' How naturally
does St. Luke describe just the confused apprehensions
which have haunted men in all ages. They think they *see*
spirits. Every hour they are conversing with spiritual
beings. Every message of affection which reaches us is a
spiritual message. Every word which depresses or elevates
us comes not from a material, but from a spiritual source.
Our consciences and our reasons are ours, because we are
spiritual ; we address the conscience and reason of other
men because we own them to be spiritual. But what we
see are the lips that move, are the hands and the feet. Our
Lord teaches them that it is so with Himself. He stands
among them, and says, '*Peace be unto you.*' That was the
voice of a Spirit speaking to their spirits. But He says,
'*Handle me, and see ; for a spirit hath not flesh and bones,
as ye see me have.*' He had an actual body. He had
brought it back from the grave. There was nothing
shadowy or fantastic in it. Now, as before, it could eat
the food which they ate. Nothing clears our minds of
the phantoms that are always floating between earth and
heaven—not really approaching either—like this simple
teaching. The Son of God speaks to the poorest men as
spiritual creatures to whom He may declare the Kingdom
of Heaven, who are capable of entering into such a Kingdom, who cannot exist without it. The Son of God says
to the poorest man, 'Brother, child of God, peace be unto
thee.' But He shows His hands and feet, that it is He

Himself. He eats the broiled fish and the honeycomb. The body is real as well as the spirit. The body is redeemed from death as well as the spirit.

V. *'And he said unto them, These are the words which I spake unto you, while I was yet with you, that all things must be fulfilled, which were written in the law of Moses, and in the prophets, and in the psalms, concerning me.   Then opened he their understanding, that they might understand the scriptures, and said unto them, Thus it is written, and thus it behoved Christ to suffer, and to rise from the dead the third day : and that repentance and remission of sins should be preached in his name among all nations, beginning at Jerusalem.   And ye are witnesses of these things.'*

It is for this that He has been preparing them through the years of teaching and discipline that He has spent with them on the Lakes of Galilee, in the streets, and in the Temple of the Holy City. They were not chosen to be His favourites. They were chosen to carry a message to the Universe. All that had been written in the days of old, all that He had spoken to them, was that they might go forth and say to Jews, to Greeks, to men at the farthest ends of the earth : ' Your Father is seeking you. ' You may turn to Him. He sends you deliverance from ' your sins.' In Jerusalem, where the greatest of all sins had been committed, where the King Himself had been slain, they were to begin their work. They were to announce, as the first token and pledge of the glorified King, that those who had been guilty of that treason were pardoned, that they might receive His highest gift, the gift of His own Spirit.

VI. That gift they were themselves to wait for : *' Behold, I send the promise of my Father upon you : but tarry ye in the city of Jerusalem, until ye be endued with power from on high.'* Every day as they went forth would show them their need of that power. If they were not messengers from a Father in Heaven, if they could not declare His will to men, if He was not working in men to do it, all they spoke would be ineffectual—their own words would confound them.

VII. *'And it came to pass, while he blessed them, he was parted from them, and carried up into heaven. And they worshipped him, and returned to Jerusalem with great joy. And were continually in the temple, praising and blessing God.'* With great joy, though this Jesus, from whom all their joy had sprung, was departed out of their sight. With joy, because that Jesus had claimed His right as the Christ, because He had shown that He had come from a Father, and had done the will of His Father. With joy, because Death and Hell were shown to be His Father's enemies, and He had vanquished them. With joy, because, being delivered from those enemies, they could serve God without fear in holiness and righteousness all the days of their life.

That was the promise in the song of Zacharias which we read in the first chapter of this Gospel. That is the promise which we have seen unfolding itself to the last words of the Gospel. I think you will see that it is what it professes to be, the Gospel of the Kingdom of Heaven. If we have been enabled to trace together the steps of the King from the message which came to the Virgin in Galilee to the time when He sat down on His Father's throne, I am sure that every event which has befallen us of sorrow and joy will have been explaining the news to us as no words can explain it, that it will have brought

evidence to us of its veracity which arguments cannot
bring.   The acts of God are the true commentaries on His
Word.   For He is with us to interpret both, who joined
the two disciples when they talked together and were sad.
He can make Himself known to us in the breaking of
bread.   He can enable us to praise and bless God through
Him whilst we are worshipping here, and in that city
where the Apostle saw no Temple, '*for the Lord God
Almighty and the Lamb are the temple of it.*'